THE POLITICAL ECONOMY
OF REGIONALISM IN AFRICA

THE POLITICAL ECONOMY OF REGIONALISM IN AFRICA

A Decade of the Economic Community
of West African States (ECOWAS)

S.K.B. Asante

PRAEGER

PRAEGER SPECIAL STUDIES • PRAEGER SCIENTIFIC

New York • Philadelphia • Eastbourne, UK
Toronto • Hong Kong • Tokyo • Sydney

Library of Congress Cataloging-in-Publication Data

Asante, S. K. B.
  The political economy of regionalism in Africa.

  Bibliography: p.
  Includes index.
  1. Economic Community of West African States—
History. 2. Africa, West—Economic integration—
History. I. Title.
HC1000.A86 1985   337.1′66   85-16740
ISBN 0-03-005902-X (alk. paper)

Published in 1986 by Praeger Publishers
CBS Educational and Professional Publishing, a Division of CBS Inc.
521 Fifth Avenue, New York, NY 10175 USA

© 1986 by Praeger Publishers

Printed in the United States of America on acid-free paper

INTERNATIONAL OFFICES

Orders from outside the United States should be sent to the appropriate address listed below. Orders from areas not
listed below should be placed through CBS International Publishing. 383 Madison Ave.. New York. NY 10175 USA

Australia, New Zealand
Holt Saunders. Pty. Ltd.. 9 Waltham St.. Artarmon. N.S.W. 2064. Sydney. Australia

Canada
Holt. Rinehart & Winston of Canada. 55 Horner Ave.. Toronto. Ontario. Canada M8Z 4X6

Europe, the Middle East, & Africa
Holt Saunders. Ltd.. 1 St. Anne's Road. Eastbourne. East Sussex. England BN21 3UN

Japan
Holt Saunders. Ltd.. Ichibancho Central Building. 22-1 Ichibancho. 3rd Floor. Chiyodaku. Tokyo. Japan

Hong Kong, Southeast Asia
Holt Saunders Asia. Ltd.. 10 Fl. Intercontinental Plaza. 94 Granville Road. Tsim Sha Tsui East. Kowloon,
Hong Kong

**Manuscript submissions should be sent to the Editorial Director, Praeger Publishers, 521 Fifth Avenue,
New York, NY 10175 USA**

For my students and colleagues in Ghana, Nigeria,
Federal Republic of Germany, and the United States

FOREWORD
by Dr. James Nti

It is indeed a pleasure for me to write the foreword to this book, *The Political Economy of Regionalism in Africa: A Decade of the Economic Community of West African States (ECOWAS).*

Africa is going through what may be termed a major economic revolution, a revolution that is quite different from the struggle for political independence. Political independence has always been viewed by African leaders as a vehicle for the development of the economies of their various countries. But as economic independence does not automatically follow political independence, there is a new struggle for the achievement of this goal.

A major goal of most developing countries is to decrease their present massive dependence on countries of the industrialized world. However, given the small populations and limited resource endowments of many African states, as well as the severe economic instability since the 1970s, African governments have come to realize that it is difficult if not impossible to go it alone in their effort to achieve this goal. Economic cooperation has therefore come to be viewed as a means to reinforce their political and economic independence as well as their collective economic strength. This has been the major reason for the formation of many intergovernmental organizations among developing countries. In West Africa these organizations range from small groupings made up of a few countries with limited goals to the Economic Community of West African States (ECOWAS) which brings together all the 16 countries of the West African sub-region with the aim of establishing an economic community.

This book by closely examining ECOWAS in relation to policy issues and problems involved in economic integration among developing countries as well as in the light of the experiences of regional economic groupings in other parts of the world, is making a real contribution to the understanding of economic integration groupings particularly in the Third World. By analyzing some of the strengths of ECOWAS as well as some of the main obstacles to cooperation in West Africa, and by making various suggestions for achieving greater success, the book is helping to enhance the conviction of some of us that ECOWAS not only has the potential, but will also in actual fact have a positive impact on the development process of the West African sub-region. By throwing the searchlight on the role, the problems, and prospects of the largest economic integration grouping in the world, this book should stimulate the thinking and provide useful information to nationals not only of ECOWAS member states but also of other developing countries as well as other persons interested in economic integration groupings.

While the ideas expressed in this book are solely those of the author and I do not necessarily accept responsibility for them, I nonetheless commend the book to all those interested in ECOWAS and economic integration groupings in general.

Dr. James Nti
ECOWAS Executive Secretariat
Lagos, Nigeria
January 1985

PREFACE

The promotion of economic cooperation among developing countries is now a well-accepted part of the international development policy. Almost all issues in the field of international economic relations are currently subordinated to the quest for regional economic associations and groupings among more or less geographically contiguous areas. Over the past two decades more than a dozen customs and monetary unions, common markets, free trade zones, and other regional cooperative arrangements have been proposed or established in Latin America, Africa, and Asia. Some of these cooperative schemes have never gotten off the ground. Others were torn apart at a very early stage by deep political conflicts. Despite the disappointments and the very slow progress that some of these schemes have made, the countries concerned continue to display a genuine desire to negotiate with each other for economic cooperation. This process has received a great deal of impetus in recent years, particularly following the economic instability of the 1970s. In recent years, therefore, attempts at regional economic integration are in the forefront of the issues with which the trade and development policies of the developing countries are concerned. The Economic Community of West African States (ECOWAS) is the most concrete African initiative in this direction.

My interest in this project was stimulated and sharpened during the summer of 1976 when I was touring some German economic research centers as a senior research fellow of the Friedrich Ebert Foundation. Anxious to know more about the newly established ECOWAS, my German fellow researchers and colleagues hurriedly organized some seminars at which I presented short papers on the organization. This interest was further developed when on my return home I selected ECOWAS as the subject of my Inter-Faculty Open Lecture delivered in March 1977 at the University of Ghana, Legon. Although this lecture was very well received, I could not for sometime undertake further research on the project as I had wished, due to my involvement in national politics until November 1979, when the German Foundation for International Development (DSE) invited me to present a paper at an international seminar on Planning Regional Economic Integration: Policies and Models in Berlin (West). The favorable reaction of

the participants to my paper on ECOWAS was more than sufficient to rekindle my interest in doing further work toward the
publication of this volume. I shall be happy if it promotes deeper
understanding and stimulates thoughtful evaluation of the process
of regional economic integration among developing countries.

A project of this kind could not have been undertaken without
financial support and moral encouragement from many people and
institutions. I should like to thank especially the Friedrich Ebert
Foundation in Bonn, Federal Republic of Germany, for its generous offer of fellowships (1976 and 1980) to participate in international seminars on regional economic integration, which also
made it possible for me to meet with officials from secretariats of
regional groupings in Africa, Asia, Latin America, and Europe.

Still another, and substantial, acknowledgment is due to a very
large number of top and middle-level government officials, businessmen, labor officials, representatives of private sub-regional
associations, and journalists as well as ECOWAS officials who
were interviewed in the course of researching and writing this
book. They gave willingly and unstintingly of their time, often
interrupting busy schedules and making an extra effort to provide
me with the needed information. I would mention in particular
Mr. J. B. Wilmot, formerly head of the ECOWAS/EEC Secretariat
at Ghana's Ministry of Finance and Economic Planning in Accra
but now Ghana's ambassador in Brussels, Belgium; Dr. J. A.
Langley, head of the Gambia Civil Service in Banjul; Messrs. J. E.
A. Manu, Director of Economic Research, and Frank Ofei, Principal Research Officer, both of the ECOWAS Secretariat in Lagos,
and Mr. Robert Tubman, Managing Director of the ECOWAS
Fund in Lome. I am greatly indebted to Dr. James Nti, Deputy
Executive Secretary of ECOWAS, for his steady encouragement to
the project from its inception as well as his invaluable support
throughout the book's evolution and, especially, for the generous
sharing of "insightful" knowledge and tolerant discussion of dis-
agreements which have done much to shape my own viewpoints.
It is indeed proper and fitting that he consented to write the
Foreword to this study.

Special thanks are due to Professor Timothy M. Shaw of
Dalhousie University in Canada, who read the manuscript, made
some necessary corrections and, above all, gave me the benefit of
his valued judgments, without--I hasten to add--incurring any
responsibility for the views expressed herein. I am equally
indebted to Professor Isebill V. Gruhn of the University of California at Santa Cruz for a quick study of the manuscript which
resulted in some valuable suggestions in matters of substance.

And once again, I owe an incalculable debt to Mr. Christopher Fyfe of the Centre of African Studies, University of Edinburgh, who throughout sent me at his own expense photostat copies of numerous documents and articles on the subject of regional economic integration. I owe immeasurable and enduring gratitude to my wife, Jane, and children--Kwabena, Yaa, Abena, and Kwame--innocent victims of my occupational diseases. The final revision of this work was done in the University of Florida, Gainesville, where I was serving as African Area Studies Consultant and Visiting Professor in the Department of Political Science and Department of History through the Center for African Studies. Special thanks are due to this university for providing me with secretarial facilities. I owe a particular debt of gratitude to Dr. Hunt Davis, Jr., Director of the Center for African Studies, for his sustained generosity, stimulation, and encouragement since my joining this university.

Finally, I am indebted to my students and colleagues who have either taught me or forced me to learn most of what is contained in my modest treasury of understanding of the intriguing, complex, and important field of regional economic integration.

S. K. B. Asante
University of Florida
Gainesville, Florida
May 1985

CONTENTS

LIST OF TABLES

LIST OF ACRONYMS

ACP	African, Caribbean and Pacific
ASEAN	Association of South East Asian Nations
CACM	Central American Common Market
CEAO	Communauté Economique de l'Afrique de l'Ouest (West African Economic Community)
CFA	Communauté financiere africaine (West African franc or French African Community franc)
EAC	East African Community
ECA	Economic Commission for Africa
ECOWAS	Economic Community of West African States
EEC	European Economic Community
LAIA	Latin American Integration Association
LAFTA	Latin American Free Trade Association
LPA	Lagos Plan of Action
MRU	Mano River Union
NIEO	New International Economic Order
TNC	Transnational Corporation
UDAO	Union Douaniere de l'Afrique de l'Ouest (West African Customs Union)
UDEAO	Union Douaniere et Economique de l'Afrique de l'Ouest (Customs and Economic Union of West Africa)
UDEAC	Union Douaniere et Economique de l'Afrique Centrale (Customs and Economic Union of Central Africa)
UNCTAD	United Nations Conference on Trade and Development
UNIDO	United Nations Industrial Development Organization

1

INTRODUCTION

ORIENTATION AND FOCUS OF STUDY

On 28 May 1975, fifteen West African countries signed the
Treaty of Lagos establishing the Economic Community of West
African States (ECOWAS for the English-speaking and CEDEAO
for the French-speaking); Cape Verde has since joined as the
Community's sixteenth member. This event represented the cul-
mination of many years of effort by these states to increase the
economic mass, and therefore the bargaining base, of their economies. Through a pooling of economic "sovereignty" their intent is
to transform their economies so as to improve the living standards
of their peoples and to extend the struggle for political decolonization into one for economic decolonization. The creation of
ECOWAS was also a response to the recognition by the West African countries that the fragmentation of the sub-region--the product of colonial balkanization--into narrow domestic markets ren-
ders a shift in the pattern of production, designed to reduce dependence, both difficult and costly. History in the last century
and a half indicates that only very large national units have a sufficient resource base, climatic diversity, and population size to
afford what Oteiza and Sercovich have termed, "an autarchic self-
reliant model."[1]

In brief, therefore, the inauguration of ECOWAS must be seen
as an attempt by the West African states to enhance their economic opportunity and to reduce their external dependency.
Thereby they hope to overcome the existing structures of neo-
colonialism and underdevelopment. The lessening of the high de-

gree of external dependence is a precondition for achieving basic structural development goals. Viewed within the context of the New International Economic Order (NIEO), ECOWAS must also be regarded as an integral part of a wider desire of the poor nations of the sub-region to eliminate, or at least to reduce, the inequalities inherent in the present international economic system. However, these effects cannot be attained automatically. Without a well-conceived and intensive effort and without adequate planning, ECOWAS could lead to the perpetuation of neo-colonialism, underdevelopment, and inequality; to increased rather than decreased external dependence. For, as Osvaldo Sunkel rightly remarked in the case of Latin America, "integration, in fact, can be either a basic instrument of national realization in Latin America; or it can be the instrument of accelerated dependence (*sucursalizacion*) of the region."[2]

On the whole, this preliminary study aims at analyzing generally some important policy issues and problems involved in economic integration among developing countries and, in particular, at examining ECOWAS closely, in light of both this analysis and of the experience gained by other developing countries in the use of integration schemes. By analyzing past trends and experiences of regional economic integration schemes in other parts of the developing world, this preliminary study of ECOWAS attempts to make some critical observations for consideration by those experts and policy-makers in West Africa who consider regional economic integration a potentially important weapon in the search for accelerated development and industrialization in the sub-region. Thus, whenever possible, this study attempts to compare aspects of ECOWAS with similar schemes in other developing areas. While this does not in any way suggest a formal comparative study, it does attempt to broaden the horizon and the general context within which ECOWAS is to operate. By so doing, the study may provide some possible alternatives to solving some of ECOWAS' myriad problems.

As the success of integration partly depends on a conscious mobilization of popular support within the integrated area, the need for a full-scale study of ECOWAS for use by businessmen, policy-makers, and government officials, officials of trade union congresses, national banks, chambers of commerce and, indeed, the general public, cannot be overemphasized. For such a study would contribute considerably to the promotion of the ECOWAS idea in the member states of the Community. Specifically, the mobilization of popular support that this volume is likely to encourage would greatly help in exercising pressure on national governments to make definite and positive commitments in favor of the Community. After all, economic cooperation goes far beyond treaty making, the negotiation of protocol, and the establishment of institutions and machinery. In writing this book, therefore, I have had in mind the needs of those who are concerned with the problems of West African economic integration in practice. I have also had in mind the needs of students in the higher forms of training colleges and secondary schools and especially, of the growing number of university students following interdisciplinary courses in which an understanding of the issues of economic integration is important. Also, the need for this book is of paramount importance because it may promote further research in the field of West African economic cooperation. It would thereby be contributing to enlarging regional understanding, stimulating thought, clarifying objectives, and promoting a sense of technocratic esprit de corps, thereby creating an atmosphere propitious to integrative moves in the sub-region.

The book does not pretend to be a definitive study of ECOWAS. In the light of its rapid and sustained development no book on this subject can be completely up-to-date. Another limitation of this study is that it does not intend to discuss the various approaches and development plans of each West African country. Neither does it attempt a detailed appraisal of the internal political, economic, and social complexity in each country, except when this is viewed as a potential source of problems for ECOWAS. On the whole, the aim of this study is quite modest: to provide as much information as possible on various aspects of ECOWAS at its present stage of development for both the general reader and students of higher educational institutions.

To a limited extent, however, this study remains an interdisciplinary effort--uniting the disciplines of politics and economics. This is not surprising because in recent years, especially in practice if not in theory, the distinction between the two disciplines is becoming more blurred. In the realm of international relations, in particular, politics can hardly be divorced from economics. For political concerns often "shape economic policy, as important economic policies are frequently dictated by overriding political interests."[3] Put another way, the behavior of governments on economic issues will be affected by political calculations. At the same time, political steps by governments must often rest on economic capabilities and are increasingly taking economic form.[4] The fact that a particular economic activity is characterized by nonpolitical behavior does not imply that politics is unimportant. Indeed, politics may have been crucial in establishing the setting within which the activity took place. This close and intimate relationship between politics and economics is particularly evident in the case of economic integration schemes. As a former president of the European Economic Community Commission, Walter Hallstein, once said in reference to the institutions and operation of the EEC: "We are not in business at all; we are in politics."[5] Political considerations are intimately involved both in the conception and in the execution of integration schemes. In the African context this element needs be stressed almost ad nauseum because economic policies in Africa must get the blessing of the politicians before they can be implemented, and where political considerations clash with economic considerations the former usually prevail. Throughout this study, therefore, attention is focused on the intimate relationship between economics and politics.

Although a number of studies have appeared recently on regional economic integration in some parts of Africa,[6] only a few comparable works would seem to have been published on the West African sub-region. Nicolas Plessz's small volume, *Problems and Prospects of Economic Integration in West Africa,*[7] is basically a pioneer study that does not adequately address itself to the recent developments in West African economic integration efforts. Also, John Renninger's *Multinational Cooperation for Development in West Africa*[8] only examines briefly the origins and prospects of ECOWAS as one of the "numerous intergovernmental organizations that exist" in the West African sub-region with which the author is concerned. To be precise, this small documentary and invaluable study is devoted to a discussion of many bilateral and other forms of association between West African countries, which, according to your point of view, support or rival ECOWAS. Another useful and invaluable scholarly study is *Industrialization in the Economic Community of West African States (ECOWAS)* published for the West African Economic Association by Heinemann Educational Books in 1980, and edited by Diejomaoh and Iyoha. As the title implies, this study is devoted almost solely to industrialization in ECOWAS and therefore it does not pay sufficient attention to the other major aspects of the Community. The volume contains a selection of papers presented at the inaugural conference of the association held in Lagos in April 1978. *Industrialization in ECOWAS* greatly contributes to our understanding of this very major aspect of the Community's goal. One volume edited by Edozien and Osagie, *Economic Integration of West Africa*[9] is a collection of articles dealing with different aspects of West African economic integration. It is not a study focusing solely on ECOWAS as such, although some of the papers devote attention to examining aspects of the Community. Similarly, Peter Robson's recently published very stimulating and scholarly study, *Integration, Development and Equity: Economic Integration In West Africa*,[10] focuses attention on the issues and experience of four main initiatives for regional integration in West Africa, including ECOWAS, to which he devotes specifically 37 pages. Thus, this is essentially a summary, and not a detailed study of ECOWAS, although it is a highly informative and extremely invaluable piece of work. Another recent title by Uka Ezenwe, *ECOWAS and the Economic Integration of West Africa*,[11] though arousing great expectations, turns out to be a very modest contribution of only two chapters (of 46 pages) devoted to ECOWAS.

Perhaps the only recently published work which concentrates solely on ECOWAS is Onwuka's *Development and Integration in West Africa: The Case of the Economic Community of West African States (ECOWAS)*.[12] The chief concern of this volume "is the process of development (of) integration as a vehicle for regional development" using ECOWAS as a case study. The main limitation of this generally interesting book is its oversimplification of some rather complex problems like the issues posed by the parallel existence of CEAO and ECOWAS as sub-regional groupings in West Africa and the ECOWAS comprehensive trade liberalization scheme. Besides, since the basic research for this volume was conducted from sources available in Britain (Preface), the author was unable to consult such extremely important primary sources as the executive secretary's semiannual or annual reports; the series of the Community's *Official Journals*; ECOWAS Policies and Programme Series; and the recent special studies sponsored by the ECOWAS Secretariat itself. The use of these primary sources would have helped in providing a refreshingly deeper insight into the general operation and fortunes of this fledgling organization. Thus, the need for a full scale study of ECOWAS, using the available primary sources for a deeper and comprehensive assessment of this first serious attempt at economic cooperation and integration in the West African sub-region cutting across divisions of language, history, and existing affiliations and institutions, for the first time in the history of the sub-region, becomes of paramount importance.

At the core of this study are three major assumptions. First, that the West African sub-region is the most varied in Africa as to size of countries, levels of economic development, and diversities of language and economic internal and external links. Second, that the member states of ECOWAS see economic integration as a means of helping to overcome the disadvantages of small size, low per capita incomes, small populations, and narrow resource bases, and of making possible a greater rate of economic growth and development. And third, that although the problems are daunting, they are not unsurmountable, given the necessary commitment and the readiness to take concerted action on all fronts.

Resting its case upon the above assumptions, this study attempts to address itself to the following crucial issues: To what extent are the West African states politically committed to ECOWAS' ideals and concepts? How adequate are the institutions set up for the realization of ECOWAS' aims and objectives? What effective measures should be initiated to combat attempts by extraregional powers, such as transnational corporations (TNCs), to take advantage of newly created regional opportunities and thus derive more benefit from ECOWAS than would the intraregional participants? In other words, how can the member states of ECOWAS extricate themselves from existing dependency relationships with their metropolitan powers? What problems are posed by the process of harmonization of industrial and commercial policies? To what extent would the disparities in national priorities, policies, and objectives be reconciled? And, finally, how can the member states of ECOWAS agree upon an acceptable distribution of benefits and costs from the Community?

To attempt to provide answers to these contentious and politically laden issues, I have adopted two research methods. First, primary data, mainly the result of in-depth discussions and first-hand observations, were collected through field investigations in some ECOWAS countries. In each country, valuable information was extracted from a partially structured questionnaire given to the staff of official bodies, representatives of export promotion organizations, chambers of commerce, trade union congresses, and financial intermediaries, as well as to public and private market intermediaries. The second method employed was to collect and systematically analyze the secondary data both published and unpublished including, for example, government or official publications, parliamentary debates, national and private newspapers, the executive secretary's reports, the series of the Community's *Official Journals*, the *ECOWAS Papers* (at the Library of the Nigerian Institute of International Affairs, Lagos) as well as the recent special studies sponsored by the ECOWAS Secretariat. The present study is thus based on both existing records and documentary materials and on an opinion survey.

The introductory chapter examines briefly the scope of the study, indicating also the theoretical framework adopted. Chapter 2 summarises first, the concept of regional economic cooperation as a key element of the New International Economic Order (NIEO) and, second, the experiences, stresses, and strains of regional economic cooperation among developing countries in recent years. In Chapter 3 some of the salient features of the neo-colonial economy of the West African sub-region have been examined. This is followed by a historical background to the creation of ECOWAS. Chapter 4 seeks to analyze the structure of ECOWAS, its main organs and decision-making processes. Chapter 5 focuses attention on issues that arise in connection with industrialization and trade liberalization in ECOWAS. In Chapter 6 the Community's attempt to tackle the problem of economic dependence is analyzed. Chapter 7 is devoted to a discussion of some of the most serious, and potentially most disruptive, problems that are likely to confront the young Community. Chapter 8 attempts a brief review of the evolution of ECOWAS over the past half decade (that is, 1977-85), while Chapter 9 concludes the study by examining not only the role of the human factor in the move toward a West African community, but also the future prospects of ECOWAS.

CONCEPTUAL AND THEORETICAL CONSIDERATIONS

One clarification of terminology might be justified at the outset. The common usage of the term "integration" is often confusing. I find some unanimity, a fair amount of consensus, but also much divergence among its users. Even the dictionary definition--"forming parts into a whole"--leaves open a wide range of ambiguity. In the economic literature, the term "economic integration" is a fashionable slogan, the meaning of which can be stretched quite far. For example, some authors include social integration in the concept, others subsume different forms of international cooperation under this heading. The term has thus been used imprecisely in common parlance. So far no single definition of "integration" has gained widespread acceptance among integration theorists. The concept has therefore provoked considerable discussion and debate in economic and political literature.[13]

By 1950, however, "economic integration" had come to be used more specifically as a term to denote a state of affairs or a process involving the combination of separate economies into larger economic regions. Defined as a process, it includes all measures that aim at abolishing discrimination between economic units from different countries. It can also be considered as a state of affairs characterized by the absence of various forms of discrimination between countries. This definition seems to be quite close to what John Pinder, with reference to the European Economic Community (EEC), has termed as the twin processes involving both *negative* and *positive* aspects of integration. While negative integration is that aspect of economic integration that consists in the elimination of discrimination against participating members, positive integration symbolizes the formation and application of coordinated and common policies in order to fulfil economic and welfare objectives other than the mere removal of discrimination.[14]

However, since it is of some consequence for the argument presented in this study, it is essential at this juncture to examine briefly the meaning of economic integration in light of African conditions. In this connection, we may rely on the analysis of Bingu Mutharika who has warned in a recent study that the peculiarity of the characteristics of the African economies and the evolution of political and other institutions "make it unrealistic to apply the term in the same sense as used in the developed countries."[15] It is necessary therefore to paint boldly and to fix firmly in our minds the economic and political realities of Africa in any discussion of African economic integration. The term may thus be defined as a process whereby two or more countries in a particular area voluntarily join together to pursue common policies and objectives in matters of general economic development or in a particular economic field of common interest to the mutual advantage of all the participating states.[16] The essence of this definition is that any scheme of economic integration must be voluntary and that each state must demonstrate its willingness to pursue certain policies in close consultation with the other states. Significantly, too, economic integration in Africa will have to be broadly based and wide in its application, at least in the initial stages, and sufficiently flexible in its practical form to embody social, cultural, political, and economic considerations.

Examined closely, ECOWAS falls within the realm of Mutharika's definition particularly in the sense that the West African states have voluntarily come together to pursue, in the words of the ECOWAS Treaty, "common policies and objectives" aimed at promoting "co-operation and development in all fields of economic activity." It goes farther to explain that, to achieve his aim, the Community "shall by stages" or progressively eliminate discrimination between the member states. At the same time, the treaty sets out to create some decision-making institutions with powers designed to implement the aims and objectives of the organization.[17] In this sense, also, the two aspects of Pinder's model of economic integration can clearly be found in the constitutional instrument of ECOWAS. It is pertinent to stress, too, that economic integration, as defined above, is used in this study not with reference to national integration in respect of the subsistence sector or to the divisions and weaknesses of dual economies in plural societies. Rather, integration refers here to inter-national (that is, continental or regional or sub-regional) economic cooperation (coordination or association as the case may be) in one form or another. It is worth noting, also, that when the term regional integration is applied to Africa in the scholarly literature it almost always assumes that "region" refers not to the entire continent but to sub-regions thereof.

Furthermore, since in this study we have been tempted to use the two competing terms, "regional cooperation" and "regional integration" interchangeably, it might be useful to differentiate between them. While, as noted above, the term regional integration has acquired several quite technical definitions, regional cooperation is a vague concept, applicable to any interstate activity with less than universal participation designed to meet some commonly experienced need. In recent years, Ernst Haas, a central figure in the neo-functionalist school of regional integration theorists, has attempted to limit the semantic confusion arising from the term "integration." Basing his early work on an analysis of Europe, Haas has argued that the study of regional integration is not the same as the study of regional cooperation. The former, in his view, is concerned with explanations of "how and why states cease to be wholly sovereign, how and why they voluntarily mingle, merge, and mix with their neighbours so as to lose the factual attributes of sovereignty while acquiring new techniques for resolving conflict between themselves." The latter, on the other hand, is concerned with the process of "getting there." In other words, regional cooperation may help "describe steps along the way" to regional integration.[18]

In this sense, therefore, the term integration may be treated as the terminal or resulting condition, the end state, or outcomes or consequences of regional cooperation activities. Hence the study of regional cooperation may be considered as a part of the study of regional integration or as a separate interest. However, the point to emphasize here is that states will either way eventually come to share individual authority with a collective mechanism or entity. I thus agree with Isebill Gruhn that whether the integration process "is perceived of as leading to the goal or as constituting the goal itself, the same consequences can result."[19] In this study, therefore, I have been tempted to regard regional integration both as a "process" and as a "terminal condition." In other words, the cooperation of West African countries in various fields of economic activity may lead to partial or complete economic integration of the sub-region.

Generally, regional cooperation may be limited to a specific project, or it may encompass the formation of a free trade area (abolition of trade barriers among member countries), a customs union (establishment of a common tariff policy toward nonmember countries), a common market (free movement of factors of production as well as of commodities within the area), or a complete economic union among the member countries.

THE THEORY OF ECONOMIC INTEGRATION REVISITED

Closely related to identification of these types of economic integration in the literature is the problem relating to the theoretical foundations on which the recent drive toward economic cooperation has been based. It is pertinent to note that, although most cases of regional economic integration are among Third World countries, research in this field has been dominated by theory based on the European experience. The EEC has thus become, in the words of Frankel, "a living laboratory for the integration theory."[20] Not surprisingly, the literature on economic integration and development has pointed out that developing countries do not satisfy the criteria of neo-classical customs union theory and that they will not reap the traditional welfare gains from integration. Hence some economists, such as Viner and Lipsey, deny that integration schemes will benefit developing countries.[21] Their argument is based upon the concepts of trade creation and trade diversion.

Viner defines trade creation as a shift in trade from high cost to low cost sources of supply within the integration area, and trade diversion as a shift from a low cost source of supply outside the integration area to a high cost producer within it. In Viner's view, if there is more trade diversion than trade creation within a customs union, then the net effect on world welfare and the welfare of the members will be negative. Since trade diversion (at least in the short run) will obviously prevail over trade creation in Third World customs union as the members shift from low cost producers in the developed world to high cost producers among their neighbors, Viner and Lipsey are opposed to the creation of customs unions among developing countries.

However, in recent years there has been a growing criticism about applying Viner's criteria and Lipsey's general conclusions to the possible effects of customs unions among developing countries.[22] Most writers concerned with the problems of Third World countries have rejected neo-classical trade theory and neo-classical customs union theory and argued that the problems of economic integration among peripheral countries should be analyzed within the context of development economies rather than as a branch of tariff theory.

This argument is based on the fact that conditions in the developing countries are strikingly different from those that exist in the developed world on which the established theoretical framework for economic integration has been based. The critical factors on which Viner's criteria and Lipsey's conclusions were based are among the ones the developing countries, such as those in West Africa, are desirous of changing through economic integration. In effect, remarked Onitiri, the renowned Nigerian economist, "the underdeveloped areas are involved in a huge effort to alter the structure of their economy and to integrate their foreign trade more closely with it than before."[23] In other words, these countries aim at changing the structure of production and trade, and then at evolving a new trade mechanism based on regional specialization. These changes are not marginal but structural. Their net effect will not be felt over a short period of time. For, as Mikesell has observed correctly, the creation of a customs union or free trade area "usually involves relatively long time periods for fruition" so that the initial impact, and perhaps the most important one, is an expectation regarding future market opportunities rather than existing trade patterns.[24] Attention, therefore, has to be paid to the long-run effects which economic integration is likely to have. Thus, in evaluating the desirability of economic integration among developing countries, the emphasis should be placed on dynamic rather than static effects. More specifically, we should be concerned with the dynamics of economic growth and stress positive effects in the creation of regional markets on the developmental pace of member countries.

Briefly, then, economic integration in the case of developing countries should be treated as an approach to economic development rather than a tariff issue. Accordingly, it combines various aspects that could improve the international trade position as well as raise the level of economic development of developing countries. Thus, it is only when we look beyond the neo-classical theory of economic integration that we can appreciate the benefits expected to be derived from such efforts. These considerations seem to be of overriding importance in the decision to integrate the economies of such developing countries as the West African states. For while there could not be sufficient justification on a "purely static analysis basis" for the creation of a West African customs union, the contrary is the case when based on dynamic grounds.[25]

On the whole, then, regional economic integration in a developing area such as West Africa is in many respects a very different phenomenon than in an economically advanced area such as Western Europe. Granted many features are the same; but many other features--important ones--are different. First, for example, we may readily point to important differences in infrastructure, market mechanisms, external dependence, administrative resources, political group structure, interdependence of social sectors, national consciousness, and ideology. Amitai Etzioni has thus argued that limited horizons, lack of administrative and political skills, and preoccupation with problems of domestic modernization all present major barriers to successful integration efforts in the developing world.[26]

Second, West European nations could afford to treat economic integration as a "matter of welfare politics" without foreclosing their "high politics option" because each started from a relatively industrialized base. The base is quite different in the developing region of the world.[27] As Nye has pointed out, integration involving developing countries seems to produce not "gradual politicization" but "overpoliticization." Such premature politicization of economic issues greatly reduces the scope for bureaucratic initiatives and quietly arranged package deals.[28] Thus conditions that may be termed requisite for successful economic integration in the developed areas cannot reasonably be applied to the developing areas. The same criteria for judging the success or failure of an integrative process cannot be applied to efforts in both the developed and developing areas. Besides, to some extent, the integrative process itself is different in developed and developing areas.

More significantly, the objectives of economic integration in developing areas are different than they are in developed areas. In the latter the overall or general objective of regional economic integration is to maintain and enhance an already existing sustained economic growth. Hence the principal economic goal is to aid the development of already established industries in highly industrialized countries through trade expansion and increased competition. In the case of developing countries, we would venture to redefine the goal of economic integration. Here, the ultimate purpose of economic integration is either to achieve an acceleration of economic growth in the partner countries, given the limited amount of scarce resources available or alternatively, to maintain the same rate of growth as before integration, but at lower cost in terms of the use of scarce resources. Put differently, regional economic integration in developing countries is seen primarily as a means of contributing to economic development. The consequences of integration are thus evaluated for their contribution to development and not necessarily to greater efficiency. Hence some economists, like Ismail Abdalla, would prefer to substitute the concept of collective self-reliance for that of economic integration, because the latter, it is contended, is "imprecise, static and irrelevant" to the development issue.[29] To this extent, therefore, regional economic integration in developing countries may more properly be called developmental regionalism, or an instrument of collective betterment, because it is designed not only to expand trade but also to encourage new industries, to help diversify national economies, and to increase the region's bargaining power with the developed nations.

UNDERDEVELOPMENT, DEPENDENCE AND INTEGRATION: THE THEORETICAL FRAMEWORK

For the most part, the theoretical framework from which this study takes its cue is the underdevelopment and dependency approach. This model provides the most useful concepts for a critical understanding of the problems of development in Africa and the Third World.[30] It seeks to explain the most pressing problems of the less-developed world in terms of relations between the developing and developed areas. Briefly, dependency is conceived as a peripheral formation and relation in the world system through which former colonies and other underdeveloped countries are exploited economically, and their backwardness is maintained over time. It thus involves a situation where effective control over the economy of a country lies outside that country. Ownership and control of the productive elements of the "national" economy are by TNCs, which do not act in the primary interests of the local country or region.

This process has shaped the political economies of the peripheral countries in such a way as to subject their development to the needs of the capitalist countries at the center. The result of such dependence for any country is continued uneven development, stagnation, unemployment, income inequality, regional disequilibria, and low integration among economic sectors. The marginalization and exploitation is effected through an apparatus of domination which, in dependent countries, takes the form of an alliance between internal privileged groups and external interests and forces, all of which benefit from the status quo.

It is through this dependency approach that we can understand both the elusiveness of development and the complexity of neocolonial structures in West Africa. It brings into focus the interrelationship of external and internal factors that enables us to enrich our understanding of the extent to which the dynamics of the international politico-economic system affect the continued underdevelopment of the West African sub-region.

Adopting the framework of dependency theory, this study attempts a critical evaluation of the extent to which ECOWAS as an economic integration scheme is sufficiently equipped in terms of resources and power to disengage, even if partially, the peripheral West African countries from inherited dependency on the former metropolitan powers and, by extension, from the existing pattern of asymmetrical economic and political relationships prevailing in the international system. The objective of dependency reduction would necessitate, first, the alteration of traditional trade and investment relationships with a view to making it possible for the West African countries to secure fuller control of their economic and political destinies. It would necessitate, second, among other things, a deliberate restructuring of the present mode of production and an adoption of regional policies to regulate external linkages in the interest of domestic development.

At its base, an important aspect of restructuring involves an increase in both the frequency and magnitude of economic exchanges between West African states, including increased trade, improved communication links, tariff reductions, industrial planning, technological acquisition, expansion of educational and technical exchanges, and the exploitation of natural resources on a sub-regional basis. The external disengagement and domestic attention to basic human needs "can be seen as compatible responses to the projections of increasing internal, continental, and global inequalities."[31] Given established transnational as well as international linkages, "disengagment externally and reorientation internally" need to be undertaken simultaneously. To sum up, then, the main objectives of ECOWAS' strategy of collective self-reliance--a logical prescription of Latin American dependency writers--are therefore to avoid dependence and to promote development.

To a great extent, then, the general thesis of this study is compatible with the main themes of the Organization of African

Unity's *Lagos Plan of Action* (LPA),[32] which falls within the *dependencia* tradition. The LPA is a major document formulated around the concepts of self-reliance and self-sustaining development and economic growth. Its main theme is on Africa's reduction of its dependence on external nations and replacement of this dependence "with a self-sustaining development strategy." On the other hand, the fundamental goals and objectives of this book are diametrically opposed to those contained in the World Bank or the Berg Report, the *Agenda for Action*[33], which is essentially a "revisionist developmentalist perspective within the modernisation *genre*." It charts no new path for Africa, breaks no new ground, offers no new perspectives. Rather, it accepts the validity of the existing approach to African development and therefore appeals for further capitalist penetration of African economies. Briefly, then, whereas the *LPA* and the present study advocate development based primarily on collective (regional) self-reliance, and therefore disengagement from the existing international economic system, the *Agenda* still espouses growth through further integration into the world economy. Thus while the *LPA* and this volume see disengagement as a prerequisite for development, the *Agenda* argues that "trickle down" will, eventually, generate growth. In essence, therefore, the perspectives and prescription of the *Lagos Plan of Action* and those of ECOWAS, as discussed in this work, are quite incompatible with those of the *Agenda*.[34]

NOTES

1. E. Oteiza and F. Sercovich, "Collective Self-Reliance: Selected Issues," *International Social Science Journal*, vol. 28, no. 4 (1976):666.
2. Osvaldo Sunkel, "National Development Policy and External Dependence in Latin America", in *Contemporary Inter-American Relations*, ed. Yale Ferguson (Englewood Cliffs, N.J.: Prentice-Hall, 1972), p. 478.
3. Joan E. Spero., *The Politics of International Economic Relations* (London: George Allen and Unwin, 1977), p. 4.
4. Barry Bracewell-Milnes, *Economic Integration in East and West* (London: Croom Helm, 1976), p. 13.
5. Cited in Dennis Swann, *The Economics of the Common Market* (Harmondsworth: Penguin, 1975), p. 11.
6. For example, Arthur Hazlewood, *Economic Integration: The East African Experience* (London: Heinemann, 1975); F. I. Nixon, *Economic Integration and Industrial Location: An East*

African Case Study (London: Longman, 1973); Abdul A. Jalloh, *The Politics and Economics of Regional Integration in Equatorial Africa* (Berkeley: University of California Press, 1973).

7. Nicholas Plessz, *Problems and Prospects of Economic Integration in West Africa* (Montreal: McGill University Press, 1968).
8. John P. Renninger, *Multinational Cooperation for Development in West Africa* (New York: Pergamon Press, 1979).
9. E. C. Edozien and E. Osagie, *Economic Integration of West Africa* (Ibadan: University of Ibadan Press, 1982).
10. Peter Robson, *Integration, Development and Equity: Economic Integration in West Africa* (London: George Allen and Unwin, 1983).
11. Uka Ezenwe, *ECOWAS and the Economic Integration of West Africa* (London: C. Hurst, 1984).
12. R. I. Onwuka, *Development and Integration in West Africa: The Case of the Economic Community of West African States (ECOWAS)* (Ife: University of Ife Press, 1982). For my review of this study see *West Africa*, 30 August 1982.
13. See, for example, Bela Balassa, *The Theory of Economic Integration*, (Homewood, Ill.: Richard D. Irwin, 1961); John Pinder, "Positive and Negative Integration: Some Problems of Economic Union in the EEC," *World Today* 24 (March 1968); and George C. Abangwu, "Systems Approach to Regional Integration in West Africa," *Journal of Common Market Studies*, vol. 13, nos. 1, 2 (1975):117-25.
14. Pinder, "Positive and Negative Integration," p. 90.
15. Bingu W. T. Mutharika, *Toward Multinational Economic Cooperation in Africa* (New York: Praeger, 1972), p. 15.
16. Ibid. See also B. T. G. Chidzero, "The Meaning of Economic Integration in Africa," *East Africa Journal* (December 1965):23.
17. ECOWAS Treaty, Articles 4-11.
18. Ernst B. Haas, "The Study of Regional Integration: Reflections on the Joy and Anguish of Pretheorizing," *International Organization*, vol. 24, no. 4 (Autumn 1970):610.
19. Isebill V. Gruhn, *Regionalism Reconsidered: The Economic Commission for Africa* (Boulder: Westview Press, 1979), p. 15.
20. Joseph Frankel, *Contemporary International Relations Theory and The Behaviour of States* (London: OUP, 1973), p. 48.
21. Jacob Viner, *The Customs Union Issue* (New York: Carnegie Endowment for International Peace, 1950); and R. G. Lipsey, "The Theory of Customs Union: A General Survey," *Economic Journal* 70 (September 1960):496-513.

22. See for example, D. Seers, "The Limitations of the Special Case," *Bulletin of the Oxford Institute of Economics and Statistics* (May 1963):83; F. Kahnert et al., *Economic Integration Among Developing Countries* (Paris: OECD Centre, 1969), pp. 15-18.

23. H. M. A. Onitiri, "Towards a West African Economic Community," *Nigerian Journal of Economic and Social Studies* vol. 5, no. 1 (March 1963):33.

24. R. F. Mikesell, "The Theory of Common Market as Applied to Regional Arrangements Among Less Developed Countries," in *International Trade Theory in a Developing World* ed. Roy Harrod and Douglas Hague (London: Macmillan, 1963).

25. Sam Olofin, "ECOWAS and the Lome Convention: An Experiment in Complementary or Conflicting Customs Union Arrangements?" *Journal of Common Market Studies*, vol. 16, no. 1 (September 1977):60.

26. Amitai Etzioni, *Political Unification: A Comparative Studies of Leaders and Forces* (New York: 1964), pp. 318-21.

27. Roger D. Hansen, "Regional Integration: Reflections on a Decade of Theoretical Efforts," *World Politics*, vol. 21, no. 2 (January 1969):261.

28. Joseph S. Nye, Jr., "Comparing Common Markets: A Revised Neo-Functionalist Model," *International Organization* vol. 24, no. 4 (Autumn 1970):831-2.

29. Ismail Sabri Abdalla, preface to "Economic Integration and Third World Collective Self-Reliance," *Third World Forum*, Occasional paper, No. 4 (1979), p. 10.

30. For a useful analysis of this, see Richard Harris, ed. *The Political Economy of Africa* (Cambridge: Schenkman, 1975); Immanuel Wallerstein, "Dependence in an Interdependent World: The Limited Possibilities of Transformation within the Capitalist World Economy," *African Studies Review* 18 (April 1974):1-27; and Colin Leys, *Underdevelopment in Kenya: The Political Economy of Neo-Colonialism* (Berkeley: University of California Press, 1975).

31. Timothy M. Shaw, "From Dependence to Self-reliance: Africa's Prospects for the Next Twenty Years," *International Journal* vol. 35, no. 4 (Autumn 1980):834.

32. Organization of African Unity, *Lagos Plan of Action for the Economic Development of Africa, 1980-2000* (Geneva: International Institute for Labour Studies, 1981).

33. The World Bank's Report, *Accelerated Development in Sub-Saharan Africa: An Agenda for Action* (Washington, D.C., 1981).

34. For a recent comparative analysis of the two documents see Robert S. Browne and Robert J. Cummings, *The Lagos Plan of Action Vs. The Berg Report: Contemporary Issues in African Economic Development* (Lawrenceville: Brunswick, 1984).

2

INTEGRATION MOVEMENTS IN DEVELOPING COUNTRIES: EXPECTATIONS AND REALITY

One of the prominent features of the contemporary international system is the heightened tendency of some state units to gravitate toward some degree of regional integration, particularly regional economic integration. This process toward economic integration, as distinct from political integration, was of relatively little importance before 1945. Although there were unsuccessful attempts in the interwar period to establish some kind of customs union in Europe, the issue of economic integration as a distinct process did not come to the forefront until after World War II, when it became very clear that the relatively small national states created in Western Europe during the past centuries no longer corresponded to the size requirements of a modern industrial economy.

Since World War II, therefore, many countries that are close neighbors or have common problems of economic development have tended to strive to maintain some degree of economic cooperation. Economic integration has become such a worldwide phenomenon that the post-world war period has been to some extent described as an "era of regional integration," or, as scholars like Haberler would have it, "the age of integration." So much is this the case that nowhere in the world today do the policy-makers and economists tackle any problem of economic development without first taking into consideration theories and trends of economic integration both at home and abroad. In most Western economic literature since 1955, the terms "integration" or "common market" have tended to become nearly synonymous with "rapid economic growth," "acceleration of economic development," or "big push."[1] For economists and social scientists today economic integration is an essential aspect of the dynamics of modern society in its continuous process of transformation. Moreover it is acknowledged as an important factor of economic development in the developing countries and of more rapid growth in the industrial ones. Vague notions about improved relations employ the term "integration" as a magic formula that can be invoked at random in order to draw the world's attention to the conditions under which joint beneficial developments can arise.

The European Coal and Steel Community (ECSC), the EEC and, to a lesser degree, the European Free Trade Association (EFTA) are undoubtedly the best known of the post-World War II regional integration efforts. The postwar progress toward integration in Europe has made a considerable impression on many countries, and the European Payments Union and the EEC are frequently, if uncritically, cited as models of integration in payments and trade, respectively, and their roles in the economic recovery and progress of postwar Europe underscored. This has encouraged, in some quarters, the idea of a simple and causal relationship between integration and economic recovery or growth.

It is against this background that during the 1950s and early 1960s, the idea of economic integration became attractive to political and economic leaders of the Third World. The potential power of the EEC triggered a desire for emulation both to reap the alleged benefits and to seek protection against the EEC's capacity to export and import goods.

The purpose of this chapter is twofold. First, to analyze briefly the dramatic resurgence of regional economic cooperation among developing countries in recent years as a key element of the New International Economic Order (NIEO). Such a background is essential because the full implications of the efforts to achieve economic cooperation in the West African sub-region cannot be fully realized unless it is seen within the context of the struggle of the developing world to achieve a new world economic order. And second, to analyze the experiences, issues, and prospects of regional economic integration schemes among developing countries.

ECONOMIC COOPERATION: A KEY ELEMENT OF NIEO

Various facets of the NIEO have been discussed extensively since the basic resolutions were adopted on 1 May 1974 by the United Nations General Assembly. The new order has been de-

picted as being primarily a movement of the majority of the
world's countries to obtain greater influence over the decision-
making processes of international economic bodies; as an economic
phenomenon calling for better distribution of the world's product
or at least as a psychological manifestation of seeking an end to
neo-colonialism as this emerges in differences in production
patterns and in income disparities between rich and poor countries
and which it is argued can be corrected only by altering the
nature of commodity trade, technology transfers, and investment
and debt relationships. The availability of literature on NIEO
obviates the need for discussion of any of these issues. What is
done here is to examine briefly the concept of regional economic
cooperation as an important aspect of the NIEO.

An issue of particular significance in the context of the NIEO
with which this study is concerned relates to the question of
cooperation amongst developing countries themselves. This concept has for long been recognized, and even reflected in certain
schemes for regional integration and cooperation. But it received
a major impetus in the General Assembly's proclamation on a
NIEO when it came to be embodied in the wider theme of what
has been called collective self-reliance,[2] which has been completely absent in the International Development Strategy for the
Second United Nations Development Decade. It is a theme that is
gaining momentum and acquiring increasing political importance
as a reflection of the growing self-awareness of the countries of
the Third World.

The concept of collective self-reliance represents a clear-cut
alternative to the present dependent type of evolution, considered
to be the crucial feature of underdevelopment. The concept,
therefore, seems to be very much connected with--and can hardly
be understood outside of--the dependency framework of interpretation for underdevelopment examined already in the introductory
chapter. Collective self-reliance has thus become an essential
component of "alternative" strategies for elimination of dependence
and exploitation which have been responsible for the distortion of
the development process throughout much of the Third World.

There are two facets to the theme of collective self-reliance as
reflected in the Programme of Action on the Establishment of a
NIEO. One is the notion of cooperation by the developing countries for the purpose of improving their collective bargaining
power vis-à-vis the outside world, of mobilizing countervailing
pressure, of acquiring muscle and applying leverage. The other
facet is the notion of intensifying trade and other linkages between themselves. This latter concept has itself two aspects. One

is intensified cooperation by groups of countries at the regional or sub-regional level in various schemes and enterprises. This study of ECOWAS and, indeed the various regional groupings discussed in the subsequent section of this chapter, falls under this facet.[3] The other is the notion--of some political significance--of cooperation across the board, so to speak, encompassing all the countries of the Third World.[4]

The concept of cooperation among developing countries embodied in the theme of collective self-reliance is further developed by the declaration and plan of action on industrial development issued at the end of the second general conference of UNIDO held in Lima in March 1975; the resolution on "Development and International Economic Cooperation" adopted by the Seventh Special Session of the General Assembly; and the resolution adopted by the UNCTAD IV Session at Nairobi in May 1976. Outside the UN and its agencies, too, cooperation among developing countries was, for example, the subject of three major meetings in 1976--in Manila, Colombo, and Mexico City. These declarations and resolutions represent, on one hand, genuine desires for a restructuring of international economic relations and, on the other, an attempt to offer a reasonable basis for cooperation among developing nations.

It must be stressed, however, that in spite of these declarations and resolutions, very little progress has been achieved when it comes to concrete measures to reorganize international economic relations on bases that are both realistic, just, and equitable. The confrontation between the developing countries and developed countries that manifested itself at the Sixth Special Session of the United Nations General Assembly; the failure of the developing countries to achieve most of the objectives that they sought for, for the purpose of restructuring the world economic order at the Fourth Session of UNCTAD at Nairobi, in May 1976;[5] the breakdown of the Paris North-South Dialogue in June 1977; the failure of UNCTAD V at Manila in June 1979; the setback of the UNIDO III in New Delhi in January-February 1980; the disappointment at Cancun in October 1981; and the frustrations at the UNCTAD VI in Belgrade in June 1983[6]--all suggest that the advanced industrial countries are not prepared to make the sacrifices necessary to achieve a New Economic Order. In these circumstances, it is essential that Third World countries consolidate their own economic base in order to be able to resist the eventual pressures and to negotiate successfully their participation in the international division of labor under more favorable conditions. The only leverage available to them is in the development of their own institutions of economic and trading cooperation. Thus, the salvation of the developing countries lies in mapping out their own strategy to solve their economic problems. They are to foster mutual cooperation so as to impart strength to their national endeavors to fortify their independence. For although each individual country might be weak, President Nyerere has said:

> Together, or even in groups, we are much less weak. We have the capability to help each other in many ways, each gaining in the process. And as a combined group we can meet the wealthy nations on very different terms; for though they may not need any one of us for their own economic health, they cannot cut themselves off from all of us.[7]

It is within this framework that the establishment of regional groupings that foster economic development through self-reliance appears essential. Such groupings embody the potential for joint action by developing countries that will strengthen their capacity to negotiate with developed countries and reduce their dependency on them. For in some form of unity, remarked Charles Pentland, there is "strength to resist exploitation and manipulation by major economic powers and multinational corporations, to resolve re-gionally shared economic and social problems, and to force struc-tural reform of the international economy."[8] Furthermore, ex-pansion of trade and financial cooperation among developing countries, coupled with increased production for their domestic markets, will undoubtedly affect the economic relations between developed and developing countries.

It is on the basis of such considerations, as well as in response to the developments of the European Communities, that common markets, customs unions, free trade areas, and other devices for economic integration of more limited scope are becoming fashion-able in the developing world. There is now hardly a geographical area in the world where some kind of economic integration scheme cannot be found. Some of the schemes have been in operation for quite some time. Many, in contrast, are of a recent vintage, and some have had a rather checkered history. The general thrust, however, is unmistakably toward the strengthening of economic relations among developing countries and the invigoration of their joint efforts to tap fully their development potential. This trend has received a great deal of impetus since the early 1970s, following the dramatic changes in the world economy and the serious repercussions that these have had on the economies of the developing countries.

REGIONAL ECONOMIC COOPERATION: BETWEEN STANDSTILL AND PROGRESS

Although the record of attempts at political and economic integration among developing countries is disillusioning, ironically, the fervor with which integration is proposed as a response to the problems of developing countries has increased in spite of the experience of integration. In Latin America in the nineteenth century and Africa in the early 1960s, the first steps were taken toward the establishment of broad continental common markets. A similar approach has never been tried in Asia, probably because of various overriding political factors. The heart of Asia is occupied by two major world powers, the Soviet Union and China; on the continent's southern perimeter are two warring but large and economically self-contained units, India and Pakistan; and military conflicts have been raging across southeast Asia for the past quarter of a century. But in both Latin America and Africa (if Latin America can be considered a continent) the continental approach seemed to be especially attractive on political grounds.

Latin America

The concept of integration in Latin America has a long if troubled history. Ever since the independence movement which led to the disappearance of the Spanish and Portuguese empires from that part of the world in the early nineteenth century, "continental nationalists" have dreamed of some form of a Latin American Union. After the failure of the early attempts at creating a political confederation, the vision of a United Latin America gave way in the mid-1880s to the idea of an inter-American system and to the rhetoric of "Pan Americanism." But the concept of Latin American integration did not die. In the late 1940s and early 1950s the movement toward regional cooperation resurfaced, this time with an emphasis on economic integration. Under the intellectual leadership and creative influence of Raul Prebisch, the executive secretary of the United Nations Economic Commission for Latin America (ECLA), the Latin American states turned to economic union to resolve the dilemma of import substitution industrialization.[9] Beset by foreign trade problems, lacking external capital assistance, and moved by the idea of spiritual and cultural unity, Latin Americans found the proposal for regional cooperation attractive.

The 1960s were the halcyon years of Latin American integration: there were "so many attempts at integration, so many problems."[10] By the mid-1970s, if not earlier, it was clear that Latin American integration was in serious trouble. After an initial surge, trade among the member states of the various economic unions stagnated at a relatively low level. For example, the LAFTA--founded in 1960 to replace the original idea of a Latin American Common Market--had been stagnating for years. It was finally dissolved on 12 August 1980 at a meeting of foreign ministers of 11 Latin American countries held in Montevideo. The ministers adopted a different, and unprecedented path to integration, agreeing to set up a new institutional framework, the Latin American Integration Association (LAIA), which was expected to supersede LAFTA from the beginning of 1981.[11]

The Central American Common Market (CACM), also established in 1960, has been paralyzed for a long time. The outbreak of hostilities between El Salvador and Honduras in 1969 wrecked the CACM, and subsequent efforts to revive it have been only partially successful. The CACM is still in a state of seemingly permanent reorganization. The Economic Union of Caribbean countries established in 1968 as a free trade union (CARIFTA) and converted in 1973 to a Common Market (CARICOM) also shows signs of disintegration. The Andean Group, established in 1969 within the LAFTA structure to advance more quickly toward a common market in the Andean sub-region, is after initial successes also subject to serious problems. It is now trying to reconstitute itself following Chile's withdrawal in 1976 over a dispute on the common treatment of foreign investment.[12] Undeniably, the economic integration schemes launched optimistically in the 1960s were largely moribund in the 1970s.

Asia

Just at about the same time that regional integration schemes were being created in Latin America, Asian economists associated with the UN Economic Commission for Asia and the Far East (ECAFE) initiated studies of the prospects for regional economic cooperation in South and Southeast Asia. ECAFE's Bangkok Resolution of 1960 calling for greater attention to international regionalism, intraregional trade promotion, and regional cooperation to achieve economic development and greater productivity was a landmark in the history of economic cooperation in Asia.[13] Since

1960, therefore, collective action at the regional level to secure national goals has become an increasingly characteristic and important feature of Asian international relations. Over the period from 1959 and 1975, regional cooperation increased dramatically in Asia. The latest and most successful attempt at regional cooperation is the declaration of Association of South East Asian Nations (ASEAN) signed in Bangkok on 8 August 1967 by five of the eleven Southeast Asian states--Indonesia, Malaysia, the Philippines, Singapore, and Thailand.[14] ASEAN came into existence as part of the settlement ending confrontation between Indonesia and Malaysia at a moment when relations between the member states were still very uneasy.

In coming to some interim conclusions, it can be said that ASEAN is showing more promise as a viable regional economic scheme than those in Latin America. It cannot be denied that the world has taken ASEAN very seriously as shown by its negotiations with the major trading countries and associations of the developed world. So far it can be said that the Association of South East Asian Nations has grown beyond its critical planning phase and has developed into the most important instrument for its member countries.[15]

Africa

In Africa, too, economic integration has been in the forefront of discussion since the massive movement toward independence in the late 1950s and early 1960s. There was immediate recognition that, while independence had been the primary goal, African countries were largely artificial by-products of the colonial scramble of the era of the 1884-85 Berlin Conference; many African countries were too small to be economically viable and the transformation of political into economic independence necessarily required concerted action.

Against this background, it is not surprising that economic integration has been seen as a means of helping to overcome the disadvantages of small size, low per capita incomes, small populations, and narrow resource bases, and of making possible a greater rate of economic growth and development. It has also been seen as a means of consolidating the political independence of African countries and thereby strengthening their overall position vis-à-vis that of the developed countries, especially the former metropolitan powers. In brief, economic integration or cooperation in general is not only desirable; it is necessary if Africa is to industrialize, develop intra-African trade, reduce her dependency on vulnerable and fluctuating overseas markets, mobilize and maximize scarce resources of capital and skills, and finally forge the way to effective African unity, both political and economic. This has been eloquently underscored by the *Lagos Plan of Action*, which recognizes the importance of regional economic cooperation and integration as necessary instruments for pursuing the objectives of national and collective self-reliance. Hence the discussion of regionalism in virtually every chapter of the *Lagos Plan*. It constitutes an integral condition for implementation of the *Plan*. And, as recent commentators like Browne and Cummings have succinctly remarked, "Obstacles or not, without regional integration the *LPA* collapses as a concept" and strategy.[16]

Even before the departure of the colonial powers African leaders had realized the significance of economic cooperation. The historic All-African Peoples Conference held in Accra in December 1958 called for the removal of customs and other restrictions on trade among African states and the conclusion of multilateral payments agreements, with a view to enhancing economic exchanges and the consequent establishment of an African Common Market.[17] Since independence, African countries have attempted various forms of collective self-reliance through regional economic cooperation as a means of accelerating their socio-economic development. According to Adebayo Adedeji, executive secretary of the Economic Commission for Africa (ECA), there were by 1977 "over 20 intergovernmental multi-sectoral economic cooperation organizations" in Africa and "about one hundred single sector multinational organizations that are meant to promote technical and economic cooperation in Africa."[18] Many of these were established in the 1960s. But the decade was also characterized by the decline of several regional groupings.

I may cite, for example, the East African Community (EAC), which experienced such acute tensions in the 1960s that by the end of the decade the level of economic integration had declined. And by June 1977 the whole structure of the EAC had disintegrated. Nor did the Customs and Economic Union of Central Africa (UDEAC) set up in January 1966 fare any better; restrictions on the opening of markets and noncompliance with its rules have sapped it of most of its energy as an integration system. Also, the cooperation agreements of the nine-member Maghreb Permanent Consultative Committee, formed in November 1965, have never been ratified. So far, concrete achievements in Africa in the fields of regional cooperation have been very modest or nonexistent. The question, then, arises, why so little progress and such faltering steps?

The problems and constraints of African economic cooperation are many, and seemingly intractable. I may mention in brief, the problem arising from the charms of national sovereignty, however exiguous; and the constraints relating to the difficulty in reaching acceptable formulas and procedures as to the way in which the costs and benefits of economic cooperation should be shared. Another important constraint is the failure of political initiatives and declared collective goodwill to be matched by practical action. Besides, as a recent study of the ECA has concluded, there are "mutual suspicion and differences of political outlook arising from heterogeneous cultures and varied colonial heritage, fear of being dominated by others and an insular view imposed by ultra-nationalism are all delicate problems which require tact and patience."[19] Political and ideological cleavages also seem to threaten even existing and otherwise viable cooperative arrangements such as the case of the defunct East African Community.

Because of these key obstacles and constraints, the creation of regional cooperation in Africa is often "no more than a declaration of intent and an indication of continental alignments."[20] Despite the rhetoric of Pan-African solidarity and the paraphernalia of elaborate decision-making structures, few groupings have advanced either unity or development. Thus regional cooperation has not been an easy panacea for Africa's inheritance of balkanization and underdevelopment.

Ironically, despite this disillusioning record, the fervor with which regional cooperation has been proposed as a response to the problems of Africa has increased tremendously in recent years. Since the early 1970s, the world recession and its severe impact on Africa's economic performance have, if anything, strengthened interest in the establishment of new regional groups and the geographical extension of existing ones. This trend was reinforced at the November 1984 OAU Addis Ababa summit where the African leaders reaffirmed in an important resolution their "solemn commitment to put together" their collective effort to implement the *Lagos Plan of Action* through the process of regional economic cooperation and integration.[21] Hence, the past several years have witnessed the re-emergence of a rash of regional integration schemes in Africa as more or less explicit challenges to the external domination of the continent inherited from the colonial era. Among the most ambitious and dynamic is the ECOWAS, which is the subject of this study. Besides ECOWAS the two newest initiatives are in Southern Africa. The first is the Southern African

Development Coordination Conference (SADCC), which was formally inaugurated in April 1980 by the signing of the Lusaka Declaration on Economic Liberation by the nine Southern African states. The second is the Preferential Trade Area for Eastern and Southern African States (PTA), which was concluded in Lusaka in December 1981 by nine out of the potential eighteen states.[22] PTA was finally launched in Zimbabwe in July 1984. The latest initiative is the treaty signed in Libreville in October 1983 to establish the Economic Community of the States of Central Africa (CEEAC), comprising the present members of UDEAC and those of the Economic Community of the Great Lakes.[23] This is intended to be the Central African equivalent of the ECOWAS.

The basic objective of these new regional integration schemes is the same: to reduce dependence of their respective member states on the external forces that seek to influence the economic policies and directions of African states; to help to improve the bargaining position of African countries, thus contributing to their development potential through the broader strategy for promoting a NIEO; and to coordinate the development programs in the different sectors and subsectors as a means of accelerating the rate of economic growth and development. The underlying premise is the desire by African states and leaders to determine as far as possible their own economic policies based on their national aspirations, natural resources, and political ideologies outside the influence of developed countries.

But what have the new regional schemes achieved so far, in only a few years of existence? Because of the recent emphasis on the concept of collective self-reliance among developing countries, it is too often assumed that any form of economic integration or cooperation will have a positive impact on development. Yet schemes such as ECOWAS, PTA, SADCC, or CEEAC will not automatically lead to accelerated development. As Shaw and Grieve have warned, regional integration "is not always an escape from Africa's inheritance of subordination," and it may not "advance disintegration from the global economy."[24] Indeed, without a well-considered and intensive effort in restructuring the economy and without adequate planning, regional schemes may lead to "regional inequalities and continued dependence."

Viewed from this "radical approach," with its focus on dependence and underdevelopment from a global perspective, just how far have the new regional initiatives attempted to fundamentally restructure both national and regional political economies as the prerequisite for integration and development? Or to what extent have they, for example, initiated efforts toward intraregional trade or horizontal exchange in order to overcome an inheritance of vertical integration with former metropolises, leading toward greater self-reliance at both national and collective levels? How far have they effectively challenged the established pattern of trade and division of labor? Given such complex problems, although regional economic integration is certainly important as a means of loosening the developmental constraints confronting African states, it is unlikely to be an easy process. It is against this background that I attempt to examine the initiatives, experience, progress, and prospect of ECOWAS as a case study.

NOTES

1. Ninon Maritano, *A Latin American Economic Community: History, Policies and Problems* (Notre Dame, Ind.: University of Notre Dame Press, 1970), p. ix.
2. Gamini Corea, "UNCTAD and the New International Economic Order." *International Affairs*, vol. 53, no. 2 (April 1977):184. (Text of the 25th Stevenson Lecture, given at the London School of Economics on December 6, 1976.)
3. For details, see Davidson Nicol et al., eds., *Regionalism and the New International Economic Order* (New York: Pergamon Press, 1981).
4. See E. Laszlo with J. Kurtzman and A. K. Bhattacharya, *RCDC: Regional Cooperation Among Developing Countries: The New Imperative of Development In the 1980s* (New York: Pergamon Press, 1981).
5. A. Adedeji, "Collective Self-Reliance in Developing Africa: Scope, Prospects and Problems" (Keynote address presented at the International Conference on ECOWAS, Lagos, August 1976).
6. See Robert Ramsay, "UNCTAD's Failures: The Rich Get Richer," *International Organization*, vol. 38, no. 2 (Spring 1984):387-97.
7. Julius K. Nyerere, *Non-Alignment in the 1970s* (Dar-es-Salaam: Government Printing Press, 1970), p. 12.
8. Charles Pentland, "The Regionalism of World Politics: Concepts and Evidence," *International Journal* 30 (Autumn 1975):602.
9. Robert D. Bond, "Regionalism in Latin America: Prospects for the Latin American Economic System (SELA)" *International Organization*, vol. 32, no. 2 (Spring 1978):402.

10. Klaus Dressel, "Latin American Economic Integration: Between Standstill and Progress," *Development and Cooperation* (May 1977):20.
11. Diana Tussie, "Farewell to LAFTA," *South* 2 (November 1980):49
12. For further details, see Rafael Vargas-Hidalgo, "The Crisis of the Andean Pact: Lessons for Integration Among Developing Countries," *Journal of Common Market Studies*, vol. 17, no. 3 (March 1979):213-26.
13. James N. Schubert, "Toward a 'Working Peace System' in Asia: Organizational Growth and State Participation in Asian Regionalism," *International Organization*, vol. 32, no. 2 (1978):449.
14. H. Monte Hill, "Community Formation within ASEAN," *International Organization*, vol. 32, no. 3 (1978):569.
15. For a critical assessment of the ASEAN see Adamo A. Castro, "The ASEAN Experience in Economic Cooperation" (Paper presented at an international seminar on planning Economic Integration: Experiences, Policies, and Models, West Berlin, November 1979).
16. Robert S. Browne and Robert J. Cummings, *The Lagos Plan of Action vs. The Berg Report: Contemporary Issues in African Economic Development* (Lawrenceville: Brunswick, 1984), p. 37.
17. Bingu Mutharika, *Toward Multinational Economic Cooperation in Africa* (New York: Praeger, 1972), p. 12.
18. Adebayo Adedeji, "The Need for Concrete Action," in *Regional Co-operation in Africa: Problems and Prospects* (Addis Ababa: African Association for Public Administration and Management, 1977), p. 10.
19. Ibid., p. 32.
20. Timothy M. Shaw, "Regional Cooperation and Conflict in Africa," *International Journal* vol. 30, no. 4 (Autumn 1975):680.
21. OAU Doc., *Resolution on Inter-African Economic Co-operation and Integration*, Addis Ababa, AHG/Res. 131 (20), November 1984.
22. For a recent discussion of SADCC and PTA see Douglas G. Anglin, "Economic Liberation and Regional Cooperation in Southern Africa: SADCC and PTA," *International Organization*, vol. 37, no. 4 (Autumn 1983):681-711; Christopher R. Hill, "Regional Co-operation in Southern Africa," *African Affairs*, vol. 82, no. 327 (April 1983):215-39; and *The Courier* 84 (March-April 1984), yellow pages xiii-xv.

23. For details of the treaty establishing CEEAC see "North-South Monitor," *Third World Quarterly*, vol. 6, no. 2 (April 1984):477.
24. Timothy M. Shaw and Malcolm J. Grieve, "Dependence as an Approach to Understanding Continuing Inequalities in Africa," *Journal of Developing Areas*, vol. 13, no. 3 (April 1979):243.

3

THE EVOLUTION OF A
WEST AFRICAN COMMUNITY

There has been no generally accepted geographical definition
of West Africa, neither has there been any universally accepted
notion of what countries constitute West Africa. While the core of
the region has not been in dispute, there has always been a considerable divergence of opinion among geographers "as to the exact
definition of its outer limits. . . ."[1] One geographer, Harrison
Church, has defined it broadly as the whole of the area lying west
of the boundary between Nigeria and the Cameroon Republic.
This would include 19 different countries and several islands.[2] In
1961 the ECA took broadly the same definition, but excluded the
islands.[3] For the purpose of this study, I have accepted the recent
definition by Professor Boateng which includes all the present 16
member states of ECOWAS, excluding the Spanish Sahara which
he considers as forming part of the sub-region.[4] These countries
cover approximately one-fifth of the land mass of the African
continent and contain about half the total population of black
Africa.

Historically, West Africa was the advance guard of the
nationalist revolution that swept away the European colonial
empires in Africa in the two decades following World War II.
Since coming into power, the new West African leaders, like their
counterparts elsewhere in Africa, had been absorbed in the immediate tasks of governing and in the urgent drive for economic
progress. The ultimate objective was to bring about the reality of
the "Nation" in the sub-region by creating independent states out
of the colonial territories. These leaders were acutely aware that
the new political units which had resulted from the breakup of the

French, Portuguese, and British colonial empires were as yet "by no means always 'Nations'; rather, they represent the shells of territorial independence in which the kernel of national identity has been planted by the independence movements."[5] It therefore became the major task of the new West African governments "to provide the soil in which the seed can grow." The most urgent of these tasks was the promotion of national unity and economic development. In the case of the latter, the governments pledged themselves to a program of modernization and development of the economy designed to bring to their people the benefits of the higher living standards that industrial and technological skills have brought to other parts of the world. This was held to be a logical sequence to the attainment of political independence.

During the period 1957 to 1962 when most of the countries in West Africa had achieved political independence, questions were raised as to whether or not political independence could bring about economic cooperation and emancipation. The radical leaders like Ghana's Kwame Nkrumah held the doctrinaire view that political unity must precede economic integration. Hence the Ghana-Guinea-Mali Union was formed from 1959 to 1963 on the initiative of Nkrumah, with an emphasis more on political rather than on rational economic considerations. This union was the first post-independence attempt to bring about a rapprochement between countries previously separated by different colonial allegiances. On the other hand, there were the moderate and conservative leaders like Houphouet-Boigny of the Ivory Coast who thought that functional cooperation when reinforced by economic integration could be a positive approach toward political unification. The lack of tangible progress in either direction shows the need for a serious re-examination of past efforts and re-evaluation of the prospects for regional economic integration in West Africa.

This chapter attempts to do three things. First, to examine the relevant features of the West African sub-region, in order to understand better the complexities of the problem. Second, to review critically the efforts at regional economic integration in the past. This is necessary, because although the actual steps that have been taken to create ECOWAS are mostly, if not all, post-1970 in origin, the idea of such a coming together is not unique to the West African independence period. Quite the contrary, West African history is littered with proposals and arrangements that were designed to foster West African unity. And finally, to analyze the main events leading to the formation of ECOWAS.

WEST AFRICA: A PORTRAIT OF NEO-COLONIAL ECONOMY

The intricacy of the economic, political, and social dimensions of the West African sub-region has been acknowledged and highlighted by previous writers on this subject. As one ECA study puts it, "The West African sub-region is the most varied in Africa as to the size of countries, degree of economic development, language and economic internal and external links."[6] Plessz, on the other hand, states that "West Africa occupies a very particular position in so far as integration is concerned,"[7] while Adedeji aptly adds that "a study of integration efforts in West Africa is inevitably a study in frustration."[8] For if Africa as a whole is badly fragmented, West Africa is even more affected than elsewhere on the continent. This is a direct result of the intense competition for trade and territorial control that took place among the European powers between the fifteenth and twentieth centuries.

West Africa represents the most heterogeneous conglomeration of states in all Africa, and has the largest number of mini-states. The 16 countries of ECOWAS constituting the West African sub-region together occupy a geographical area of 6,141,153 square km., and share among themselves a total population of almost 150 million in 1980. They, however, vary considerably both in size and population. Cape Verde, the smallest of them, has an area of only 4,033 square km. and a population of less than half a million. The corresponding figures for Niger are 1,267,000 square km. and 5.3 million (1980), while Nigeria has a total land area of 923,768 square km. and an estimated population of 84.7 million, representing nearly 60 percent of the sub-region's total population. Table 3-1 illustrates the various sizes of the ECOWAS countries as well as the population, income, and growth. Except for Ghana, Guinea, the Ivory Coast, Nigeria, and Senegal a vast majority of the population in ECOWAS countries live in the rural areas and/or cities with population of less than 500,000 people. In countries such as Ghana, Guinea, and Senegal urban population has increased tremendously.[9]

Other significant characteristics of West Africa are first, the level of poverty and, second, the standard of living in the sub-region which is one of the lowest in the world.[10] The average GNP was about $760 per capita in 1980, including subsistence incomes. Seven of the 16 member states of ECOWAS are officially listed among the 30 least developed countries of the world. These are Benin, Cape Verde, Gambia, Guinea, Mali, Niger, and Burkina Faso. In all, 13 of the 16 ECOWAS members are listed among 42

TABLE 3-1. ECOWAS: Population, Income, and Growth (GNP--1980)

Country	Population (m.) 1980	Area ('000 sq.km)	Population density (inhabitants per sq.km)	Rate of population growth 1970-80	Aggregate ($m.)	% of sub-group	% of ECOWAS	Per capita ($) 1980	GNP per capita (% real av. annual growth) 1960-80	Real GPD growth (% average annual growth) 1960-70	Real GPD growth (% average annual growth) 1970-80
CEAO											
Ivory Coast	8.3	322	25.8	5.0	9,550	56	8	1,150	2.5	8.0	6.7[a]
Burkina Faso	6.1	274	22.3	1.8	1,280	7	1	210	0.1	3.0	3.5
Mali	7.0	1,240	5.6	2.7	1,340	8	1	190	1.4	3.3	4.9
Mauritania	1.5	1,031	1.6	2.5	660[b]	4	1	440[b]	1.6[a]	NA	1.7
Niger	5.3	1,267	4.2	2.8	1,760	10	2	330	-1.6	2.9	2.7
Senegal	5.7	196	29.1	2.8	2,560	15	2	450	-0.3	2.5	2.5[a]
	33.9	4,330			17,150	100	15	510			
Mano River Union											
Guinea	5.4	246	21.9	2.9	1,590	45	1	290	0.3	3.5	3.3
Liberia	1.9	111	17.1	3.4	1,000	28	1	530	1.5	5.1	1.7
Sierra Leone	3.5	72	48.6	2.6	980	27	1	280	*	4.3	1.6
	10.8	429			3,570	100	3	330			
Other ECOWAS countries											
Benin	3.4	113	30.1	2.6	1,050		1	310	0.4	2.6	3.3
Ghana	11.7	239	49.0	3.0	4,920		4	420	-1.0	2.1	-0.1
Nigeria	84.7	924	91.7	2.5	85,510		75	1,010	4.1	3.1	6.5
Togo	2.5	57	43.9	2.5	1,020		*	410	3.0	8.5	3.4
Guinea-Bissau	0.8	36	22.2	NA	130		*	160	NA	NA	NA
The Gambia	0.6	11	54.5	3.1[a]	150		*	250	1.7	NA	NA
Cape Verde	0.3	4	75.0	2.0[a]	100		*	300	NA	NA	NA
Total ECOWAS	148.7	6,143			113,600		100	760			

[a] 1970-79

[b] The estimates of GNP and growth rate for Mauritania should be treated with reserve. Alternative World Bank estimates (e.g., Atlas) suggest a substantially lower GNP ($530m.) and a negative annual growth rate (-0.7%).

*less than half total unit shown.

NA not available

Source: World Bank, 1981 World Bank Atlas (Washington, D.C.: The World Bank, 1982) and World Bank, World Development Report 1982 (New York: Oxford University Press, 1982).

countries that are at the greatest disadvantage in the world economy.[11]

One other important feature in West Africa is the artificiality of the frontiers or national boundaries. For if frontiers are artificial and arbitrary on the African continent in general, they are absurd and capricious in this sub-region. They run inward from the coast, cutting across tribal, cultural, and linguistic borders. Thus, for example, the Ewe-speaking people are still divided between the Republics of Ghana and Togo; some Yoruba speakers live in the Republic of Benin while the majority of their kinsmen are Nigerians. To this may be added the great African political divides: French, English, and Portuguese-speaking regions and, until the EEC-ACP Lome Convention of February 1975, the EEC associates and nonassociates.

Since independence the economies of the West African countries have exhibited a variety of structural characteristics that reflect and reinforce the sub-region's dependency on the capitalist world system. As these economies have been structured to meet the needs of that system, their performance since the early 1960s must be evaluated within this context. Salient aspects of the structural characteristics of the economies are reviewed in this section, though the discussion is by no means exhaustive.

A significant aspect of this structural dependence is that all the West African countries do not only belong to one or other of various currency and trading groups; they also exhibit the continuity of the presence of the metropole in most sectors. Thus, though "Independence in Africa meant a change of the dramatis personae in the state; it did not involve the general re-establishment of national control over the economy or society. . . .The new ruling classes, especially in the more dependent countries, were able to rule only through collaboration with external interests. . . ."[12] This trend has effectively conditioned the development of the West African countries and consequently delayed the emergence in many of any signs of building-up developmental capacity for autonomous decision making. Since the ex-colonial powers in West Africa employ different methods to maintain neo-colonial control, it is useful to group the ECOWAS countries according to the metropolitan power with which they are linked. France and Britain being the dominant ex-colonial powers in West Africa, the analysis will concentrate mostly on them and their former colonies.

One of the ECOWAS groups--and perhaps the one whose dependence on the former metropole is most pervasive and intensive--is composed of the former French colonies whose monetary system, with the exception of Guinea, are very closely linked to the French franc. Their membership in the franc zone is central to the whole issue of France's relations with its ex-colonies. It is this link which has so far given Paris almost total economic, financial, and ultimately, political control. The surrender of these states to monetary control from France in effect deprives them of the right to exercise an essential component of their sovereignty. Not only has this placed serious constraints on their monetary independence, it has also created the conditions for privileged trading ties between France and these countries, "favouring of French capital and dependence on foreign capital . . ." and reinforced the relative power of the French enterprises already in existence, and the continuation of dependence on export commodities to the international market.[13]

One noticeable result of this control from Paris is that movements in the exchange rate of the French franc--as occurred in late 1969 and early 1974, or any French devaluation, which is decided exclusively by Paris--automatically affect the trading balance and the balance of payments of these countries by increasing their already considerable external debt. On the other hand, these states can neither revalue nor devalue their currencies independently. Furthermore, as a consequence of the existence of a fixed parity with the CFA franc, the franc zone has created an avenue for the free transfer of capital. There is no control over the repatriation of capital abroad and this is a basic impediment to any accummulation of capital domestically. It has enhanced the position of foreign capital in the banking system and has naturally left an open path for French capital into the country. Given the structure of foreign capital present in all the embryonic industrial sectors of Francophone Africa, this free transfer has encouraged the investment of TNCs based in France through local subsidiaries; this has again stimulated the outflow of capital.[14]

Besides, the structure of the economies of these countries is characterized by the paucity of indigenous control over key sectors. Countries like Senegal and the Ivory Coast have a very high proportion of foreign firms and technical assistants. In the case of the former, a critical Senegalese has observed that industrialization remains largely in foreign hands, which has meant retaining overseas linkages rather than generating domestic ones.[15] Similarly, the much-heralded boom that the Ivory Coast has enjoyed since the 1950s has been superficially propelled for the benefit of the expatriate population who dominate the entire economy. Moreover, both development efforts and investment decisions are largely determined by the interests of metropolitan investment as well as those of the Westernized elites--the so-called "comprador class" or "auxilliary bourgeoisie" who control the political machinery and collaborate with the foreign capitalists to deplete the resources of the territory.[16] As Samir Amin has argued in a revealing study, the type of growth that the Ivory Coast has experienced over the years "does not automatically result in an economic take-off, but in an increased external dependency and the blocking of growth." He has characterized the Ivory Coast example as "growth without development."[17] In other words, there has been negligible "spill over" from growth to development.

B. The second ECOWAS group of countries comprises the four Anglophone states of the Gambia, Sierra Leone, Ghana, and Nigeria, which have been members of the sterling bloc, and still share membership in the Commonwealth. On the eve of independence, each of these countries acquired independent currencies issued by their respective central banks. Although the strength of the economy of each depends on levels of foreign exchange reserves and balance of payments, each country still maintains a sterling link. Unlike France, Britain is more thoroughly integrated into the growing world-imperialist system. The British have not chosen the technique of continued direct involvement in their former colonies; instead they have allowed for a concentration of effort by TNCs. Resources are extracted and employed for the benefit of Britain in particular, and international capitalism in general, without the more overt use of direct national power over the internal affairs of former dependencies. Consequently, the former colonies of Britain give the appearance of having greater control over their own destinies than do those of France. This illusion is quickly dispelled, however, by the realization that the economic dependence of both groups on externally based capitalism is roughly equivalent. For example, while French monopolies control 95.7 percent of Niger's economy, 87.4 percent of Senegal's, and 80 percent of Ivory Coast's; according to 1974 UN sources on TNCs, British monopolies control 87 percent of the Gambia's economy, and 84.4 percent of Sierra Leone's. In Nigeria, foreign monopolies continue to control 65 percent of all industrial investment and a similar percentage holds true for Ghana as well.[18]

In addition to the French- and English-speaking groups, there are today four ECOWAS countries that do not belong to either international community but stand in a more or less isolated position. These countries are Liberia which belongs to the dollar area and uses the U.S. dollar as legal tender; Guinea which has established its own separate central bank and national currency; and

Guinea-Bissau and Cape Verde which have their currencies linked to that of Portugal.

Of considerable significance is the trade pattern of the ECOWAS sub-region.[19] For if trade dependence is a characteristic feature of developing countries, such dependence is chronic in the ECOWAS countries. As Table 3-2 shows, trade of the sub-region with developed countries for the period 1968-74, for example, averaged about 87.0 percent of total trade while intraregional exchange for the same period was on the average about 3.4 percent only. As detailed below in this study, the channels of the ECOWAS countries are geared toward enhancing trade with former colonial powers in particular and with the industrial countries in general. The direction of trade between them follows the lines and patterns of dependence. As Kwame Nkrumah painfully remarked, "Our trade . . . is not between ourselves. It is turned towards Europe and embraces us as providers of low-priced primary materials in exchange for the more expensive finished goods we import."[20]

On the whole, therefore, it can be said with justification that the destiny of the ECOWAS countries is still in large measure shaped outside the sub-region and inside the sub-region by foreign forces. Even the much-heralded Lome Convention of February 1975 between the EEC and the African, Caribbean, and Pacific (ACP) countries has not, in the last resort, created a qualitatively new relationship between industrial Europe and the developing ECOWAS countries.[21] The central problem for the sub-region, therefore, has always been how the ECOWAS countries can break free from the historical conditions in which they find themselves. For since all social systems seek to ensure their continued existence, it follows that dominant countries will try to retain the bases of their dominance over others and thus see to it that dependent countries do not follow their "dream of independence." This, then, is the crux of the matter. By the early 1970s, when dislocations in the international economy revealed the extreme vulnerability of almost all the countries in the sub-region, the West African governments were faced with a choice between continuing to support the inherited structure of dependence individually or beginning to build collectively an integrated economy. By creating ECOWAS in May 1975, the West African countries appeared to have opted for the latter strategy. But whether ECOWAS as an institution can really transform the West African economies from a dependent structure responsive to the external demands of the world market to an integrated economy responsive

TABLE 3-2. Share of Intra-West African Trade* in Total External Trade (U.S. $ million)

Description of Trade	1968	1969	1970	1971	1972	1973	1974
(a) Total trade with all countries of the world	3,846.6	4,546.6	5,683.4	6,684.5	7,503.5	10,548.5	21,435.3
(b) Intra-regional trade (ECOWAS)	144.8	133.9	162.3	236.4	241.9	428.3	975.3
(c) (b) as % of (a) (average for the period)	3.8	2.9	2.9	3.5	3.2	4.1	3.7
(d) Exports to all countries of the world	2,017.6	1,392.2	2,954.3	3,397.2	4,126.4	6,094.5	13,902.3
(e) Exports to countries in the sub-region (ECOWAS)	75.1	66.1	86.2	140.4	127.1	231.1	411.3
(f) (e) as % of (d) (average for the period)	3.7	2.8	2.9	4.1	3.1	3.8	3.0
(g) Imports from all countries of the world	1,829.1	2,154.5	2,728.5	3,287.3	2,277.1	4,454.0	7,533.0
(h) Imports from countries within the sub-region (ECOWAS)	69.7	67.8	76.1	96.0	114.8	197.1	384.0
(i) (h) as % of (g) (average for the period)	3.8	3.1	2.8	2.9	3.4	4.4	5.1

*Excludes Guinea-Bissau

Source: I.M.F., I.B.R.D., Direction of Trade 1968-1972, 1969-1973, 1970-1974.

to domestic needs and resources is the subject of the subsequent chapters of this study.

ECONOMIC INTEGRATION: THE RATIONALE

During the early years of independence, each of the West African governments took some steps to promote industrial development as a means of bringing about a much greater rate of economic growth than was achieved in the past under colonial rule. They made studies, prepared development programs, created development agencies, appropriated funds, negotiated loans, and offered various incentives or inducements to investors. However, these efforts were not rewarded, and for various reasons.

First, many of the development plans invariably failed to indicate a well-integrated and coordinated approach. Most of them discussed the progress of individual industries or individual projects in a disjointed fashion, apparently ignoring the fact that most industries are interrelated and interdependent.[22] Second, these development plans tended to be inward-looking, and to refer to measures for increasing economic growth within the country concerned. It was not easy for a minister drawing up a plan for industrialization to decide that a particular industry should be set up in a neighboring country, particularly if it was one that enjoyed high prestige in terms of technology and the sophistication of its products. Consequently, none of the development programs initiated during the early 1960s attempted to coordinate industrial development in one country with the industrial growth of the neighboring states.

And third, and perhaps more significantly, the small size of the West African markets, the unlikelihood that West African manufacturers could ever compete in the world market with those of the major industrial nations, and the scarcity of developmental resources limited the degree and type of industrialization (and thus economic development and improvement of living standards) that the countries could achieve. With the possible exception of Nigeria, not one of the states in the sub-region is a large enough economic unit capable of creating and sustaining an integrated modern economy with high levels of productivity. Thus the establishment of a great many industries was precluded and many of the industries that could be established were doomed to be small-scale, high cost, economically inefficient operations requiring a great deal of expensive governmental protection. Hence, the prospect was dim to nonexistent that the 16 countries, each acting on its own, could improve economic conditions and achieve economic development. And so, in West Africa, as indeed in Africa in general, the 1960s were a disappointment:

> It is now more than a decade since most African countries attained political independence. But no African country is, as yet, within striking distance of self-sustaining growth and economic independence. The basic structure of the economies and the welfare of the majority of the people remain unchanged.[23]

The policy of industrialization and modernization, which has been the major objective of the West African governments, calls for the creation of modern industrial installations. In order for these industries to be reasonably efficient they will have to operate on a relatively large scale and will have to find outlets for products on relatively large markets. A larger market would allow industries to expand production and to take advantage of economies of scale, thus reducing prices. Price reduction would lead to increased consumption. Goods that were luxuries or semiluxuries would become items of mass consumption. In the larger market, too, some manufacturers who operate inefficiently under the protection of national tariffs and government subsidies would have to become competitive or go under. Other industries that could not develop at all in the small national markets would have an opportunity to do so in the larger market. It is worth stressing, also, that there are at present certain industries established in the sub-region that operate at less than full capacity due to narrow national markets. Ghana's Akosombo Dam project and Ivorian breweries are cases in point. Conceivably, market integration in the sub-region would lead to the rationalization and mobilization of the existing level of excess capacity through vertical specialization of the production processes between plants in the same industry.[24] Above all, the creation of a larger market would make the sub-region more attractive to investment capital. It would be a more profitable and a more promising area for industrial investment.

In brief, therefore, this search for wider markets which can accommodate large-scale industries or at least provide an adequate home-demand base partly explains the recent attempts to promote economic integration of the West African sub-region. Economic integration in West Africa must therefore be seen as a method of providing a more viable basis for economic growth and, more especially for industrialization.

Another outstanding feature of the West African setting is the unemployment and underemployment of resources, particularly human resources. Many of the sub-region's economic problems and limitations stem from the existence of mass unemployment and underemployment. Estimates for 1970 indicate that the unemployment rate was as high as 17 percent in Ghana, 15 percent in Sierra Leone, and 14 percent in Nigeria. Indications are that the trend is upward.[25] To this may be added the lack of income or extremely small income which has restricted the demand for manufactured goods, has bred deplorable living conditions, has contributed to health and educational problems, and has had a retarding effect on the economy in general. With the creation of ECOWAS it is possible that, after the transitional period of 15 years when the customs union would become fully operational, job opportunities would be created following the integration-induced investment in industry; national and per capita income would increase as a result; living conditions would improve.

I may perhaps mention, also, that the rationale for West African economic integration is primarily, but not exclusively economic. To some extent there is also a political rationale. There is presently a hope--among some an expectation--that by integrating their economies the West African countries would in time enhance their bargaining power on economic issues (particularly those concerning trade) vis-à-vis the developed countries, especially the former metropolitan powers. There is also the hope--again, among some an expectation--that through economic integration the West African countries would at some point in the future increase their political strength and influence in African affairs and in the international community at large.

However, as James Cochrane has warned, it is "dangerous to attempt to rank the importance of various objectives or goals" of an economic integration scheme. For very often no "ranking or hierarchy" exists in reality.[26] This warning notwithstanding, it appears that the political rationale or objective of West African economic integration is secondary in terms of importance to the economic rationale. The West African economic integration movement was proposed and is being pursued for essentially economic reasons. Although of apparently secondary importance as motivational factors, political objectives cannot be dismissed or wholly ignored. They have made some contribution and provided some measure of motivation. After all, it was through the initiative of some West African political leaders that the idea of ECOWAS was conceived.

To conclude, West African countries effectively need integration to achieve the development implied by the existence of sufficient markets, a vigorous economic life, technological progress and the shoring up of their cultural values; to strengthen their national sovereignty, making them more independent, granting success to their relationships of interdependence and enabling them to be better equipped to face the unjust exploitation to which others seek to submit them. Thus the West African countries do not envisage integration as an exclusively economic undertaking, but rather as a multifaceted enterprise.

THE IDEA OF A WEST AFRICAN COMMUNITY: ORIGINS

It is perhaps necessary to cast ECOWAS in a proper historical perspective. For the idea of West African economic and/or political integration in one form or another is not a product of recent manufacture. Its roots go deeper than are usually appreciated, and are complex in character. Like the erstwhile East African Community, ECOWAS has a background of varied experience.

Historically, there is evidence of a movement toward a West African community even as early as the mid-nineteenth century. The history of nationalism in West Africa is full of references to this vague, artificial, and imaginary entity. Africanus Beale Horton of Sierra Leone, for example, had as early as 1867, advocated the "self-government of Western Africa."[27] Like the West African middle class of the mid-nineteenth century, Horton saw nationalism in the context of the whole of West Africa. But by far the most important and the most influential theoretician and prophet of the idea in the late nineteenth and early twentieth centuries was Edward Wilmot Blyden. A West Indian by birth and a Liberian by adoption, Blyden was not only the ideological father of the idea of West African unity, he also spearheaded the cultural nationalism that accompanied it.[28] After his death in 1912, J. E. Casely Hayford, the great Ghanaian pan-Africanist and the staunchest disciple and ideological heir of Blyden, revived the West African community dream, this time giving it an organizational form. Casely Hayford initiated the move toward the formation of the National Congress of British West Africa in March 1920. The Congress which symbolized the idea of a West African unity had both political and economic objectives.[29]

While in Europe in the 1920s and 1930s, the prime minister of France, Aristide Briand, coined the name "Common Market" and submitted a detailed scheme for a European union to the League of Nations Assembly in 1929;[30] in East Africa, arrangements for a customs union were completed in 1927 between Kenya, Uganda, and Tanganyika (the former name of Tanzania);[31] and in West Africa, the stalwart nationalist politicians preached the idea of a West African unity. J. B. Danquah of Ghana, then a vice-president of the West African Students Union in Great Britain, for instance, persistently maintained that the larger future of Africa could be read in the light of West African progress and prosperity: "You cannot make a nation of Africa," declared Danquah in 1926, "but by securing unity in West Africa. . . . You thereby raise the general standard of African welfare and lay down an ideal of life which the African in East and South will strive to realise."[32] Like Casely Hayford, Danquah believed that if Africans were to survive, West Africa must become a nation and that it must unite under the sentiment of national progress. Similarly, during this period, I. T. A. Wallace Johnson, an outstanding Sierra Leonean militant anticolonialist and pan-Africanist, ceaselessly urged West Africans to unite and recognize their common nationality. This was exemplified in his foundation and leadership of a West African Youth League first in Ghana and later in Sierra Leone.[33] Although in the late 1920s, Kobina Sekyi, a Ghanaian lawyer, philosopher and nationalist politician, advocated the extension of the National Congress of British West Africa to include, as he put it, "our brethren in French West Africa," the organization remained essentially an English-speaking West African affair.[34]

Taking his cue from Kobina Sekyi, with whom he was in close touch on matters affecting West Africa, Kwame Nkrumah throughout the 1940s advocated the idea of West African economic and political unification which should include the British, French, Portuguese, and Spanish territories, as well as Liberia. Nkrumah's concept of West African unity contained a wide variety of values: unity to find appropriate African solutions to problems and prevent the intervention of non-African powers, unity to express a common outlook, unity to bring about the rapid termination of colonial rule, and unity to lessen the weaknesses caused by underdevelopment. As a result of Nkrumah's efforts, the 1945 Pan-African Congress held in Manchester, to which he was joint-secretary, recommended the creation of a West African Economic Union.[35]

Although throughout the 1950s the idea of a West African economic cooperation was variously discussed, it was in 1961 that Nnamdi Azikiwe, then the governor-general of the Federation of Nigeria, proposed a scheme of a West African Common Market as an economic factor that could bring about unity in the sub-region.[36] However, this idea of forging a wider West African grouping as advocated by Azikiwe, Kwame Nkrumah, and other pan-African nationalists before them, was not seriously pursued during the early independence period. The political structure of the West African sub-region with all the linguistic and colonial structures involved hardly encouraged, after independence, an early movement toward a comprehensive integrative system. Aside from Guinea-Bissau and Cape Verde Islands, which gained independence recently in 1974 through a protracted liberation struggle, the legacies of colonialism clearly show in the groupings in West Africa along metropolitan linguistic lines: the Anglophone and Francophone barriers. It may be instructive to briefly review some of these arrangements.

THE EARLY POST-INDEPENDENCE EFFORTS

It is worth noting that the variety of economic groupings and associations established in West Africa during the first decade of independence were principally among the Francophone countries. While they preserve or revive pre-independence ties, there were others that were designed "to bolster new political alliances through commercial and economic agreements." On the other hand, partly because the British administrative structure did not give a sense of economic unity, the English-speaking West African countries have never really come together for the purpose of an economic association after attaining independence.

Among the Francophone countries, however, the period since independence has witnessed the evolution of a variety of regional groupings. The earliest attempt toward evolving an economic union was made in June 1959 when Benin, Ivory Coast, Burkina Faso, Mali, Senegal, Mauritania, and Niger signed a convention in Paris creating the West African Customs Union (Union Douaniere de l'Afrique de l'Ouest--UDAO) with headquarters at Abidjan in the Ivory Coast. The union soon ran into difficulties principally on the grounds that member states were unable to agree on a formula for the distribution of the customs revenue collected on imports. It was replaced in June 1966 by UDEAO (Union Douaniere et Economique de l'Afrique de l'Ouest) with the same membership. UDEAO lacked vigor, and the practical and visible achievements of the organization were less than had originally been hoped for. Not surprisingly, therefore, at the summit meeting of the UDEAO member states held in Bamako on 21 May 1970, a new organization--the West African Economic Community (CEAO--

Communauté Economique de l'Afrique de l'Ouest)--was launched
by a protocol agreement. The main treaty establishing the community was signed in Abidjan on 17 April 1973. The Community
began to function on 1 January 1974. The major objectives of
CEAO are first, to improve the infrastructure of the area as a
whole by cooperation in the development of transportation and
communication; second, to promote and accelerate the joint industrialization of the member states; and third, to facilitate trade
among members in both manufactured products and raw materials.[37] These objectives were to be implemented by the Conference of Heads of State, the Council of Ministers, and the General
Secretariat.

It seems appropriate at this stage to review briefly some of the
striking features of this first phase of West African cooperation
efforts. One striking observation during the period under review
was the inability of the Anglophone and Francophone West African countries to break their colonial heritages, and to form effective economic groupings that cut across them. Thus many of the
organizations formed during this period were in actuality con-
tinuations of colonial groupings. The few attempts made toward
the establishment of organization involving both the Francophone
and the Anglophone countries proved to be far less successful than
the efforts made among the Francophone countries. We may
recall, for example, the short-lived Ghana-Burkina Faso and the
Ghana-Guinea-Mali experiments, as well as the fruitless efforts
made in 1963 to integrate the economies of Senegal and Gambia.
Similarly, the West African free trade area initiated in 1964
between Liberia, Ivory Coast, Guinea, and Sierra Leone did not
get off the drawing board.

A noticeable feature of this first phase of cooperative activities is the increasing desire on the part of the West African countries "to grasp and act on the basis of the concept of collective
economic activity." Paradoxically, however, this phase witnessed
some deterioration rather than progress in the field of effective
regional integration in West Africa. No solid foundations for a
united West Africa were laid, despite the countless expressions of
fidelity to the principles of pan-Africanism and West African
unity. Significantly, too, very little was achieved by the various
regional groupings in French-speaking West Africa. As Abangwu
succinctly sums up, "Despite the plethora of preambular pledges,
signing of integration protocols, treaties, conventions and agreements that has characterized intra-regional transactions in recent
years, these have proved to be largely ineffective."[38] The complex

political problems connected with the process of nation-building significantly affected the efforts toward economic integration in the sub-region during this early period.

For with the disappearance of the imperial overlords, a resurgence of identification on the basis of smaller ethnic units erupted in one African country after another. There developed what Ali Mazrui has termed "the ideology of the paramountcy of ethnic interests" or simply retribalization.[39] West Africa, our own sub-region of study, was not unaffected by these developments. In the case of Nigeria, the largest and the most populated country of the sub-region, retribalization attained tragic dimensions especially from the mid-1960s. In the early independence period, therefore, individual African states were first faced with the urgent task of consolidating indigeneous people living within their respective boundaries into one nation. In sum, state-nation-building can be described as a process toward national unification.

It was this issue of nation-building with which West African states were faced immediately after their independence from the colonial yoke that greatly militated against the effort toward regional economic integration during the phase under review. For, as Haas has briefly stated, "Countries which are poorly integrated internally make poor partners in a regional integration process because of the reluctance of leaders to further undermine their control at home."[40] It was the same complex problems relating to the nation-building process that also explain the rapid political change in the sub-region during this period. This change also affected integrative efforts by creating a climate of uncertainty. Furthermore, as an important aspect of this process of nation-building, this first generation of West African leaders was required to satisfy the rising expectations and aspirations of their people by showing some concrete (or visible) evidence of their political independence or making possible some immediate benefits accruing from their new status. This prompted many of these leaders to direct attention to national priorities and, as it happened, to initiate narrow and shortsighted national policies in the economic and other spheres. Some of these policies such as, for example, the introduction of national currencies and the establishment of national air and shipping lines, led, in turn, to what Abangwu has rightly termed, the prevalence of "Micro-statism rather than supranationalism."[41] This phenomenon created obstacles to the process of sub-regional economic integration, obstacles that in fact did not exist during the colonial period.

In spite of the dismal failure to form effective economic groupings even for a limited number of countries within the West

African sub-region, efforts were diverted during the mid-1960s toward the formation of a larger grouping. It is on these efforts initiated under the auspices of the ECA that I focus attention in the second phase of the historical development of the idea of the Economic Community of West African States.

THE TORTUOUS ROAD TO ECOWAS

The idea of an economic grouping embracing all the states in West Africa emanated from the ECA, which since its establishment in 1958 has played a vital role in fostering the economic development of Africa through economic cooperation. At its first meeting held in December 1962, the ECA's Standing Committee on Industry, Natural Resources and Transport decided to render assistance to governments in promoting sub-regional cooperation in the development of industries on the basis of international specialization and in the harmonization, where appropriate, of industrial development plans, through studies and field investigation.[42]

The first major step at evolving an economic community embracing the two language groups in West Africa took place in 1963 when, in accordance with the 1962 decision noted above, an ECA mission was sent to the West African sub-region to assess the possibilities of industrial development with primary emphasis on projects serving more than one country. This led to the Lagos Conference on Industrial Co-ordination in West Africa held in November 1963. However, it was not until October 1966 that the first major step toward the formation of ECOWAS was taken at a Conference on Economic Cooperation in West Africa held in Niamey. At this meeting, which was attended by 11 states in the sub-region, several recommendations were adopted regarding the establishment of economic cooperation among the member states of the sub-region.[43]

The Niamey meeting was followed by the momentous West African Conference on Economic Cooperation held in Accra, Ghana, from 27 April to 4 May 1967. Robert Gardiner, the executive secretary of the ECA, presented the document embodying the Articles of Association which were agreed upon in Niamey in October 1966, to the meeting for adoption and signature thus inaugurating the Economic Community of West Africa. At this meeting Gardiner cautioned that:

Many branches of economic activity are closed to the majority of West African countries owing to their small economic size. In this situation the countries of the sub-region must find means to consolidate their economies into more viable units. This need not involve the formation of full-fledged common markets, although increased trade will have to be a central component of any programme of economic co-operation. It is probably premature at this stage to envisage that *all* West African Governments would immediately agree to arrangements entailing a high degree of co-operation of important elements of economic policy with *all* their neighbours in the sub-region.[44]

The Accra Conference subsequently adopted the Articles of Association for the Establishment of an Economic Community. The agreement was signed by 12 of the 14 states in the West African sub-region. These were Republic of Benin, Ghana, Ivory Coast, Liberia, Mali, Mauritania, Niger, Nigeria, Senegal, Sierra Leone, Togo, and Burkina Faso. Only Guinea and Gambia were absent.

It was during this period that at a meeting in Bamako of the four heads of state of the Organization of Senegalese River States it was recommended that a regional grouping that should embrace the whole of West Africa be created. Accordingly, the head of state of Mauritania was mandated to go on a mission to all the heads of the 14 states of West Africa. This mission was quite a success. For in April 1968 nine heads of state of the West African sub-region--Gambia, Ghana, Guinea, Liberia, Mali, Mauritania, Nigeria, Senegal, and Burkina Faso--met in Monrovia where the protocol establishing the West African Regional Group was signed. There were two important decisions taken at the meeting: one was that Nigeria and Guinea should prepare priority studies of possible areas of cooperation between and among the member states of the proposed community, and the other mandated Liberia and Senegal to prepare a draft treaty and an accompanying protocol on a customs union.

Since the signing of the protocol in April 1968, progress became very slow on the question of reaching an agreement on a treaty for the establishment of the Economic Community of West Africa. Although in June and November 1968, officials of the governments of Nigeria and Guinea met in Lagos and Conakry respectively to prepare their report which was then submitted to the 14 West African states for study, the second meeting of the Interim Council of Ministers which was to consider the draft treaty and the protocol on customs union did not meet. Consequently, neither of these documents was considered, let alone adopted. The enthusiasm for the creation of the Community was dampened after the Monrovia summit. The result is that between 1968 and 1972 no action was taken on this matter.

THE FAILURE OF ECA-INSPIRED EFFORTS

Many reasons could be given for the failure of the ECA-inspired efforts to bring about an effective sub-regionwide economic grouping. In the first place, the attempts did not take sufficient cognizance of existing realities and therefore tended to be over ambitious. A second significant reason for the failure of the ECA-sponsored efforts can be traced to the different economic groupings within West Africa of the pre-Lome Convention era. The Commonwealth, French, and EEC preferential arrangements had constituted serious drawbacks to the efforts at regionwide cooperation among West African states. They often gave rise to conflicts of interest. For example, where the arrangements entailed the granting of reverse preferences by West African countries, as was the case under the Yaounde Convention, economic contact among some of the countries was usually affected adversely.

There was, also, the other grouping--the Commonwealth West African countries--which during the negotiations for the Yaounde Convention turned down association with the EEC at the September 1962 London Commonwealth Conference. Their central reasons for rejecting Common Market association appear to have been uncertainty as to the details of what the Yaounde Convention might entail for inter-African economic affairs and the fear that association with the EEC would involve them politically and/or militarily in European cold war disputes.[45] Some of their leaders, in particular Ghana's Kwame Nkrumah, denounced association as a neo-colonial device allegedly aimed "to create a bitter schism among the independent African states or else cajole them into the fold of the European market, in the same old imperialist relationship of the European rider on the African-horse." Nkrumah called the EEC "a new system of collective colonialism which will be stronger and more dangerous than the old evils we are striving to liquidate."[46] Although later in 1966 Nigeria for various reasons signed a trade agreement with the EEC, this was never implemented; by September 1968 Nigeria had decided to abandon altogether its efforts to become an associate member of the EEC.[47]

The two Yaounde Conventions only reinforced the special accords that France and its African colonies had signed on the eve of their independence, accords that constituted another great obstacle to West African cooperation. An important aspect of this was to steadily discourage the formation of federations or unions that brought together French- and English-speaking African states. Rather, France supported economic cooperation among countries in the franc zone. No doubt France was aware that her special position with her former colonies declined in importance as the weight of oil-rich Nigeria continued to increase.

Aside from the French factor in West African cooperation efforts was the crisis in Nigeria during this period. Indeed, this crisis which developed into a civil war from 1967 onwards should be considered as another significant reason for the failure of the West African Regional Group to implement the agreements that had been signed. The war years--1967-70--were years of worry, doubts, concern, and difficult choices. These years did not create the requisite atmosphere for cooperative endeavors along economic, political, and social lines. Although the Nigerian government signed the nine-nation Monrovia Protocol on a West African Economic Community, its main objective at the time was to utilize fully the formal gathering of the West African states in promoting an understanding between Nigeria and neighboring states in the war against Biafra.

By the end of the civil war in 1970, all the complex problems and factors that had halted the progress on the creation of an economic grouping in the West African sub-region would seem to have dwindled into insignificance. I have noted how France's control over its ex-colonies had been an obstacle to economic and other forms of interaction between the Francophone states and other parts of West Africa. I have also mentioned how this control was further ensured through associate membership of the Francophone states in the EEC.

By the early 1970s, French influence in Francophone West Africa appeared to be diminishing, at least on the surface. For with the departure of President de Gaulle from the Elysee Palace in 1969 and his death the following year, the cover provided by this venerated father figure over the reality of decreasing French attention to the policy of cooperation was removed.[48] A growing number of Francophone states--in particular, Benin, Mauritania, and Niger--began to denounce the numerous cooperation agreements with France as "neo-colonial" and "strait-jacket" and infringing their sovereignty. The demands for reforms in the agreements not only showed a desire for greater independence from

France; these demands also became less and less polite. Mauritania which led the way insisted on its Arabness and, on 31 December 1972, Nouackhott unilaterally announced that the old accords were null and void.[49]

The dilution of the French factor as an impediment to greater sub-regional cooperation in West Africa was significantly reinforced by the Lome Convention which replaced the Yaounde regime in February 1975. The EEC might have contributed to past trade and economic divisions within Africa but the Lome Convention, in a real sense, reunited African nations in a common endeavor. By bringing together the French- and English-speaking African states, the 18 months of negotiations culminating in the Lome Treaty forged a sense of common destiny and the need for cooperation on mutually beneficial economic issues. If all the countries in West Africa could come together to sign an agreement to promote trade with the EEC, it ought to be possible for them to conclude an agreement for the same ends within the subregion. "The psychological attitudes, the face to face encounters in the course of the negotiations, and indeed the Convention provisions," observes Isebill Gruhn, "brought about the political climate and economic structure which allowed ECOWAS to be concluded."[50] Thus, although the obstacles for inter-West African states cooperation and coordination might have been swept under the rug in the year of Lome, Lome no doubt produced an air of compromise, optimism, and self-confidence which was badly needed at the time for the creation of the ECOWAS scheme.

More significantly, the end of the civil war brought about a renewal of confidence in Nigeria as the dominant economic power in the West African sub-region. Since 1970 the federal government of Nigeria has placed emphasis on greater cooperation with her neighbors than was the case during the Balewa era. Thus, whereas, for example, in 1962 Nigeria "cold-shouldered the formation of an economic union of Dahomey and Togo," the federal government came out strongly after the war in favor of such a grouping. In pursuit of the policy of establishing a sub-regional grouping, Nigeria initiated a powerful campaign soon after the end of the hostilities for the creation of a West African economic community.[51] By the end of 1970 the federal government had contacted all the other West African countries about the possibility of following up the decisions of the Monrovia summit of April 1968 by taking concrete steps to bring about the realization of an economic community in the region. Although only a few countries showed a positive enthusiasm for this move, the federal government forged ahead.

"A LIVING THING IS BORN"

In April 1972, the heads of state of Nigeria and Togo decided to revive the idea of an economic community that would cut across linguistic and cultural barriers. To this end General Gowon of Nigeria and President Eyadema of Togo signed a treaty providing for the setting up of what the Togolese president called "an embryo" of a West African economic community. The political purpose of initiating the Nigerian-Togo agreement was to show that a small, relatively poor country can engage in economically rewarding relationship with a large and rich country. This may reduce the fear of domination on the part of smaller, poorer states which may be contemplating membership in an expanded regional economic community. Furthermore, the Nigeria-Togo agreement showed that official language differences need not constitute an insurmountable barrier to trade and economic relationship among the states in the West African sub-region.

Because of the practical difficulties that had been experienced in the past, and drawing lessons from previous efforts, Nigeria and Togo agreed on the principles that would guide their efforts. These were the adoption of a pragmatic and flexible approach, the pursuit of objectives capable of early realization, the adoption of an open-door policy which would enable all the countries in the sub-region to become members of the community and the setting up of necessary institutions to deal with specific issues that require immediate attention. The adoption of these principles no doubt reflected an understanding of the need to fashion instruments which would be workable in the peculiar circumstances of West Africa, and not necessarily those that had proved admirable in the sophisticated economies of the industrialized world.[52] As a first step, a joint Nigeria-Togo official delegation toured all the countries in the sub-region in July and August, 1973. A committee of expert officials of both countries thereafter prepared a detailed draft, which was later submitted to a Ministerial Conference of the 15 countries in the West African sub-region held in Lome, Togo, from the 10 to 15 December 1973. At this historic conference, Adebayo Adedeji, the Nigerian counterpart of Raul Prebisch of Latin America or Jean Monnet of France, who was then the Federal Commissioner for Economic Development and Reconstruction in Nigeria, solemnly declared:

We are here today to explode the myth that differences in language, culture, and economic level necessarily render impossible the achievement of meaningful co-operation in

West Africa. We have precedents to guide us. It is a fact
of history that after the Second World War, bitter enemies
such as Germany and France are now working together
under the umbrella of the EEC. Luxembourg, a relatively
small country, is also co-operating with economic giants
like France and Germany. In the EEC, there are as many
as nine languages. And these countries are no less heterogeneous culturally. . . . Today, the EEC is the richest economic grouping in the world because its members have
learned to share their technological and scientific know-
how which has accelerated their economic growth. . . . If
the EEC has taken so many years to develop to the height
that it has now reached, we in West Africa must be realistic.[53]

Although the analogy with the EEC may not be altogether ac-
curate, in that the historical context in which the EEC was born is
significantly different, also that the member states of the EEC
were not only already developed industrially, but had had a long
tradition of separate nationhood, the basic arguments of Adedeji
can hardly be disputed. Many a time we tend to consider the
linguistic, cultural, and economic diversity of the countries of the
sub-region and their different colonial experiences as constituting
powerful obstacles to cooperation in West Africa. These seemingly
insurmountable barriers have tended in the past to discourage efforts toward economic integration in the sub-region, whereas
slightly similar objective conditions have not obstructed the creation of the EEC. Perhaps what seemed to be lacking in the case
of West Africa was pragmatism in approach, coupled with failure
to identify areas of cooperation that were urgent and where some
measure of success could be achieved.

There was also the need for discipline, dedication, and above
all, the necessary political will to integrate, and the will to explore
new and dynamic methods to give meaning and content to West
African cooperation.

The Lome ministerial conference was "a positive success." The
15 participating states--including Guinea-Bissau which three
months earlier had unilaterally declared its independence from
Portugal in September 1973--recognized the need to get the organization functioning in those areas that were immediately practical and capable of yielding demonstrable results, such as the
setting up of infrastructure like communications, technical
cooperation, and trade. After calling on Nigeria and Togo to
draw up detailed proposals for the future shape of the community,

the conference then outlined a timetable for the evolution of the Economic Community of West African States.

On 27 and 28 May 1975, the heads of state and government of the 15 states finally assembled in Lagos to sign the treaty establishing the Economic Community of West African States. This marked an important milestone in the economic history of West Africa, representing, as it does, a major breakthrough in efforts at economic cooperation in the area. As General Yakubu Gowon, head of the federal military government of Nigeria, rightly declared in his opening address:

> This is a momentous day, marking as it does the fulfilment of many hopes; the result of efforts on the part of leaders from all corners of West Africa; another major and concrete step in giving practical effect to aspirations which we all share and which, in various previous meetings, conferences and groups, we have all endeavoured since the beginning of the last decade, to bring to fruition. . . . The Economic Community which we are striving to establish will be a living organism evolving in its own unique way and growing over the years.[54]

The ECOWAS Treaty came into effect on 23 June 1975, when seven states--Ghana, Guinea, Ivory Coast, Liberia, Nigeria, Togo, and Burkina Faso--ratified the agreement. By early July, the Gambia, Benin, and Niger also ratified, bringing the number of ratifications to ten. In November 1976 at Lome, five protocols to be annexed to the ECOWAS Treaty were signed. Furthermore, decisions were taken on the locations of the headquarters of the Community at Lagos and of the Fund at Lome. It was also decided that the executive secretary be nominated by Ivory Coast and the managing director of the Fund by Liberia.

This chapter has attempted to review the main events leading to the formation of ECOWAS. Economic integration negotiations, whether in developed or developing areas, entail hard and sometimes difficult decisions for the participating units. National interest is involved, and sometimes it is threatened. In the main, the ECOWAS negotiations were characterized by pragmatism and hard bargaining on the part of the countries involved. The governments of these countries did not just give in or give away whatever was asked simply to further the process of West African economic integration. They looked out for their own well-being. The following chapter attempts a brief analysis of the Lagos

Treaty emphasizing the decision-making institutions of the
ECOWAS scheme.

NOTES

1. E. A. Boateng, *A Political Geography of Africa* (Cambridge:
   Cambridge University Press, 1978), p. 103.
2. R. J. Harrison Church, *West Africa* (London: Longman, 1963),
   p. xxv.
3. ECA, *Economic Bulletin for Africa* (Addis Ababa), vol. 1, no.
   1 (1961):17.
4. Boateng, *Political Geography of Africa*, p. 105.
5. L. Gray Cowan, *The Dilemmas of African Independence* (New
   York: Columbia University, 1965), p. ix.
6. ECA, *Elements of Model Convention for Sub-regional Common Markets in Africa*, E/CN, 14 WPI/1 (Addis Ababa,
   1965), p. 76. See also Douglas Rimmer, *The Economies of
   West Africa* (London: Weidenfeld and Nicolson, 1984), pp. 1-
   3.
7. Nicholas Plessz, *Problems and Prospects of Economic Integration in West Africa* (Montreal: McGill University Press,
   1968), p. 13.
8. Adebayo Adedeji, "Prospects and Regional Cooperation in
   West Africa" in *Prospects and Problems of Regional Cooperation in Africa* (Nairobi: English Press, 1969), p. 67.
9. *A Critical Appraisal of the Economic and Social Conditions in
   the West African Sub-region*, prepared by the Nigerian Institute of Social and Economic Research (NISER), and the
   Ivorian Centre for Economic and Social Research (CIRES),
   March 1979.
10. According to Diaby-Ouattara, executive secretary of
    ECOWAS, the per capita income of the West African Com-
    munity in 1974 was about U.S. $270 compared to the world
    average of $1,422, the European average of $3,313, the Latin
    American average of $953, the Asian average of $479, and
    the African average of $366. (Paper presented at the inaugu-
    ral conference of the West African Economic Association,
    Lagos, April 1978).
11. See *A Critical Appraisal of the Economic and Social Con-
    ditions In the West African Sub-region.*
12. Timothy M. Shaw and Malcolm J. Grieve, "Dependence as an
    Approach to Understanding Continuing Inequalities in

Africa," *Journal of Developing Areas*, vol. 13, no. 3 (April 1979):236.

13. Alex Rondos, "How Independent is Francophone Africa after Twenty Years?," *West Africa*, 1 September 1980.
14. Alex Rondos, "Franc Zone and French Africa," *West Africa*, 8 September 1980.
15. Rita Cruise O'Brien, "Factors of Dependence: Senegal and Kenya," in *Decolonisation and After: The British and French Experience*, ed. W. H. Morris-Jones and Georges Fisher (London: Frank Cass, 1980), p. 287.
16. M. B. Akpan, "Neo-colonialism: The Political Economy of Combating Dependent Modernisation in West Africa"'(Paper presented at the Conference on the New International Economic Order, Lagos, September 1977).
17. Samir Amin, "Capitalism and Development in the Ivory Coast," in *African Politics and Society*, ed. I. L. Markovitz (New York: 1970), p. 288.
18. John Kwadjo, "Collective Self-reliance . . . or Collective Neo-colonialism?" *West Africa*, 15 September 1980.
19. For details see International Trade Centre UNCTAD/GATT, "The Profiles and Potentials of External Trade of Members of the Economic Community of West African States," in *ECOWAS Trade, Customs and Monetary Study Projects* (Geneva: December 1979).
20. Kwame Nkrumah, *Africa Must Unite* (London: Panaf Books, 1963), p. 160.
21. For an extended discussion see S. K. B. Asante, "ECOWAS, the EEC and the Lome Convention," in *African Regional Organizations*, ed. Domenico Mazzeo (Cambridge: Cambridge University Press, 1984), pp. 171-95.
22. Andre Simmons, "Economic Planning in Africa," *Economic Impact* 2(1976):69.
23. Cheikh A. Diop and Puis Okigbo, "Technical Cooperation Among African Countries," (DP/TCDC/RAF/11, 1976), p. 1.
24. Uka Ezenwinyinya, "The Economic Community of West African States: Problems and Possibilities", *Nigerian Journal of International Affairs*, vol. 2, no. 1, 2 (1976):106.
25. Uka Ezenwe, "The Way Ahead for ECOWAS," *West Africa*, 20 September 1976.
26. James D. Cochrane, *The Politics of Regional Integration: The Central American Case* (New Orleans: Tulane University Press, 1969), p. 48.
27. Africanus Horton, *West African Countries and Peoples* (London: W. J. Johnson, 1868), p. iii. For a recent biography

of Horton, see Christopher Fyfe, *Africanus Horton: West African Scientist and Patriot 1835-1883* (London: OUP, 1972).

28. Hollis Lynch, *Edward Wilmot Blyden: Pan-Negro Patriot, 1832-1912*, (London: OUP, 1967), p. 250.

29. Colonial Office (Public Record Office, London) 554/54/2760: Resolutions of the Congress of British West Africa Held in Accra, Gold Coast, 11-29 March 1920.

30. Anthony J. C. Kerr, *The Common Market and How It Works* (New York: Pergamon Press, 1977), p. 5. Also, Dennis Swann, *The Economics of the Common Market*, (Harmondsworth: Penguin, 1975), p. 13.

31. Arthur Hazlewood, *Economic Integration: The East African Experience* (London: Heinemann, 1975), p. 22.

32. *Wasu* (London: Journal of West African Students Union in Great Britain) 2 (December 1926):40.

33. For details see S. K. B. Asante, *Pan-African Protest: West Africa and the Italo-Ethiopian Crisis, 1934-1941* (London: Longman, 1977), Chaps. 5, 6.

34. Kobina Sekyi, "The Parting of the Ways" (1927):23, in "Sekyi Papers," Acc. 464/64, Cape Coast Regional Archives, Ghana. Also see S. K. B. Asante, "The Politics of Confrontation: The Case of Kobina Sekyi and the Colonial System in Ghana." *Universitas*, vol. 6, no. 2 (New Series) (November 1977):15-38.

35. For further details see S. K. B. Asante, "Kwame Nkrumah and Pan-Africanism: The Early Phase, 1945-1961" *Universitas* (New Series), vol. 3, no. 1 (October 1973):36-49.

36. Bingu W. T. Mutharika, *Toward Multinational Economic Cooperation in Africa* (New York: Praeger, 1972), p. 12.

37. For details see S. K. B. Asante, "CEAO/ECOWAS: Conflict and Cooperation in West Africa", in *The Future of Regionalism in Africa*, ed. R. I. Onwuka and A. Sesay (London: Macmillan, 1984); and also Mousa N'Gom, "CEAO: The West African Economic Community," *Courier* 44 (July-August 1977):49-50.

38. George Abangwu, "Systems Approach to Regional Integration in West Africa," *Journal of Common Market Studies* 13 (1975):123.

39. Ali A. Mazrui and Hasu H. Patel, eds., *Africa: The Next Thirty Years* (London: Julian Friedmann, 1974), p. v.

40. Ernst B. Haas, "The Study of Regional Integration," *International Organization*, vol. 24, no. 4 (Autumn 1970):619.

41. Abangwu, "Systems Approach to Regional Integration," p. 124.

42. ECA, *Report of the West African Industrial Cooperation Mission* E/CN. 14/246, January 7, 1964, p. 1.

43. See also Isebill V. Gruhn, "The Economic Commission for Africa," in *African Regional Organizations*, ed. D. Mazzeo (Cambridge: Cambridge University Press, 1984), pp. 41-47.

44. Opening statement by R. K. A. Gardiner, executive secretary of the ECA at the West African Sub-regional Conference on Economic Cooperation held in Accra, Ghana, 27 April to 4 May 1967, E/CN. 14/9, Annex VII.

45. Isebill V. Gruhn, "The Lome Convention: Inching towards Interdependence", *International Organization*, vol. 30, no. 2 (Spring 1976):244.

46. Kwame Nkrumah, as quoted in William Zartman, *The Politics of Trade Negotiations between Africa and the European Economic Community: The Weak Confront the Strong* (Princeton, N.J.: Princeton University Press, 1971), p. 215.

47. A detailed examination of Nigeria's relations with the EEC during this period is a subject of a doctoral thesis by Lemuel Owugah, "Nigeria and the European Economic Community: A Case Study in Decision-Making 1960-1973" (University of Toronto, 1978).

48. Ladipo Adamolebun, "Cooperation or Neo-colonialism-- Francophone Africa," *Africa Quarterly*, vol. 18, no. 1 (July 1978):40-41.

49. Geoff Varley, "France's Year in Africa, 1972," in *Africa Contemporary Record, 1972-73*, ed. Colin Legum (London: Rex Collins, 1973), p. 10.

50. Isebill V. Gruhn, "The Lome Convention," *International Organization*, vol. 30, no. 2 (Spring 1976):261.

51. For details see O. J. B. Ojo, "Nigeria and the Formation of ECOWAS," *International Organization*, vol. 34, no. 4 (Autumn 1980):571-604.

52. "West Africa Finds a New Future", Speeches by heads of state during the ECOWAS inaugural meeting in Lagos, 27-28 May, 1975 (Lagos: Federal Government Printers, 1975).

53. Adebayo Adedeji, "The Evolution of a West African Economic Community" (Text of an address presented at a Ministerial Conference on ECOWAS, Lome, Togo, 10-16 December 1973).

54. General Yakubu Gowon, opening address in "West Africa Finds a New Future" (Formal meeting of ECOWAS heads of state in Lagos on 27 May 1975).

4

ECOWAS:
INSTITUTIONAL FRAMEWORK AND
DECISION-MAKING PROCESS

This chapter generally attempts to accomplish two things.
First, to examine the aims and objectives of the ECOWAS scheme
and highlight the main provisions of the treaty. And second, to
focus attention on the decision-making institutions and the
decision-making process of the organization. These two important
aspects of ECOWAS are not mutually exclusive. For while the
first step in economic integration is to identify aims and possibilities, the actual process of integration can only be facilitated by
suitable institutional foundations and formulations.

THE MAIN TREATY PROVISIONS

The Community, as reflected in the ECOWAS Treaty contain-
ing 64 articles arranged into 14 chapters, has as its central objectives the promotion of "co-operation and development in virtually all fields of economic activity, particularly in the fields of
industry, transport, telecommunications, energy, agriculture,
natural resources, commerce, monetary and financial questions and
in social and cultural matters, for the purpose of raising the
standard of living of its people, of increasing and maintaining
economic stability, of fostering closer relations among its members
and contributing to the progress and development of the African
continent" (Article 2).
There are perhaps seven principal objectives discernible from
the foregoing all-embracing if not fuzzy set of objectives. These
can be listed as: elimination of customs duties; abolition of quan-

62

titative and administrative restrictions on trade; establishment of a common customs tariff and a common commercial policy; the abolition of obstacles to the free movement of persons, services, and capital; the harmonization of agricultural and industrial policies; the establishment of a fund for cooperation; and the harmonization of monetary policies. The treaty provides some specific goals and specific provisions for realizing these declared objectives. These are in the areas of trade, monetary cooperation, and cooperation in the field of industrialization. It is envisaged that the establishment of the customs union would take a transitional period of 15 years after the treaty has come into force. Within this period all existing customs and other barriers to free trade would have been gradually whittled down and finally eliminated, giving way to common customs, tariffs, and nomenclature for the Community against outside countries.

In addition to the free movement of goods, services, and capital, the treaty seeks to bring about the free movement of persons; that is, citizens of member states should be able to visit, and reside in, each other's territories with very few restrictions. Also enshrined in the treaty are harmonization of economic policies and, where appropriate, joint development of industrial and other projects. At present the members of the Community have separate, sometimes divergent policies in the various economic sectors. Some have controlled centralized economies while others run their economies on fairly liberal lines. For an integrated and balanced economy to be achieved within the Community there must be approximation or harmonization of policies. Hence the treaty sets out ways and means of forging economic cooperation and development among member states in various economic fields. In the field of industrial cooperation, for example, provision is made for the exchange of feasibility studies, report on performance of foreign business groups, the initiation of joint studies for the identification of viable industrial projects, and the financing of research in the exchange of technology. It also provides for the harmonization of industrial policies in order to avoid dissimilar policies, by exchanging industrial plans.

Unlike the defunct East African Common Market, the ECOWAS Treaty has no provisions for a Development Bank. Chapter 5 which states the objective for industrial harmonization and development is silent on this. Moreover, Chapter 7 which deals with cooperation in monetary and financial matters leaves to the Trade, Customs, Immigration, Monetary and Payment Commission recommendations concerning the harmonization of fiscal policies among member states. Only Chapter 11, Article 50 establishes a fund for Co-operation, Compensation and Development. This Fund will be used to finance projects in member states, provide compensation to members where necessary, guarantee foreign investments in member states, and help develop the poor member states. It will be established from contributions by member states based on their economic strength, assessed as a factor of GNP and population; from the income of Community enterprises; and from receipts from bilateral, multilateral, and other foreign sources and subsidiaries and contributions of all kinds from all sources. The ECOWAS Fund is thus meant to serve the same objectives as contained in the provision for the East African Development Bank (Article 52 of Lagos Treaty and Annex 5 of Kampala Treaty). Except for their mode of operation, the ECOWAS Fund can be described as a direct equivalent of the East African Development Bank as well as the UDEAC Solidarity Fund.

It must be added that the provisions of the treaty and the protocols are couched in general terms. This strategy was adopted by the founding fathers so as to make it possible for them to achieve the much needed consensus on general principles and enable them to sign the basic documents that would create ECOWAS as a subregional institution. However, to facilitate the implementation of the treaty, it has become necessary to examine the basic documents with a view to making the necessary modifications or amendments of some basic provisions and important articles. For example, the provisions of Article 13 of the treaty have been extended so as to make the "Consolidation of Tariff Barriers" applicable to nontariff barriers. Similarly, Article 27 of the treaty has been modified in order to provide for a Protocol of Freedom of Movement, Right of Residence and Establishment and the redefinition of the concept of "Community Citizen." Also some amendments, modifications, and additions have been made in respect of the Protocol on Rules of Origin provided under Article 11.

THE INSTITUTIONS OF THE COMMUNITY

The process of integration necessitates creation of suitable institutions to deal with the complex problem of linking the economic destinies of several nations. Indeed much of the success of the EEC is attributable to the wide range of institutions which have been instrumental in translating its programs and policies into action. The Treaty of Rome established clear provisions not only for setting up these organs, but for a gradual transfer of initiative from member states to these supranational entities. A significant result of these built-in provisions is that integration among the member states of the Community has become a "continuous process, whose scope is expanding along a previously determined time-path."[1] It is the continuity of this process which to a large extent has consistently increased the stake of the member nations in European Community programs.

While the institutions of ECOWAS are not so elaborate, the Lagos Treaty recognizes the development of adequate institutional machinery as an essential condition for successful coordination of development policies. In addition to providing a forum in which opinions on matters of common interest can be exchanged, the institutions created by the ECOWAS Treaty are of particular importance to the implementation of joint decisions for cooperation. The coordination of industrial development policies and the harmonization of national development plans provided for in the treaty cannot be achieved if there are no adequate institutional arrangements to take the coordinating role. It is in light of this, and especially of peculiar African conditions, that all formal institutions created by the ECOWAS Treaty have their part to play in the functioning of the Community. It is the totality of these activities which constitutes the Community method in decision taking; this depends upon a modus vivendi existing between the units to allow the processes to operate.

The highest decision-making organ of the Community is the Authority of Heads of State and Government which is charged with administering and directing the integrative movement of the Community. In other words, "The Authority," as often referred to in the treaty, is to have a general direction and control over the performance of the executive functions of the Community. Composed of one representative from each member state, this supreme organ of the Community which meets at least once a year, has authority to adopt whatever policies it regards as necessary and appropriate. The Authority is the only organ empowered to suspend a member state and establish additional commissions as it deems necessary.

As the role of the Authority is limited to "the highest policy-making in very few important matters," the general administration of the Community, including even budgetary matters, is entrusted to the responsibility of other institutions of the Community, particularly the Council of Ministers. Thus, the Authority is not saddled with many decision-making issues except in very selected cases. This has the advantage of insulating the operation of the Community, at least for some time, from the impact of a strained relationship between any two or more states. One other advantage is that this arrangement leaves the actual operation of the Community to a group of experts or technocrats who not only owe allegiance to the Community but are also committed to its success or viability.[2]

In making the Authority of Heads of State and Government the supreme organ of the Community, the ECOWAS Treaty is merely adopting the practice of the existing economic, and even political, cooperation schemes in Africa. It often is considered necessary in the continent to involve the highest level of political representation, usually the heads of state and/or government. Under the UDEAC Treaty, for example, the executive functions are carried out by the Council of Heads of State, which is the supreme organ of the organization and has wide powers and responsibilities in the formulation of policies for the attainment of the treaty objectives. Similarly, in the East African Treaty, the East African Authority was the supreme organ of the defunct East African Community and was composed of the three presidents of Kenya, Uganda, and Tanzania. It was responsible for the general direction and control of economic decisions in accordance with the provisions of the treaty.

On the other hand, unlike African systems of economic cooperation, none of the regional economic groupings in Latin America involves the heads of state and government in the institutional machinery responsible for administering and directing the integrative movement. The Andean Common Market, for example, has at the top of its institutional structure the Mixed Commission, an intergovernmental body resembling a diplomatic conference which meets three times a year. Similarly, the Latin American Economic System (SELA) established in October 1975 has as its supreme body the Latin American Council which is composed of one representative (not head of state or government) of each member state. This, however, does not make these organizations completely insulated from political pressures. The Andean Common Market, for instance, has not been able, despite its unique organizational machinery, to insulate the decision-making process from the politics of national interest. The Mixed Commission is sensitive to national priorities, and it has frequently modified technical proposals of the Junta, an independent secretariat of supranational officials.[3] Perhaps the only significant difference here is that the African regional economic schemes, such as ECOWAS, have more direct political involvement in their operation than those of Latin America.

The ECOWAS Authority of Heads of State and Government is assisted by another political body, the Council of Ministers--made up of two representatives of each member state--who act in an advisory capacity to the Authority, as well as give directions to all subordinate institutions of the Community. The Council of Ministers is also charged with the responsibility of keeping "under review the functioning and development of the Community in accordance with the Treaty" as well as making recommendations to the Authority on harmonious functioning and development of the Community. Its decisions are binding on all the subordinate organs of the Community.

The third most important institution of ECOWAS is the Executive Secretariat of the Community established in Article 8 of the treaty. It is the machinery of execution headed by an executive secretary who is appointed by and is directly responsible to the Authority and who can be removed from office by the Authority on the recommendation of the Council of Ministers. The executive secretary is the principal executive officer of the Community and head of the Secretariat which is responsible for the day to day running of the Community and its institutions. He is assisted by two deputy executive secretaries responsible for the two branches of the Secretariat: administrative and economic matters respectively.

There are four technical and specialized commissions in ECOWAS, namely, the Trade, Customs, Immigration, Monetary and Payment Commission; the Industry, Agriculture and Natural Resources Commission; the Transport, Telecommunications and Energy Commission; and the Social and Cultural Affairs Commission. Each of these commissions is composed of experts from all the member states and their duty is to draw up programs in their relevant fields of competence and assess the implementation of such programs. There is provision for the creation of any other specialized and technical bodies should the need arise. Taking advantage of this provision, the Authority of Heads of State and Government at its annual summit meeting held in Freetown in May 1981 approved the establishment of a Defence Council consisting of Ministers of Defence and Foreign Affairs of member states; and a Defence Commission comprising a chief of staff from each member state.

Finally, like many other economic groupings, the ECOWAS Treaty makes provisions for the setting up of a tribunal. The founding fathers were acutely aware that differences in the interpretation of the provisions of the agreements for cooperation might raise serious problems of implementation. Therefore it becomes necessary to have a multinational body that can guide the economic grouping in any matters that may result in a conflict of interest. Hence a tribunal of the Community is provided for to see to the correct interpretation and application of the provisions of the treaty and the protocols and also to solve any dispute that may arise. Whereas some economic groupings attach little importance to the need for a separate organ responsible for enforcing community law, others like the EEC regard this as an "integral part of the institutional structure."[4] In Organisation Commune Africaine et Mauricienne (OCAM) and the Maghreb, for example, the treaties are not explicit on these matters, and often disputes arising between member states are left to be solved through a series of dialogues and consultations.[5]

The ECOWAS Tribunal is important at least in two respects. First, it would assist in clarifying matters whenever there is disagreement arising essentially out of technical problems in interpreting the treaty. It would appear, however, that the Tribunal would find it extremely difficult to resolve disputes arising from misunderstandings or misinterpretations which are consciously provoked to serve national interests. The strength of the Tribunal is limited in the sense that it has neither the "powers of the sword" nor of the purse but instead those of impartiality and technical competence. Second, the role of the Tribunal in offering advisory opinion on technical and legal matters may minimize the dangers of a tendency toward politicization of nonpolitical issues by states in disagreement under the treaty. Besides, like Article 12 of the League of Nations Covenant, the involvement of the Tribunal in a dispute can occasionally serve as a cooling off period. In other words, this can buy the necessary time to cool tempers of states involved in the dispute. It is, however, doubtful whether the Tribunal can effectively handle matters involving delicate national interests.

Such in brief are the institutions of the ECOWAS Treaty. The treaty clearly demonstrates a hierarchy of authorities where the Authority of the Community is not only the live wire of the organization but of the Community itself. To a lesser degree, the Council of Ministers is also vested with enormous powers, for example, in relation to definition of products originating in member states (Article 15, clause 3), and with making financial regulations for the applications of provisions relative to the Community's budget (Article 53, clauses 3 and 5).

THE DECISION-MAKING PROCESS

The decision-making process would seem to constitute one of the most contentious areas of regional economic groupings. This process sometimes creates tensions between the formal institutions of a grouping. A clear case in point is the most critical struggle between the council and the commission of the EEC which formed an element in the political stagnation affecting the Community during 1965 and 1966 from which the commission emerged chastened. In the African context, in particular, decision making is bound to raise questions that may not be relevant to and cannot be answered on the basis of European experience. For, whereas in the case of the EEC the success of the Community is based "on the inherent confidence of member nations in their ability to meet the challenges of integration," the situation is quite the reverse in the case of African regional groupings. Although African countries do recognize the prospects and benefits that can be derived from integration, they are nevertheless extremely cautious in negotiating binding commitments. To a large extent, the consciousness of newly won independence tends to influence the general approach to economic integration as well as the details of the integration. This is clearly reflected in the ECOWAS decision-making process.

The structure of the institutions of ECOWAS shows that decisions have to be taken at various levels: initially technical commissions and then the Council of Ministers culminating in the final consideration of any major issue by the Authority of Heads of State and Government. There is no provision for voting under the treaty, neither is it made quite clear which institution is empowered to make a formal proposal as a first step in the decision-making process. In the case of the EEC, for example, a Community decision normally arises as a result of a formal proposal from the commission to the council, which must itself make the decision whether to accept or reject the proposal in accordance with the agreed procedure. However, under Article 27 of Protocol 4, annexed to the ECOWAS Treaty, it is provided that each member state on the board of directors of the Fund "shall have one vote. All matters before the Board of Directors shall be decided by a simple majority."

It must be stressed, however, that apart from the Fund, at each level of decision making the unstated principle of unanimity applies. In fact, it is stated in Article 6(b) of the treaty that at the deliberations of the Council of Ministers, if any member state opposes or objects to any matter, no decision may be taken and the issue should automatically be referred to the Authority for its ruling. In other words, the Community's institutions should at each level strive to appease each member state--the interests of each one must be taken care of. Thus, even in practice, voting does not take place in the meetings of the board of directors of the Fund. This is due to the fact that the same ministers who attend the Council of Ministers do participate in the deliberations of the board of directors of the Fund and they are invariably conscious of the provisions of Article 6(b) of the treaty. Thus the rule of unanimity applies to all the deliberations of the Council of Ministers.

Unanimity is the rule in most cooperative and integration groups. Unanimity rule, however, has its merits and demerits. A recent United Nations study of the problems of economic integration among developing countries has argued that, although the primary purpose of the rule is to obtain as much support as possible from all members, unanimity applied without discrimination at all levels of an organization--as we have noticed in the case of ECOWAS--"exposes it to many dangers." It can become a major obstacle to positive action by the organization. The constant need for complicated deals, and the arduous efforts to arrive at a compromise indispensable for decision, often lead to immobility and obscure the text or resolutions. Thus a compromise is often reached at the expense of precision and in favor of a confused text which is difficult to interpret.[6]

Another drawback of the application of the unanimity rule is the slowness of the decision-making process and the fact that each member is able to paralyze the process by using its veto. Consequently, there is a certain contradiction between these constraints and the need for an effective decision-making machinery in a modern economy, especially as this rule is still applied in several regional groupings in the developing countries such as CACM and UDEAC which have reached an advanced degree of integration. In the case of CACM, for example, although the Executive Council, like the Commission of the Andean Common Market, takes its decisions by majority vote, unanimity is required for all important decisions in the Economic Council. This unanimity requirement, combined with the necessity for ratification by the member statesa practice adopted by ECOWAS--renders the decision-making process a slow and inadequate one. It is not unknown for this slowness to produce such a time lag that, when the decision comes into effect, the situation has changed to the extent that the decision applied is no longer in keeping with the actual circumstances.

In UDEAC, the unanimity rule in the council sometimes has the drawback of delaying the settlement of certain matters. As long as a single member state objects to any matter, no decision is adopted. The matter has to come repeatedly before the council until unanimous agreement is reached. A similar repetition of issues was also occurring in the erstwhile EAC at all levels. In both groupings this has effects which, according to the matter involved and the viewpoint taken, "can be regarded either as delays or as maturing periods."[7]

The application of the unanimity rule in ECOWAS does not necessarily imply that this would in practice constitute an obstacle to the functioning of its institutions. It has so far not done so even in the case of UDEAC. The unanimity rule, on the other hand, implies the existence of a considerable measure of goodwill making it possible to find acceptable compromises and to bear the losses resulting from a common decision "without recourse to the veto." Even in the case of both the Executive Council of CACM and the Commission of the Andean Group which have adopted the use of majority rules, members have preferred, on many occasions, to seek a consensus. Similarly, the EEC in 1965 reached an agreement recognizing that "unanimity would continue to be used" whenever a member considered the matter under discussion to be of vital national importance. Subsequently the Community's Council of Ministers has used "unanimous voting as its general rule" with the normal understanding that a member may abstain from voting on a matter which is not of vital interest to it, but which it would rather not support, without preventing the other members from agreeing to the policy.[8] Perhaps at its present stage of integration, it is in the interest of ECOWAS to continue to adopt unanimity or consensus especially with regard to the important policy decisions, if not necessarily in the case of administrative and operational actions.

It is not surprising, therefore, that the Authority at its fifth ordinary annual meeting held in Cotonou in May 1982 shelved a discussion of the subject as proposed by the executive secretary of the Community. Dr. Ouattara in his annual report to the summit complained about the long delay in "arriving at decisions and getting them implemented, even on issues that are not of very vital importance to the security of a country." The executive secretary then called for a distinction to be made on issues where unanimity or consensus or majority decisions is necessary; and also what decisions can end at Commission or Council or Authority level to become enforceable and which ones "need to be ratified." In the interest of progress, he suggested a review of the decision-making process of the Community so as to enable ECOWAS to "combine thoroughness with speed of action" and thereby remove the tendency to frustrate those member states "who are eager and have taken the trouble to ensure that the Community moves ahead."[9] While the soundness of the executive secretary's suggestion cannot be disputed, the Authority found itself unable to tackle this sensitive subject, which was excluded from the final communique issued at the end of the summit.[10]

The unanimity rule notwithstanding, the powers of the Community to bind member states to its decisions are almost non-existent, irrespective of the level at which such decisions are taken. For decisions become binding only after ratification, usually by at least seven signatory states. This is in marked contrast to what obtains in other similar organizations where the decisions become binding upon signature. In the EEC the final product of a decision-making process will generally be a directive, a regulation, or a decision. These types of acts of the Community are, however, quite distinct.

An EEC directive, for instance, only sets out an objective to be achieved such as, for example, uniform safety standards for commercial vehicles; but this comes into force only after the member states have enacted national legislation to achieve this objective. On the other hand, a EEC regulation becomes law throughout the Community as soon as it has been published in *Official Journal* of the Community. A decision simply settles "a particular issue, often of some urgency."[11]

Of particular importance to note, also, is the fact that the Treaty of ECOWAS does not create a supranational body, as the neo-functionalists would wish to see. Perhaps I should at this point pause to define what is meant by supranationalism. Dennis Swann has explained that supranationalism can refer to a "situation in which international administrative institutions exercise power" over, for example, the economies of the nation states. In the case of ECOWAS, it would have meant the Executive Secretariat at Lagos--that "stateless body," to quote General de Gaulle's reference to the EEC Commission--being endowed with powers over the economies of the 16 member states, such powers being exercised independently of either the Authority or the Council of Ministers. Alternatively, supranationalism can refer to a situation in which ministerial bodies, when taking decisions (to be implemented by international administrations) work on a majority voting system rather than by insisting on unanimity.[12]

Applied to ECOWAS, one can hardly see any evidence of supranationalism. This view is reinforced not only by several

ECOWAS Treaty provisions, but also by the way some of the institutions have been functioning since the treaty came into force.
For example, Article 3 of the treaty provides that "Member States
shall make effort to plan and direct their policies with a view to
creating favourable conditions for the achievement of the aims of
the Community; in particular, each Member State shall take all
steps to secure enactment of such legislation as is necessary to give
effect to the Treaty." A careful examination of this Article would
seem to suggest that the Community is not intended to be supranational. And, as noted already, while the decisions and directions of the Authority of Heads of State and Government "shall be
binding on all institutions" of the Community, they cannot be
binding immediately on member states themselves. It will appear,
however, that the only cases where an institution of the Community can take binding decisions on member states are under Article
54 dealing with budgetary matters and Article 56 relating to procedure for settlement of disputes. That the treaty has not created
a supranational body is shown by two decisions recently adopted
by the Community. The first was the Protocol on Non-Aggression
Pact and the second, the general conventions on privileges and immunities of ECOWAS, which were adopted on 22 April 1978.[13]

INTEREST GROUPS AND DECISION-MAKING PROCESS

A significant aspect of the ECOWAS decision-making process
worth examining here concerns the extent to which the Community provides a forum for exchange of views with interest groups
or private sectors in the West African sub-region--employers'
associations, chambers of commerce, trade unions, etc.--who are
directly interested in and likely to be directly affected by many of
the provisions of the treaty and policies of the Community. Some
of the obvious questions to be raised include the following: What
organ has the Lagos Treaty created within the decision-making institutions for consultation with the private sector, both business
and labor? To what extent do the broad masses of the people of
West Africa participate in or influence the decision-making
process? Or is the idea of West African economic integration to
be "sold" to a reluctant, an uncommitted, and skeptical private
sector and working population?

Theoretically, the importance of the role of interest groups in
promoting integration has been stressed ad nauseum by neo-functionalist scholars like Haas and Lindberg.[14] According to such
neo-functionalist theorists, by participating in the policy-making

process, interest groups are likely to develop "a stake in promoting further integration" in order to acquire economic payoffs and additional benefits from maintaining and stimulating the organization through which certain demands can be articulated and goals attained. This implies that in the integration process interest groups can play an instrumental role in the maintenance of the integrative system. Through their involvement in the policy-making process of an integrating community, these groups will "learn" about the rewards of such involvement and undergo attitudinal changes inclining them favorably toward the system. The result of this process is quite significant for the growth of the integrating community. For while the interest groups would be interested in working steadily toward the perpetuation of the system, the decision makers would in turn develop an interest in being responsive to demands of these groups. Through this process, the supportive clientele of the integrating community, which is of paramount importance for its growth and operation, would be wide and considerable. Thus the interest groups can enhance the position of responsive institutions.

Given the importance neo-functionalists attach to the role of interest groups in promoting integration, it is not surprising that discussions leading up to the establishment of the EEC considered the formal involvement of economic and social groups in the policy-making process. Hence within the European Communities channels have been developed through which economic and social interests participate in discussions, although it is far less clear what influence they can exert on the outcome. The main formal channel provided for under the Rome Treaty is the Economic and Social Committee (ESC) set up under Articles 193-198. According to Article 193 the ESC shall consist of representatives of the various categories of economic and social life, in particular, representatives of producers, agriculturists, transport operators, workers, merchants, artisans, liberal professions, and the general interest. In practice about one-third of the members are trade unionists. It was thought that this body would provide a stimulus to interest groups to participate directly in Community discussions, from which support for policy proposal would flow. But the ESC has not developed as an institutional resource for mobilizing opinion at the supranational level to respond to interest group demands. Consequently, recent commentators like Lodge and Herman do not assign any great weight to its role in the EEC decision-making process, yet this does not entirely diminish the significance of its existence as a forum for the articulation of interest group positions.[15] It is worth noting that neo-functionalist premises have been realized for the EEC outside of ESC, that is, through channels other than the ESC. Interest groups have pressurized supranational policy and decision-makers through alternative mechanisms found to have been more effective than the ESC. By 1965 there were 231 regional offices of business and trade associations and 117 regional agricultural associations with offices in Brussels.[16]

This experience of the EEC is not reflected in the institutional structure of ECOWAS. Indeed, ECOWAS can rightly be criticized for not having any popular roots, and because the personalities and institutions controlling it have little contact or involvement with the man in the street. The whole institutional structure can be described as a brain child of the elite, and there is no organ through which interest groups can bridge, as neo-functionalists suggest, the elite-mass gap. Being intergovernmental in nature, key ECOWAS decision makers are generally the top-level political elites and bureaucrats. Participation in the decision-making process by the staff of the Executive Secretariat is minimal while the various parliamentary bodies play, if at all, a very peripheral role. Not only is the bulk of the people virtually ignored but also, and perhaps more importantly, organizations representing business interest--employers' associations or chambers of commerce--are not included on a regular and formal basis even though they do make their presence felt individually, indirectly, and informally. Although the Federation of Chambers of Commerce in West Africa participated meaningfully in the negotiations leading to the establishment of the Community,[17] to date only observer status has been accorded it by the Community.[18]

Indeed, in general, participants in the decision-making process within African regional organizations are the political elite, the bureaucratic elite, and representatives of foreign interests. Hence the broad masses of the people are excluded from effective participation in the economy as both producers and consumers. This low level of economic mobilization of the broad masses of the people means that they are unlikely to be involved in regional integration efforts based on functionalist strategies. This implies, therefore, that regional groupings in Africa will be between only a tiny fraction of the population of the states concerned.[19]

ECOWAS, however, is not an exception. Both UDEAC, and especially the defunct EAC, did not establish any forms of consultation with the private sector; therefore they did not in principle associate persons other than official experts with their work. These two groupings have no organs whose membership consists of representatives of the economic and social sectors. Put differently, neither the EAC nor UDEAC provided for a separate and continuous committee of experts or for the formal involvement of private individuals or groups in the decision-making process. Indeed, at the meeting of heads of state and government of UDEAC held in Yaounde in January 1967 it was firmly resolved that UDEAC decisions must be made entirely at the intergovernmental level, thus closing the door to business groups within the region to have any right to participate formally in UDEAC decision making.[20]

By contrast, however, the association of independent or private experts and representatives of professional organizations or the private sector with the preparation and implementation of decisions, through advisory bodies or ad hoc groups, are to be found, with some variations, in all the Latin American groupings. In the case of CACM, for example, the private sector is closely associated with the activities of its institutions through various working parties. However, it is perhaps within the Andean Group that consultation through such bodies as the Consultative Committee and the Economic and Social Advisory Committee has been firmly institutionalized and formalized. For although the erstwhile LAFTA allowed for private sector consultation through various advisory committees, consultative committees, and sectorial meetings, that consultation was not formalized as it is in the Andean Common Market.[21]

Interest groups, however, need not necessarily be in favor of the integration process. In general, many of these groups remain a weak force, as Werner Feld concluded in his study of European interest groups.[22] In many cases the types of interests that are aggregated at the regional level tend to be very general, with more specific interests and structures remaining at the national level. For instance, as Nye has emphasized, despite the existence of regional trade union secretariats in Brussels, the idea of collective bargaining at the European level in response to the creation of a European market has not taken hold--in part because of divisions in the labor movement but also because of the importance of national governmental power in collective bargaining.[23] Besides, many interest groups could conveniently be opposed to it. A characteristic case in point was the opposition mounted by the Venezuelan private sector against the country's entry into the Andean Common Market. The private sector was extremely effective in turning its interests into government policy. Specifically, Federation de Camaras (Federation of Chambers), the best organized pressure group in Latin America representing 168 Venezuelan trade associations and federations, stoutly opposed its country's membership in the Andean Group. Consequently, although the Andean Pact was signed in 1969, Venezuela did not join the Andean Common Market until 1973.[24]

In spite of these observations, the argument favoring the importance of interest groups or the private sector as relevant actors in promoting integration remains valid. These groups, lacking in authoritative decision-making capacity, should not lead to the interpretation that they are unimportant. They may prove to be very significant. By building in the involvement and collaboration of the private sector, these groups may well play a vital role, as they have done, in the case of the EEC. In his examination of the role of the trade unions as an interest group in the European Community, Colin Beever has come to the conclusion that, as far as general Community policy is concerned, the unions in the EEC countries, with the exception of the World Federation of Trade Union (WFTU), have almost unreservedly supported the principles of European integration and the Common Market itself "and have . . . pressed for more progress and a greater degree of supranational power to be given to the Community institutions." They claim that they are the true defenders of the principles of the Rome Treaty, and have never wavered in this belief.[25] Similarly, in the 1969 crisis of CACM, for example, it was the Federation of Chambers of Commerce and Industry of Central America which issued a statement defending the Common Market. Furthermore, in addition to representing a shift of political activity toward the regional level and a potential source of regional pressure on national governments these nongovernmental groupings themselves have elite socialization effects.[26]

In this regard, the failure to involve the private sector in ECOWAS decision-making processes appears to be more serious than may readily be appreciated. For in the final analysis, cooperation among West African countries is not or rather should not be just the concern of governments. If the political will to cooperate, to pool sovereignty is the "subsoil in which we must nurture the tree of collective self-reliance," the intellectual inputs in terms of ideas and especially the sustained pressure of the working population and organized opinion on their government to push ahead "is the water which must continually nurture the growth of the tree."[27]

This chapter has attempted a brief assessment of the main provisions of the ECOWAS Treaty as well as the decision-making process of the Community. An attempt has also been made in the course of this assessment to indicate where necessary the differences and similarities between ECOWAS and other regional groupings. In general, however, if the institutional structures of the ECOWAS and those of such African regional groupings as the defunct EAC or UDEAC are shown in an organizational chart or table, it becomes immediately apparent that regional integration schemes in Africa are almost structurally quite similar. ECOWAS, no doubt, is the largest economic integration grouping in the world in terms of the number of countries which are members. While size can make for stability when viewed against the background of the collapse of the EAC, it could be a great disadvantage to be too unwieldy, particularly so in ECOWAS because of the nature of the decision-making process. Be this as it may, the institutions and the decision-making process discussed in this chapter are intended to help put into practical expression the aims and objectives of ECOWAS as enshrined in the Lagos Treaty. The following chapter attempts a detailed examination of the two principal objectives of ECOWAS: industrial development and trade liberalization.

NOTES

1. R. H. Green and K. G. Krishna, *Economic Cooperation in Africa: Retrospect and Prospect* (Nairobi: OUP, 1967), p. 44.
2. S. A. Akintan, *The Law of International Economic Institutions in Africa* (Leyden: A. W. Sijhoff, 1977), p. 185.
3. W. P. Avery and J. D. Cochrane, "Innovation in Latin American Regionalism: The Andean Common Market," *International Organization*, vol. 27, no. 2 (Spring 1973):203
4. For details, see A. M. El-Agra, ed., *The Economics of the European Community* (Oxford: Philip Allan, 1980), pp. 27-28.
5. Bingu Mutharika, *Toward Multinational Economic Cooperation in Africa* (New York: Praeger, 1972), p. 63.
6. UNCTAD, "Current Problems of Economic Integration," TD/B/422 (1974), p. 162.
7. Ibid.
8. El-Agra, *Economics of the European Community*, p. 21.
9. ECOWAS Doc., ECW/CM/XI/2, *Annual Report of the Executive Secretary, 1981-1982* (May 1982).
10. Details of the communique are provided in ECOWAS DOC., ECW/HSG/V/4 (29 May 1982).
11. Anthony Kerr, *The Common Market and How It Works* (New York: Pergamon Press, 1977), p. 56.
12. Dennis Swann, *The Economics of the Common Market* (Harmondsworth: Penguin, 1975), p. 17.

13. For the examination of these decisions adopted by the Community to stress its nonsupranational character, see Oyewola Jemlyo, "The Treaty Law of the Economic Community of West African States (ECOWAS)" (Paper discovered in "ECOWAS Files, 1977"--Library of the Nigerian Institute of International Affairs, Lagos).

14. E. B. Haas, *The Uniting of Europe: Political, Social and Economic Forces, 1950-57* (Stanford: Stanford University Press, 1958); L. N. Lindberg, *The Political Dynamics of European Economic Integration*, (Stanford: Stanford University Press, 1963).

15. J. Lodge and V. Herman, "The Economic and Social Committee in EEC Decision-Making," *International Organization*, vol. 34, no. 2 (Spring 1980):266-84.

16. Stephen Holt, *The Common Market* (London: Hamish Hamilton, 1967), p. 66.

17. For details see Chief Henry Fajemirokun, "The Role of the West African Chambers of Commerce in the Formation of ECOWAS" (Paper presented at the ECOWAS Conference, Lagos, August 1976).

18. ECOWAS Doc., C/DEC 1/5/79, Decision of the Council of Ministers Relating to the ECOWAS Federation of Chambers of Commerce, *Official Journal* 2 (June 1980):11.

19. Abdul A. Jalloh, "Regional Integration in Africa: Lessons from the Past and Prospects for the Future," *Africa Development*, vol. 1, no. 2 (1976):48-53.

20. Abdul A. Jalloh, "The Politics and Economics of Regional Political Integration of Equatorial Africa" (Ph.D diss., University of California, Berkeley, 1969), p. 300.

21. Avery and Cochrane, *Innovations in Latin American Regionalism*, p. 205.

22. Werner Feld, "National Economic Interest Groups and Policy Formation in the EEC," *Political Science Quarterly*, vol. 81, no. 3 (September 1966):392-411.

23. Nye, "Comparing Common Markets: A Revised Neo-Functionalist Model," *International Organization*, vol. 24, no. 4 (Autumn 1970):809.

24. For details see, Roger W. Fontaine, *The Andean Pact: A Political Analysis*, vol. 5, of *The Washington Papers* (Beverly Hills/London: 1977), pp. 33-4. See also W. P. Avery, "Oil, Politics, and Economic Decision Making: Venezuela and the Andean Common Market," *International Organization*, vol. 30, no. 4 (Autumn 1976):541-71.

25. R. Colin Beever, *Trade Unions and Free Labour Movement in the EEC* (London: Chatham House; PEP, 1969), pp. 18-19.
26. Nye, "Comparing Common Markets," p. 809.
27. Adebayo Adedeji, "Collective Self-reliance in Developing Africa: Scope, Prospects and Problems" (Paper presented at the Conference on ECOWAS, Lagos, 23-27 August 1976).

5

INDUSTRIALIZATION AND
TRADE LIBERALIZATION
IN ECOWAS

Undoubtedly, the basic economic motivation for the economic integration efforts of the West African states is industrialization. It is in the context of national industrialization, coupled with trade expansion and long-run economic growth generally, that individual member states of ECOWAS are likely to identify their economic interests with the Community. Similarly, the basic instrument for integration is the liberalization of tariffs. All the West African countries recognize that the expansion of trade which can follow on the opening up of markets is vital to their development. This has become particularly important because of the great dependence on export earnings as the major source of exchange earnings and government revenues. Indeed, development of trade and industrialization are linked together as engines of growth. But the main reason for agreeing to the partial relinquishment of sovereignty, seemingly inherent in any attempt to achieve integration, is the hope of turning to account the economies of scale offered by the new economic region for the purpose of establishing industries with greater vertical integration and modern technology. Underlying economic cooperation there is thus the hope of crossing a new economic and technological frontier, which would generate a far-reaching transformation in economic structure. In this chapter, then, I intend to analyze the ECOWAS strategy for industrial development and trade expansion.

INDUSTRIALIZATION AND DEVELOPMENT IN ECOWAS

In its broadest sense, Clarence Zuvekas has recently defined the term "industrialization" as the process of transforming raw materials, with the aid of human resources and capital goods, into consumer goods; new capital goods which permit more consumer goods (including food) to be produced with the same human resources; and social overhead capital, which "together with human resources provides new services to both individuals and businesses."[1] Conceived of in this way, industrialization technically may denote the organization of production in business enterprises, characterized by specialization and a new division of labor, involving the application of technology and mechanical and electrical power to supplement and replace human labor. In this chapter, however, we are concerned with a much narrower concept of industrialization--the process by which an economy develops from one that predominantly produces agricultural products to one in which industry represents an important share of total economic activity. It is seen not only as a way of accelerating economic expansion but also as a way of bringing about a more general structural transformation of the society.[2]

Industrialization is thus widely accepted by both the developed and the developing countries as the "centre piece of the development process." Apart from the material benefits that industrialization can bring, there is a general belief, as Pierre Moussa once put it, that "the factory chimney has mythical value; it expresses a people's success on earth, their ability to cope with the modern world."[3] Industrialization, however, should not be considered merely as a question of economics, of selecting projects that can be proved to be viable in commercial terms and guaranteed to provide employment for a certain number of workers. Industrialization concerns people and the way they live. Thus for many politicians and planners in developing countries, industrialization (narrowly interpreted) and development have been synonymous with one another. This close relationship between industrialization and development has been stressed by Chenery and Syrquin who state that "Not only is there a strong statistical association between the rise of industry and the level of per capita income, but virtually all countries that have achieved high living standards by any measure have also industrialised to a substantial degree."[4] On the other hand, industrial progress can also hinder the process of general economic development. Economists like Little, Scitovsky, and Scott, for instance, have observed that if countries "pursue wrong industrialisation strategies, this can jeopardise prospects of successfully achieving the overall goals of economic development."[5]

The West African sub-region is one of the least economically developed regions of the world. Despite the fact that recent years have witnessed considerable efforts by member states of ECOWAS to industrialize, the contribution of the industrial sector to the structure of gross domestic product in the two United Nations Development Decades has been marginal. According to a recent ECOWAS study, the average share of manufacturing industry in the gross domestic product of the sub-region has increased marginally from about 8.2 percent in 1970 to about 8.4 percent in 1976. This proportion is still far less than the level achieved by the North African sub-region. The West African sub-region's share is also below the average for the whole of developing African countries. However, the 6 percent rate of growth of value added in manufacturing in the period 1970-76 for the ECOWAS sub-region is the highest for any sub-region in Africa in the same period. The level of achievement of the individual countries of the sub-region varies from country to country. While, for example, five countries in the sub-region achieved a growth rate of less than 3 percent and seven countries achieved growth rates of between 3 and 8 percent, four (Ivory Coast, Niger, Nigeria, and Senegal) achieved growth rates of over 8 percent thus surpassing the target set in the strategy for the second United Nations Development Decade.[6]

On the whole, however, even though upon the attainment of political independence industrialization has been a major economic policy in all ECOWAS countries, the record of achievement has been dismal especially when studied against the background of the resources that have been poured into this sector. The low contribution of the industrial sector to gross domestic product has been a major concern of almost all the member states of the Community. The concern of Nigeria over this state of affairs, for instance, is reflected in the country's 1975-80 national development plan.[7]

A cursory look at the geographical distribution of industries in the West African sub-region would tend to disclose certain similar features about its industrial centers. One noticeable feature is the unevenness of the distribution of industries in each country. Generally, most of the industries are centered around national capitals that are relatively more developed in terms of infrastructural facilities and where large urban populations which provide ready markets for the products of the industries are concentrated. A classic case in point is the concentration, as data for 1975 suggest, of about two-thirds of value added by Nigerian manufacturing around Lagos, the national capital. Similar conditions prevail in Liberia where virtually all manufacturing activity is centered around Monrovia.[8] Available evidence also indicates the concentration of manufacturing establishments in the greater Accra region of Ghana which alone in 1970 had over 60 percent of the country's total number of factories.[9]

This disparity in the location of industries in the sub-region is even more noticeable when studied across countries. For the industrial locations are a reflection of differences in national resources endowment and levels of industrial development in the individual member countries of ECOWAS. Thus, while industries are concentrated in the fairly developed countries like Ivory Coast, Ghana, Nigeria, and Senegal, there are almost none in the Gambia, Cape Verde, Guinea-Bissau, or Mauritania.

The type of manufacturing industries established in the sub-region as a whole is in the rudimentary stage and covers items ranging from the production of raw materials to the processing of primary products. The manufacturing sector is thus generally dominated by low technology industries such as food processing, beverages and tobacco, beer and soft drinks, textiles and clothing, rubber processing and rubber footwear. Thus even though the sub-region is adequately endowed with natural resources, there is almost complete absence of highly sophisticated technology or heavy engineering industry for the production of industrial and agricultural machinery and equipment. It is only in very few countries that industrial production covers such products as chemicals, petroleum products, non-metallic mineral products, and basic metals and metal products. While "crafts" actually dominate the industrial sector in some ECOWAS countries, relatively heavy industries such as oil refining, motor car assembling, electronics, and electrical equipments can be found in only a few countries such as Ghana, Ivory Coast, and Nigeria.[10]

One other salient feature is the basic similarity of the products produced by industries in the sub-region. This situation has resulted in the products being more competitive than complementary to one another. Besides, as most of the industrial plants are relatively very small they produce exclusively for their national markets. The implications are that these plants produce under quasi-monopolistic, inefficient, and high cost conditions within the protected national markets. A good number of them tend to operate below capacity. The result of such excess capacity has been wastage of scarce resources, duplication of plants, and fragmentation of production which ultimately increase costs of production and the prices of the end product.

Another area of concern is the degree of foreign involvement and inputs in the industrial sector of the sub-region. Generally, most of the industries rely heavily on foreign capital and imported raw materials. Although since 1970 there have been shifts toward the utilization of cheap and abundant domestic raw materials, imported capital and technology are still very important because of the relatively underdeveloped capital goods industry and relatively low absorptive capacity for modern technology. As noted in the ECOWAS special study on industrial development, the utilization of high-level foreign technology and capital is featured in the large-scale import-substitution industries such as brewing, chemicals industry, and especially oil refining and motor vehicle assembly plants. These industrial activities also employ high-level manpower which is often imported.[11]

Besides, the ECOWAS study on industrial development has noted a number of constraints that inhibit industrial development and industrial cooperation in the sub-region. The most crucial of these constraints, as stated already, is the Lilliputian national markets. Other major constraints to industrialization in the sub-region may include supply of raw materials, acute shortage of manpower in the skilled, managerial, and professional cadres, and the problems of inadequate infrastructures. The supply problem of imported raw materials is highly correlated with balance of payments difficulties. The problem is complicated in many cases by the shortage of foreign exchange.

The handicap in terms of national market size and lack of raw materials is compounded by inadequate infrastructures like water and electric power supply. This is much more serious in the Sahel than it is along the coast. The shortage of water affects the agricultural sector, thus compounding the problem of supplying raw materials to agro-based industries. Besides, there are a number of constraints that inhibit cooperation in the industrial field of the sub-region. The most important of these "is the bias in most countries against the manufactured goods from the neighbouring countries." Following such a bias, economic policy measures are taken to protect domestic industries. The protection of the industries against competition from intraregional industries thus limits the extent of the market.[12]

It is the general awareness of these problems of industrialization, coupled with the need to focus on more effective industrial policies in the sub-region, which greatly motivated the initiatives taken to create a sub-regional Community. Accordingly, an important provision is made in the ECOWAS Treaty for the establishment of an Industry, Agriculture and Natural Resources Commission charged with the responsibility of directing the Community toward evolution of more effective policies for industrial development and harmonization.

ECOWAS INDUSTRIAL POLICY

Cooperation in the field of industrial development is fundamental to the success of ECOWAS. Nearly all the member states of the Community are at the rudimentary stages of industrialization such that rapid industrial development is now being emphasized by these developing nations. Thus the sub-region is in the process of industrial transformation. In pursuit of this important objective, the ECOWAS Treaty sets out guidelines on which cooperation in industrialization in the sub-region would be based. Specifically, Industrial Development and Harmonisation are the subject of Chapter 5 (Articles 28-32) of the ECOWAS Treaty which consequently deals with the issue of industrial integration in the sub-region.

To implement the ECOWAS provisions on industrial cooperation, it has become necessary for the Community to formulate an industrial policy which, as the French economist Pierre Uri once commented, is something that no country or regional grouping can do without.[13] Generally, industrial policy is concerned with the development of industrial capabilities that will both reflect and improve the economic and social environment within which industry operates. Stated simply, industrial policy embraces all acts and policies of the state in relation to industry, that is, all aspects of state attitudes toward industry in its economic, social, and environmental setting. Formulation of this policy has been a common feature of regional economic communities committed to the creation of a single market; legal, fiscal, and financial harmonization; improvement of management techniques and minimization of unemployment arising from industrial change; and greater community solidarity in external economic relations. Defined in the context of regional economic community, industrial policy is a strategy designed to develop industrial activity in such a way that the single market presaged by the creation of a customs union will become a reality--by establishing a single industrial base for the community as a whole. Coordination of the industrial policies of countries participating in a regional integration scheme should be highly beneficial. As Komiya has remarked, in many of the industries in which an extensive industrial policy is called for, "economies of scale are a strategic factor in successful industrial development."[14] Then, too, if an industry in its early stage of development can have an integrated regional market instead of just a national one as its base, it would be easier for it to establish itself.

The ECOWAS "Industrial Policy and Programme" was approved by the Council of Ministers in Dakar in November 1979.[15] The policy emphasizes three major factors. The first factor relates to the identification of critical industrial sectors which lend themselves to harmonized efforts by ECOWAS member states in their development. To this end some criteria have been outlined for consideration in the selection of projects. For example, the selection should be influenced by the strategic nature of industries concerned, based on the economic and social needs of the populations of the sub-region. Other considerations may include the employment effect of the industry as well as its viability from the technical, financial, and commercial points of view. On the basis of these criteria, the Council of Ministers has identified ten priority sectors for consideration. These are food processing, building and construction materials, wood processing, telecommunications and electronics, petrochemicals, pharmaceuticals, iron and steel, and automobile and related industries.[16]

The second important element of the ECOWAS industrial policy and program is focused on the establishment of Community enterprises. This is a step that could be the key to rapid industrial development regionally. The protocol relating to the Community enterprises has created the legal basis for regulating the establishment and operation of regional multinational industrial projects. The enterprises approved under the protocol are designed to contribute to the development of the Community in general and in particular the industrially less advanced areas of the Community.[17] The ECOWAS regional company is to serve essentially two different functions. It is to be the vehicle through which the priority sectors of industry in the ECOWAS community are developed. Furthermore, this corporate framework is to be available for the general industrialization of the region also outside of the priority sectors. The third and final aspect of ECOWAS industrial policy is concerned with the location of regional industries, a process that is guided by two principles: the requirement of an equitable distribution of the benefits derived from Community action, and the objective of a balanced development of the sub-region. To this end, the ECOWAS industrial policy will focus special attention on the even distribution of regional industries over the 16 member states and the identification and location of at least one major regional enterprise in each member state.

PROBLEMS AND POSSIBILITIES

On the whole, the ECOWAS industrial policy, as briefly out-lined above, looks quite attractive and impressive. If effectively implemented, it would have an overall effect on the economic activity of the sub-region, an effect that would extend far beyond industrialization. The program takes into consideration the disparities in the level of development of the sub-region, and the need to satisfy the preference for industrialization of each member state through the greatest possible use of the economies of scale offered by the economic activities. In such cases, the goal is intraindustrial specialization within the area, which would enable the Community and each of its member states to develop in interdependent lots, a vertically integrated industry which will have a powerful impact on overall development.

The priority industrial sectors identified for consideration are just the dynamic ones required for an industrial "take off" of the sub-region. Appropriately, these are the very basic industries listed for development under the *Lagos Plan of Action*'s "short-term objectives up to the year 1985."[18] Equally laudable is the regional company concept embodied in the industrial policy. This is indeed a manifestation of the desire of the West African countries to move toward autonomous development and lessened dependence on the industrialized world. Also worth noting is the plan for harmonization of policies and incentives envisaged in the industrial policy. Experience in Africa and other parts of the world suggests that harmonization of policies and incentives among member states is essential for the eventual success of economic integration. In all probability, the need to harmonize policies is greater in the industrial sector than in any other sector.

But it is important to recognize the great difficulties in formulating, implementing, and administering an appropriate industrial policy. Like the phenomenon of integration as a whole, industrial policy is by its nature fraught with conflicts and tensions. For although our definition of industrial policy is by no means a comprehensive one (it would be necessary to add such elements as the environmental aspects of industrial development, the supply of energy and raw materials, and so on) it will be apparent immediately that the question of industrial development is inextricably enmeshed with broad questions of social, economic, and political objectives. In other words, industrial policy may appear to be a distinct functional task but in reality cannot be developed in isolation from social policy, regional policy, or the general methods used by governments for managing their economies. A few of the difficulties associated with industrial policy, especially in a market economy, are worth stressing here.

In the first place, the member countries of a regional grouping usually have different views on the future outlook of industrial development and it would not be easy for them to agree on which industries in which countries should be protected and by what policy measures. Second, intraregional coordination of industrial policy is likely to create a serious opposition of interests with regard to the distribution of industries. An active industrial policy within a regional grouping "usually means greater international division of labour" among the members, and the countries "may not be able to agree on the pattern of intra-regional specialisation," especially where "strategic" industries are involved. There is the likelihood of some member countries gaining much while others gaining little, or even losing under a certain arrangement.[19] Finally, the strategies of industrial development often stem from ideological and philosophical orientations. Here, it must be stressed that the relationship between government and industry may vary considerably from one country to another. Certain types of intervention that are acceptable in one country may not be acceptable in other countries. Development plans can thus not be harmonized without reconciling the social, political, and economic divergencies that account for disparate policies in the first place. These considerations suggest that attempts to pursue a coordinated, intraregional industrial policy, as detailed in the ECOWAS Treaty, may encounter much greater difficulties than are involved in a national industrial policy.

It is for this reason that even the EEC, the most advanced regional grouping in the world, has had little success in coordinating its members' national industrial policies. According to Hodges, the industrial policies pursued (or eschewed) in the member states of the European Communities "have been as diverse as the different relationships among governments, trade unions and business enterprises prevailing in each country." EEC discussions of the Memorandum on Industrial Policy (often called the Colonna Report) of March 1970 revealed a general disagreement on the fundamental philosophy underpinning development toward economic union. In particular this provoked a clash between the liberal philosophy of market economy based on competition, advocated primarily by the German government, and the French predilection for direct intervention and planning.[20] There was thus a division between partisans of a liberal policy and those advocating a more interventionist strategy. Consequently, the EEC has still not been able to develop a comprehensive policy for industrial development at the Community level.

Among developing countries, also, many regional groupings have incorporated members with significantly different economic systems. This is the case, for example, with the defunct East African Community, the Permanent Consultative Committee of the Maghreb, and the Arab Common Market. Like the EEC, the attempt by the Andean Common Market to harmonize economic policies between its member states that have not only different political systems, but completely different approaches to development, has had a serious effect on the overall evolution of the Andean integration process. This became particularly critical after the 1973 military coup in Chile, when the military junta adopted a laissez-faire policy that was impossible to reconcile with criteria of regional planning, regional tariff protection, and common rules toward foreign investment stipulated in the Cartagena Agreement which created the Andean Community. Although the withdrawal of Chile from the Andean Pact solved the impasse, it cannot be said that the rest of the Andean countries, with their differences in approaches to development, have succeeded in harmonizing their industrial policies.

The respective experiences of the EEC and the Andean Common Market with regard to implementation of industrial policies would seem to have some significance for ECOWAS. For whereas a meaningful harmonization of industrial policies is predicated on sharing of a common ideology and consequently common socio-economic objective, the disparities among member states of ECOWAS in political ideologies and philosophies reflecting their overall approach to economic policy and their assignment and use of policy instruments are most striking. How, for example, will it be possible to adjust tax incentives for private foreign investment in the People's Republics of Benin and Guinea, which have aligned themselves with scientific socialism, and in Nigeria and Ivory Coast, which are oriented toward capitalism? How will it be possible to harmonize their development plans? While all countries of ECOWAS have established development planning in some form, the degree of official intervention in economic processes differs significantly from country to country.

Generally, three approaches to planning in the Community can be distinguished. The first involves comprehensive planning procedures covering the entire economy, in some cases down to the level of individual enterprises. This approach is often accompanied by the prevalence of public ownership of major firms and industry, commerce and finance, as well as by the predominance of cooperative agricultural production over private production. There is thus a discernible trend toward increasing governmental intervention in shaping the development of national industrial capabilities, usually with the objective of making sure that an independent and viable national capability is preserved in every significant industrial sector. Countries that appear to fall into this category of economies are Benin, Cape Verde, Guinea, and Guinea-Bissau. Economic policy in these countries generally involves a rather heavy reliance on official intervention in the workings of market forces, notably in the form of price controls. This is also the case in Ghana, where, however, the planning procedure is less comprehensive and public ownership less prevalent.

There is also a second group of ECOWAS countries that rely to a substantial degree on overall economic planning, but unlike the countries belonging to the first group, these countries confine themselves largely to macroeconomic planning. Moreover, only strategic enterprises such as power companies and major productive firms are partly or fully state-owned. Finally, price controls are the exception rather than the rule. Countries belonging to this group are primarily the member countries (except Benin) of the West African Monetary Union (WAMU), as well as two other French-speaking countries in the Community--Mali and Mauritania. The approach of these countries to economic planning in many respects resembles the French system of "planification."

There is yet a third group of countries that rely to a large extent on the workings of market forces and private initiative although this does not exclude public ownership of selected enterprises. As the IMF special report on ECOWAS has emphasized, the essential reliance on market forces "does not imply that development planning and price controls are completely absent." Planning is concentrated primarily on public sector expenditure and on moderate fiscal incentives aimed at influencing the structure of private sector investment and production, while price controls are more often than not limited to strategic commodities and are in some cases applied during certain phases of the business cycle only.[21] ECOWAS countries falling into this category are the Gambia, Liberia, Nigeria, and Sierra Leone, with Liberia probably being a country with the least degree of official intervention in the economy.

The three different approaches to planning in the Community or the coexistence of ideologically diverse states within the single West African trading bloc raises issues relating to the role of foreign private investment, relationships with third parties, and a number of other aspects of social and economic policies. Yet the

ECOWAS Treaty's market-oriented conception is silent over how to deal with the increasing role of governments in shaping the structural and sectoral evolution of industry.

Closely related to the problem of ECOWAS industrial development is the orientation of the present trade pattern of member states. In the following section, therefore, attention is devoted to the pattern of trade in West Africa as a necessary background to the study of the ECOWAS trade liberalization program. While several previous studies have made some detailed references to the subject, it is nonetheless instructive to highlight briefly some strikingly relevant aspects.[22]

WEST AFRICAN TRADE PATTERN

One striking feature about the trade patterns of West Africa is that the level of exports and imports and the relative importance of various ECOWAS countries in overall regional trade vary widely. By far the largest importer and exporter in the region is Nigeria. The data for 1977 indicate that Nigeria accounted for about two-thirds of both total imports to and exports from the region.[23] By contrast, Cape Verde accounted for about 0.01 percent of total exports and about 0.26 percent of total imports. Between these two extremes, most countries in the sub-region have exports and imports that range between 1 and 3 percent of total exports and imports, respectively.

Intraregional trade is relatively low, accounting for less than 3 percent in 1977 for either exports or imports. As noted already, a common feature of West African trade is that most of the foreign trade of individual countries in the sub-region is carried out with non-West African countries. The orientation is toward the industrial countries of Europe, the United States and Japan. The overall import profile reveals the heavy dependence of the ECOWAS countries on trade with Europe. While for most of the French-speaking countries, about one-third of their imports originate in France, over 40 percent of the imports of the two Portuguese-speaking countries originate in Portugal. Similarly, the English-speaking countries of the Gambia, Ghana, Nigeria, and Sierra Leone obtain about a quarter of their imports from the United Kingdom, while Liberia obtains about the same proportion from the United States. Thus, the major trading partners of ECOWAS are the developed market economies whose shares of ECOWAS' exports and imports were about 80 percent during the period from 1966 to 1975. On the other hand, ECOWAS' trade with the centrally planned economies is relatively low, averaging 3 and 5 percent of exports and imports, respectively.[24] All this may be explained partly by the fact that the economies of the sub-region were established principally to serve as sources of raw materials for the factories of the various metropolitan countries. The attainment of political independence by these countries since the early 1960s has not substantially changed their trade pattern.

There are, however, two sets of factors that can also be considered responsible for this relatively low level of intraregional trade. The first includes factors that currently act as an impediment to intraregional trade. These include the noncomplementary production structure of the member countries of ECOWAS. The economies of most of these countries are heavily concentrated in the production of primary agricultural and mineral products which constitute a substantial part of their exports. And since they are highly competitive in agricultural products (that is, each country is almost self-sufficient), the demand for each other's primary products within the sub-region is quite limited. On the other hand, the import demand of these countries is primarily for processed foodstuffs, durable consumer goods, intermediate goods, and capital goods--most of which can only be supplied at present by the industrialized countries.

The dominance of trade between the ECOWAS countries and the developed countries in the total trade of the Community has necessitated continued attention to the efficiency of the transportation and communications system between these two groups of countries. By contrast, transportation and communications within ECOWAS have been largely neglected until recently. The lack of adequate intraregional road, railway, and air transport networks has resulted in prohibitively high transportation costs and acts as a major impediment to intraregional trade.

Even if the above major obstacles are alleviated, there is the second subset of factors that will assume more importance as disincentives to intraregional trade. These include trade barriers such as tariffs, export taxes, and quantitative restrictions. It must be emphasized that currently most ECOWAS countries depend heavily on customs receipts for government revenue. All this, together with the desire to protect domestic industries, results in an inordinately high level of tariffs. In most ECOWAS countries, no distinction in tariff application is made in favor of imports from other ECOWAS member countries. Accordingly, the current tariff structure does not appear to provide any special incentive to import from countries in the sub-region rather than from outside.

These, then, are some of the crucial issues that demand a very close attention in any effort at trade liberalization in West Africa. The extent to which intrasub-regional trade develops over the years will depend to a large extent on the alleviation of the current factors limiting intrasub-regional trade. As examined below, the problems involved are without doubt complex and daunting.

TRADE LIBERALIZATION IN ECOWAS

Trade liberalization constitutes a significant aspect of a regional economic grouping. A country participating in such a scheme benefits from the elimination of barriers to its exports on the part of the partner countries. This removal of restrictions would ensure the development of intraregional trade in a significant manner. It is also of special importance for the developing West African countries whose exports of manufactured goods often suffer discrimination in developed country markets such as those of the EEC, despite the provisions of the Lome Convention.[25] Also, since the major objective of ECOWAS, like any other regional economic grouping, is to combine elements of greater intraregional trade liberalization with some element of protectionism against third countries outside the grouping, it is only economically rational that countries within this economic framework should try and adopt both a common tariff nomenclature and also a common customs tariff. A common tariff is indeed the backbone and distinguishing characteristic of any customs union. It is an essential tool of cumulative economic growth in any regional grouping.

Adoption of a common tariff on imports from third countries and the harmonization of other measures affecting imports and exports will eliminate distortions in competitiveness among the partner countries provided the exchange rates are free to adjust. It will also offer some protection to nascent industries within the integrated community. The removal of tariff divergencies following the adoption of a common customs tariff will encourage a full utilization of the enlarged West African market. A common customs tariff and harmonization of the tariff nomenclature will greatly minimize the problem of unrecorded trade so characteristic in the sub-region. While smuggling cannot be completely eliminated in this area, it is common knowledge that an added incentive is provided by divergencies in the tariff structure which create price differentials between countries, as commodities tend to be traded unrecorded from a low-tariff-wall country to a high tariff one.

It is in light of these considerations that the Lagos Treaty provided for a detailed program for trade liberalization. The main juridical framework for trade liberalization within ECOWAS is provided by Article 2, Sub-section 2 and its relevant protocols which stipulates among other things that the Community shall by stages ensure the elimination as between the member states of customs duties and other charges of equivalent effect in respect of the importation and exportation of goods; the abolition of quantitative and administrative restrictions on trade among member states; and the establishment of a common customs tariff and a common commercial policy toward third countries. These general aims of the treaty are explained in a detailed and programmatic form in the third chapter of the ECOWAS Treaty, which lays down a 15-year timetable for the liberalization of intra-Community trade and the formation of the customs union.

The implementation of this program began soon after the Community had become operational. A significant step toward trade liberalization was taken at the ECOWAS summit of heads of state and government held in Lagos in April 1978. This meeting took the all-important decision to make 28 May 1979 the starting date of a two-year period during which member states were obliged to refrain from imposing new customs duties or taxes and from increasing existing ones. The freeze was required to help both member states and the Community to prepare for the subsequent phases of the trade and customs cooperation program. But the crucial decision was taken in May 1980 when the Community adopted in Lome a Trade Liberalisation Programme in conformity with Articles 12 and 13 of the Treaty.[26] In accordance with this momentous decision, all tariff and non-tariff barriers to unprocessed products were to be totally eliminated as from the end of the two-year consolidation period, that is, 28 May 1981 without compensation to any member state. With regard to industrial products, it was decided that Community-designated priority goods imported into the four more industrially-advanced member countries of Ghana, Ivory Coast, Nigeria, and Senegal be completely liberalized over a four-year period starting 28 May 1981. Tariffs on such products imported into the remaining 12 less industrially-advanced ECOWAS countries were to be completely removed over six years, commencing on 28 May 1981. It was decided, also, that tariffs on all other industrial products imported into the four more industrially-advanced countries be completely removed over a six-year period beginning on 28 May 1981; while for the less advanced member states an eight-year period, starting from 28 May 1981, was specified. Thus the pace of tariff reduction was to vary according to the priority given to an industrial product and the country into which the product was being imported. The higher the priority accorded a product and the more industrialized the country, the faster the tariff elimination would be effected.

Also to be noted is the decision on trade liberalization which called for elimination of non-tariff barriers to intra-Community trade ahead of the tariff elimination program if the latter exercise was to be effective. For this reason, it was resolved that elimination of all types of non-tariff barriers should begin on 28 May 1981 and be completed by all ECOWAS countries within four years. However, at the Cotonou summit in May 1982, the Community introduced some modifications and decided that foreign exchange restrictions on current transactions shall only be eliminated after the problems of currency convertibility have been resolved.[27] Like the CEAO, the Community has not as yet adopted a common external tariff, which is the third phase of the trade liberalization scheme, to provide a uniform measure of protection to ECOWAS industries.

To facilitate the process of trade liberalization, the Community has made three important decisions. The first which relates to the "Rules of Origin for Community Trade" defines the products originating from member states that qualify for trade liberalization within the Community. This is an extremely important aspect of any regional integration scheme, particularly "one in which, initially, national tariffs are high and disparate." Closely related to this is the second decision which is concerned with determining the desirable level of national participation in the equity capital of industrial enterprises whose products benefit from preferential duty. Accordingly, at the May 1980 summit, the required minimum levels of participation were specified.[28] These were amended at the May 1983 Conakry meeting which set national equity participation to be 20 percent from May 1983; 40 percent May 1986; and 51 percent May 1989. The third decision is related to a scheme for compensation for revenue loss as a consequence of the implementation of the trade liberalization program. Briefly, the relevant mechanism states, among other things, that compensation will be paid only in respect of losses resulting from tariff reduction on imported Community-originating industrial products.[29] The scheme provides for the payment through the ECOWAS Fund.

On the whole, the ECOWAS program for trade liberalization, as the executive secretary of the Community has commented, is undoubtedly "one of the most immense and complex undertakings of the Community."[30] A successful implementation of this program during the ten-year period (May 1979-May 1989) would culminate in the creation of a free trade area in the sub-region. The program is destined to regulate on a gradual basis the vast potential ECOWAS market which now consists of some 150 million consumers. It is designed to contribute to the overall Community objective of a rapid economic development of member states through, inter alia, its taking advantage of the market potentials that are not available to a single country but only generated by the creation of an economic union. For the elimination of barriers to have the desired effect and impact, the program covers both trade liberalization proper and trade promotion issues. To this end, the Community would undertake a series of trade promotion measures including market research, establishment of a trade newsletter and bulletin, joint action in product presentation--labeling, packaging, and advertising--as well as organization of trade fairs and seminars. Through such means, prospective traders, exporters, and importers would be adequately informed of trade possibilities.
The trade promotion aspects of the program would also enable the export promotion councils and chambers of commerce, and manufacturers' associations in each ECOWAS country to maintain closer ties and contacts among themselves for the purpose of disseminating information on trading opportunities to traders and businessmen.

PROBLEMS AND PROSPECTS

There is no doubt, however, that the implementation of ECOWAS' ambitious trade liberalization program will not be as easy as it appears on paper. Indeed, trade liberalization programs initiated by integration schemes among developing countries have generally not lived up to expectations. As Balassa has noted, the CACM provides the only case where tariffs on intra-area trade were abolished and a common external tariff was adopted. Although as a result of this, trade among the member countries increased rapidly, with the average annual rate of growth exceeding 30 percent between 1961 and 1968, this development was short-lived. For following the unilateral introduction of fiscal incentives by member countries and the withdrawal of Honduras from the CACM, the rate of increase of intra-area trade among the remaining member countries declined also.[31]

Similarly, in the erstwhile LAFTA, the target date for completely freeing trade was repeatedly postponed and the annual negotiations on tariff reductions, carried out on an item-by-item basis, slowed down after a few years and have made practically no progress in recent years. Although in the Andean Common Market tariff reductions are proceeding according to schedule, quantitative restrictions on intra-area trade have been largely retained and the establishment of the common tariff has been postponed.

This gloomy picture is not different with regard to integration schemes in Africa. In the defunct East African Community, for example, the common tariff was preserved although member countries followed different policies with regard to duty drawbacks on machinery and equipment. Similarly, although the Central African Customs and Economic Union has a common external tariff, additional taxes may also be imposed by the individual member countries and differences in tax rates provide a protective element in intra-area trade. In the CEAO, too, agricultural trade has been freed, but tariff reductions on manufactured goods will be subject to future negotiations on an item-by-item basis. On the other hand, the Regional Co-operation for Development (RCD) group did not envisage general trade liberalization, but only the freeing of trade on items produced by common enterprises. These examples would seem to point to the nature of problems that ECOWAS is likely to encounter in the implementation of its trade liberalization program. It may be instructive to analyze some of these complex problems.

First, in a purely national context, the tariff can be viewed as a taxation instrument available to national authorities to be deployed in the raising of revenues or the allocation of national economic resources, based solely on national considerations. In that context the tariff carries with it certain degrees of flexibility. It is this degree of national flexibility that tariff harmonization removes from the national authorities and its removal imposes some element of constraint on their freedom of action, since the common tariff is established by agreement of the partners: likewise, any changes to it can only be by common consent. However, the extent to which this could be a serious constraint on national freedom of action depends largely on the consultative machinery that could be established within institutions of the ECOWAS, the speed at which they are able to operate especially in periods of emergency and other crises, and the nature of the safeguards that may be incorporated to meet such emergency situations.

A second hurdle worth considering is the marked differences in the importance and structure of tariffs and quantitative restrictions that existed between the ECOWAS countries before the entry into force of the treaty. The national differences include varying degrees of reliance on tariffs or import restrictions, varying scope and coverage of import charges and fiscal taxes, differences in customs and statistical nomenclatures and standards of statistical compilation, differences in the basis of customs valuation, differences in trading philosophies and marketing arrangements, as well as in the basis of exchange control arrangements. For the purposes of trade liberalization, all these disparities have to be harmonized, or at least their existence should be taken into account. On the whole, the lack of "a uniform Community system of customs and of internal indirect taxes," as well as the lack of a clear distinction in the tax systems of several ECOWAS countries between imports duties and internal indirect taxes would no doubt constitute some serious problems in the course of the implementation of the trade liberalization program.[32]

Besides, a characteristic feature of the majority of the ECOWAS countries is that a significant proportion of their revenue is derived from indirect taxes--mainly import and export duties. Consequently, a great deal of importance is attached to customs duties in their countries as a share in their foreign trade and GDP as well as their share in total government revenue. United Nations sources for 1973 indicate large variations in the degree of dependence of ECOWAS countries on customs duties as a source of government income.[33] In that year (1973) in the Gambia, for example, more than 50 percent of total government revenue was originating from customs duties. Although this was somewhat less in Benin (49 percent), Burkina Faso (47 percent), Sierra Leone (37 percent), and Ivory Coast (35 percent), customs duties nevertheless constituted a very important source of income to the government in these countries.

This problem is compounded by the fact that 10 out of the 16 ECOWAS member states are simultaneously members of some West African regional groupings such as the CEAO (1973), Mano River Union (1973), and the Cape Verde/Guinea-Bissau Free Trade Area (1976). These groupings also aim at an elimination of tariffs on trade and sometimes even call for the granting of preferential treatment in their trade. Even before the CEAO Treaty came into force, intratrade between its present member states was running at a level much higher than the average level for the rest of ECOWAS.[34]

Progress toward a customs union in West Africa must be viewed against the background of these two disturbing factors-- the importance of the differences in the level and structure of customs duties in the Community and the complicating factor of adherence to more than one regional organization with a separate trade agreement by a number of countries. It is not surprising, then, that the ECOWAS countries were unable to start immediately with the implementation of phased programs as envisaged in the treaty.

Although information about the extent to which member states have so far complied with the regulations for a duty standstill is not immediately available, there is much evidence to suggest that the implementation of the trade liberalization program is not making significant headway. For example, a questionnaire prepared and dispatched by the Executive Secretariat in October 1980 to all member states was not given due attention. The questionnaire's purpose was to enable the Community to assess the effect of the trade liberalization scheme on member states that belong to both ECOWAS and CEAO and also to facilitate the formulation of measures to be taken to protect priority industries within the Community. All the efforts by the Secretariat "through writing and personal contacts to have the replies to this questionnaire . . . have proved futile."[35] Yet for both political and economic reasons, the ECOWAS approach to trade liberalization should be compatible with that of the subgroupings which also involve some member countries. Similarly, the attempt to introduce into use the common customs nomenclature or the harmonized customs documents of ECOWAS as a prerequisite for a smooth application of the trade liberalization program has not been encouraging. For quite a long time none of the new customs documents "has been effectively implemented by any Member State."

On the whole, the rate of implementation of the Community policies and measures relating to the trade liberalization program leaves much to be desired. As would be noted later, it was not until May 1983 that a single trade liberalization scheme was finally adopted. Although these teething problems, particularly the inordinate delay in responding to Community demands, are not entirely unexpected in an international organization of this size and variety, there is nevertheless the need for greater determination and the requisite political goodwill by member states directed toward the achievement of the objectives of the Community's trade liberalization scheme. Undoubtedly, effective implementation of trade liberalization can give a valuable stimulus to investment, stimulate measures of cooperation in production, and generally assist to develop other measures to expand production.

But trade liberalization schemes per se may be inadequate in increasing intra-Community trade. For the extent of the benefits to be derived from it is likely to depend significantly on the taking of parallel measures to expand industrial production and, especially, to improve distribution through improved communications and transport arrangements as well as the removal of monetary and financial obstacles to trade. Accordingly, a transport program, which has as its objective the coordination of transport and communications within the sub-region was adopted at the May 1980 Lome summit. This summit also decided to establish a "Special Fund" for telecommunications which is to be annexed to the ECOWAS Fund. The Community has also initiated measures on monetary cooperation as enshrined in Articles 37 and 39 of the ECOWAS Treaty. A bold decision was taken at the May 1983 Conakry summit which mandated the late President Sekou Toure of Guinea to carry out necessary studies aimed at the creation of an ECOWAS Monetary Zone.[36]

By these measures, the Community may be said to be providing the necessary infrastructure so that the expected major directional shifts in trade flows can be accommodated effectively. If these necessary parallel measures are effectively implemented, trade liberalization can be expected to afford considerable developmental benefits in the form of new expanded agricultural and industrial production, new technologies, additional employment, and infrastructural improvements.

EQUITABLE DISTRIBUTION OF COSTS AND BENEFITS

A principal policy issue that confronts ECOWAS in the process of industrialization and implementation of its trade liberalization program is the issue of equity in the distribution of benefits. The critical importance of the "distribution" function has been stressed in most of the current literature on integration efforts among developing countries. This refers to the capacity of the integration system to deliver certain benefits to the least developed members of the scheme and, by so doing, help "counteract the effects of unequal gains and polarization resulting from a laissez-faire approach to freeing trade. . . ."[37] Indeed, for most if not all integration schemes, it is the distribution of industry that is the key indicator of equality as far as political leaders are concerned. For it is better prospects for industrialization that tend to be a major incentive for common markets, and each country is intensely concerned with industrialization for status as well as welfare reasons. For not only does the industrial allocation question have a bearing upon intra-system resource distribution but in addition, the employment and thus multiplier effects that are created by new industry, and the prospect that it in turn will "serve to attract further investment to the area by virtue of spin-offs of improved local skills, technology and infrastructure."[38] Given this brief background, it would be seen that much of the success of the ECOWAS industrial policy and program and the trade liberalization scheme would crucially depend upon the Community's approach to this troublesome matter of "distribution" function.

The usual pattern in most economic communities is that the distribution of the benefits among nations tends to be unequal when developing countries with different degrees of industrialization begin an integration process. For there is a tendency for industry to cluster to take advantage of existing external economies, factor input endowments, and market structures. In the CEAO, for example, industry, commerce, and services are concentrated in and around Abidjan and Dakar. Similarly, Nairobi had the concentration of all the industrial and commercial activities of the defunct East African Community. Thus where there is little or few poles of growth this tends to create serious imbalances in the distribution of industry.

The experience acquired in efforts to achieve economic cooperation is rich in examples of formulas that have failed to induce the participation of all member countries in the regional industrialization process. And this has significantly affected the progress of many an integration scheme. In the CACM, for instance, it was the problem of unbalanced development that became the source of a series of political crises beginning in 1965.[39] The West Indian Federation broke up in 1962 over this issue, and its successor, the Caribbean Free Trade Association, has yet to demonstrate its ability to give proportional satisfaction to all its members. Nearer home in Africa, the collapse of the East African Community bears out this point.[40] Chad decided in 1968 to withdraw from membership of UDEAC and to agree to close links with Zaire mainly because of the dissatisfaction over UDEAC's inability to work out a formula for measuring the costs and benefits from integration and to agree on an equitable distribution of industrial projects.[41] And within the West African sub-region itself, the West African Customs Union (UDAO) and the Customs Union of West African States (UDEAO) broke down over the problems arising from the distribution of costs and benefits.

This situation, then, poses some crucial challenges to the member states of ECOWAS. How, for example, can they agree upon an acceptable distribution of the benefits from the Community's industrial cooperation program and trade liberalization scheme? How can this be implemented? How, also, can the obvious gaps be bridged between say, the more industrially-advanced countries of Ghana, Ivory Coast, Nigeria, and Senegal on the one hand, and the less industrialized ECOWAS members like Benin, Mali, Niger, and Burkina Faso on the other? Which countries would be required to give up what, when, and for what rewards?

The ECOWAS Fund for Co-operation, Compensation and Development is at present the most concrete manifestation of the Community's concern with promoting a fair and equitable distribution of the benefits of economic cooperation and with eliminating disparities in the levels of development of its member states, insofar as they depend on finance. The problem here is that ECOWAS has no resources of its own for the operation of the scheme and would therefore have to depend on the prompt payment by member states of their assessed contributions. As Robson has rightly remarked, the experience of CEAO--and indeed of ECOWAS itself in other areas--makes it obvious that "promptness in meeting financial obligations towards the Community cannot yet be invariably relied upon."[42] For example, arrears of payments of annual contribution for the effective running of the Community, some of which go back to 1978, stood at more than $10 million and, in spite of repeated efforts, only three member states managed to make partial payments of their assessed contributions to the budget for the 1982 fiscal year. Sources at the ECOWAS Secretariat indicated that by the end of 1983 about $23.5 million was owed in delayed contributions.[43]

Thus, although the ECOWAS Treaty gives weight to the need to promote a fair and equitable distribution of the benefits of cooperation, it is doubtful whether the measures proposed, especially in the area of fiscal compensation, are, in practical terms, adequate enough to make the less favored partners altogether willing to make such sacrifices in the interest of the overall growth of the Community. The experience of regional economic groupings among developing countries with compensation schemes has not been satisfactory. In both the EAC and UDEAC, the recipient countries argued that the sums they were receiving were insufficient to compensate them for the lack of new industry.[44] Against this background, therefore, unless some other "positive integration measures" operating in favor of the less advanced ECOWAS members are introduced, the protection of the interests of these countries would be limited. They may not really profit from the opportunities offered by the Community's trade liberalization and industrial policy programs.

The key point worth emphasizing in relation to this critical issue of equity in the distribution of benefits is that the political capital favorable to integration arising from West African aspirations for regional unity would soon be exhausted "unless the distribution problem is effectively resolved." For since leadership, as it is obvious in the sub-region, is nationally based, it tends to evaluate the gains accruing from integration in predominantly national terms. The severity of the economic problems faced by some of the national leaders and probably the lack of resources available to them, invariably predisposes the leadership to seek immediate and dramatic gains from integration. Integration thus "is not and can hardly be viewed by the leadership as a collective venture" in which the development of the whole is a good thing, but rather as a means to enhance national capacity. The leadership goal is legitimate and pragmatic, but once the developing goals are not being realized under the conditions of immediacy specified by leadership, the legitimacy of the integrative system becomes seriously questioned and the result is either stagnation or disintegration of the integrative effort.[45] Thus even if the political rhetoric were to indicate that some member states see ECOWAS primarily or solely as a step toward the eventual political union of Africa, the Community would command the loyal support of all members and succeed only if each member is likely to be better off inside the Community than it would have been outside it.

This chapter has focused attention on industrialization and trade liberalization which to a large extent is the main rationale for the establishment of ECOWAS. It has been noted that the Community has initiated some extensive and laudable schemes with a view to implementing the industrialization and trade liberalization provisions of the treaty. In some areas actual implementation has reached a fairly advanced stage. However, it would be premature at the present state of the Community's development to assess the viability or otherwise of these measures. An attempt has therefore been made to analyze some of the crucial problems and challenges that ECOWAS is likely to encounter in the course of implementing its industrialization and trade liberalization programs. Finally, the chapter has also analyzed the potentially most disruptive problems about the issue of equitable distribution of benefits and costs from industrialization and trade liberalization in ECOWAS. In the next chapter, attention is focused on one very crucial issue that seems to underlie the whole development process: the issue of dependency or neo-colonial mesh. Would trade liberalization and industrialization in ECOWAS lead to a process of dependent development, dominated by foreign corporations and interests through their control of capital, technology, and markets?

NOTES

1. Clarance Zuvekas, *Economic Development: An Introduction* (London: Macmillan Press, 1979), p. 242.
2. ECOWAS Doc., ECW/Work/P/8186: *ECOWAS Medium Term Industrial Programme, 1981-86*, Lagos, 1981.
3. Cited in K. M. Barbour, "Industrialization in West Africa--the Need for Sub-Regional Groupings within an Integrated Economic Community," *Journal of Modern African Studies*, vol. 10, no. 3 (1972):357.
4. H. B. Chenery and H. Syrquin, "Comparative Analysis of Industrial Growth." Cited in V. P. Diejomaoh and Milton A. Iyoha, eds., *Industrialization in the Economic Community of West African States (ECOWAS)* (Ibadan: Heinemann, 1980), p. 32.
5. I. Little, T. Scitovsky, and M. Scott, *Industry and Trade in Some Developing Countries: A Comparative Study* (London and New York: Oxford University Press, 1970).
6. For details see *Critical Appraisal of the Economic and Social Conditions in West African Sub-Region, Appendix IV*, "Industrial Development," ECOWAS (March 1979).
7. *Nigeria--1975-80 National Development Plan*, p. 147. Cited in I. I. Ukpong, "The Infrastructural Base for Industrialization in ECOWAS," in *Industrialization in ECOWAS*, ed. Diejomaoh and Iyoha (Ibadan: Heinemann, 1980), p. 228.
8. Diejomaoh, "State, Structure and Nature of Manufacturing Production," in *Industrialization in ECOWAS*, ed. Diejomaoh and Iyoha (Ibadan: Heinemann, 1980), p. 50.
9. Kodwo Ewusi, "Scope, Structure and State of Industrialization in Ghana," in *Industrialization in ECOWAS*, ed. Diejomaoh and Iyoha, p. 72.
10. *Critical Appraisal of the Economic and Social Conditions*.
11. Ibid.
12. Ibid.
13. Pierre Uri, "Industrial Policy: Location, Technology, Multinational Firms, Competition, and Integration of Product Markets," in *Economic Integration: Worldwide, Regional, Sec-*

toral, ed. F. Machlup (London: Macmillan Press, 1978), p. 140.

14. Ryutaro Komiya, "Comments on Industrial Policy," in *Economic Integration*, ed. F. Machlup (London: Macmillan Press, 1978), p. 152.
15. ECOWAS Doc., ECW/CM.VI/2, *Report of the Executive Secretary to the Council of Ministers*, Dakar (26-28 November 1979).
16. *ECOWAS Policies and Programme Series*, No. 2 (1981), p. 9.
17. ECOWAS Doc. ECW/1ANC/111/2, *Draft ECOWAS Protocol Relating to Community Enterprises*, Lagos (1981).
18. O.A.U., *Lagos Plan of Action*, para. 67.
19. Komiya, "Comments on Industrial Policy," p. 152.
20. Michael Hodges, "Industrial Policy: A Directorate-General in Search of a Role" in *Policy-Making in the European Communities*, ed. H. Wallace, W. Wallace, and Carole Webb (New York: John Wiley and Sons, 1978), p. 115.
21. ECOWAS Doc., ECW/MONEP/2, *Currency Convertibility in the Economic Community of West African States*, Report by IMF, Lagos (1980) pp. 16-17.
22. See, for example, Uka Ezenwe, "Trade and Growth in West Africa in the 1980s", *The Journal of Modern African Studies*, vol. 20, no. 2 (1982):305-22; and Foloyan Ojo, "Trade Expansion and Economic Co-operation in West Africa: The Role of ECOWAS" (Paper presented at the Conference on ECOWAS, Lagos, August 1976).
23. The author has to some extent relied on the recent report by IMF, *Currency Convertibility in the Economic Community of West African States*, pp. 27-35. Details of regional trade of the ECOWAS is provided in Michael Idi Obadan, "Regional Trade of the ECOWAS: Characteristics, Problems and Prospects" (Paper presented at the Third Bi-annual Conference of the West African Economic Association, Freetown, Sierra Leone, April 1982).
24. Obadan, "Regional Trade of the ECOWAS."
25. For further discussion see S. K. B. Asante, "Lome II: A Machinery for Updating Dependency?," *Intereconomics* 4 (July-August 1981).
26. ECOWAS Doc., A/DEC 18/5/80, *Official Journal* 2 (1980).
27. ECOWAS Doc., A/DEC 4/5/82.
28. Indigenous ownership and participation was fixed along a progressive scale at 20 percent from 28 May 1981; 35 percent 28 May 1983; and 51 percent 28 May 1989; ECOWAS Doc., A/DEC 15/5/80, *Official Journal* 2 (June 1980).

29. Further details are provided in ECOWAS Doc., A/DEC 19/5/80, Decision of ECOWAS Heads of State and Government relating to the application of the compensation procedures for the loss of revenue suffered by member states as a result of the trade liberalisation programme, *Official Journal* 2 (June 1980).
30. ECOWAS Doc., ECW/CM/ix/2 Rev. 1, *Annual Report of the Executive Secretary, 1980-1981*, (May 1981).
31. Bela Balassa, "Types of Economic Integration," in *Economic Integration: Worldwide, Regional, Sectoral*, ed. F. Machlup (London: Macmillan Press, 1978), p. 26.
32. Peter Robson, *Integration, Development and Equity: Economic Integration in West Africa* (London: George Allen and Unwin, 1983), p. 116.
33. *Statistical and Economic Information Bulletin for Africa*, No. 9 U.N.E./CN.14/SE IB.9; *International Financial Statistics*, IMF, (January 1978). Details in Table I, UNCTAD preliminary report on *Trade Liberalisation Options and Issues for the ECOWAS*, p. 39.
34. UNCTAD, *Preliminary Report on Trade Liberalisation Options and Issues for ECOWAS*, p. 21.
35. *Annual Report of the Executive Secretary, 1980-81.*
36. ECOWAS Doc., ECW/HSG.VI/4/Rev.1, *Final Communique of the Sixth Summit Meeting of the Authority of the ECOWAS Heads of State and Government Held in Conakry, Guinea, May 28-30, 1983.* Decision A/DEC 6/5/83 relating to studies for the creation of a single monetary zone for the sub-region.
37. W. A. Axline, "Underdevelopment, Dependence, and Integration: The Politics of Regionalism in the Third World," *International Organization*, vol. 3, no. 1 (Winter 1977):94.
38. John Ravenhill, "Regional Integration and Development in Africa: Lessons from the East African Community," *Journal of Commonwealth and Comparative Politics*, vol. 17, no. 3 (1979):230.
39. Stuart I. Fagan, *Central American Economic Integration: The Politics of Unequal Benefits* (Berkeley: Research Series No. 15, Institute of International Studies, University of California, 1970), p. 1.
40. Thomas S. Cox, "Northern Actors in a South-South Setting: External Aid and East African Integration," *Journal of Common Market Studies*, vol. 21, no. 3 (March 1983):298. See also Arthur Hazlewood, "The End of the East African Community: What are the Lessons for Regional Integration Schemes?"

Journal of Common Market Studies, vol. 18, no. 1 (September 1979).

41. Lynn K. Mytelka, "A Geneology of Francophone West and Equatorial African Regional Organizations," *Journal of Modern African Studies*, vol. 12, no. 2 (June 1974):304; and her article "Fiscal Politics and Regional Redistribution," *Journal of Conflict Resolutions*, vol. 19, no. 1 (March 1974):138-60.

42. Robson, *Integration, Development and Equity*, p. 109.

43. "Budget for ECOWAS," *West Africa*, 2 January 1984.

44. See for example, P. Ndegwa, *The Common Market and Development in East Africa* (Nairobi: East African Publishing House, 1965), p. 106.

45. J. Ruggie, "Collective Good and Future of International Collaboration," *American Political Science Review*, vol. 66, no. 3 (September 1972):874-93.

6

ECOWAS AND THE
QUESTION OF DEPENDENCY OR
NEO-COLONIAL MESH

From a stance of structural change, the two operative concepts of the previous chapter--industrialization and trade liberalization --may be closely linked to the extent to which they can enhance the economic opportunity of West African states and thereby help reduce their external dependency. In particular, industrialization of a basically agricultural, primary export-oriented economy should be seen as the means by which the chains of dependence forged during the colonial period could be broken, matching the newly acquired political independence with economic independence. It must, therefore, be viewed as an economic strategy and political rallying point in any effort toward overcoming external dependence. It is, in short, the most direct route of escape from *dependencia*.

On the other hand, as noted above, although the countries of the West African sub-region have been "independent" for a little over two decades now, the basic structure of their economies and the welfare of the majority of their people remains almost unchanged. None of the countries is, as yet, within a striking distance of self-sustaining growth and economic independence. Yet the creation and maintenance of meaningful political independence requires the attainment of "national political economics." A state whose economy is characterized by concentrated external dependence can hope to have neither a significant degree of control over the rate of growth and nature of allocation of domestic resources nor a high level of external credibility from which to bargain.

To illustrate, the type of industrialization undertaken in the post-independence ECOWAS countries has usually been within the context of multinational enterprise and has been shaped by that context. Thus, for example, 58 percent of the paid-up capital of Nigerian manufacturing activities in 1971 was foreign-owned;[1] and 85 percent of "modern" manufacturing sector in Senegal was foreign-owned in the early 1970s.[2] A significant feature of the industrial development of all the CEAO countries in particular is its dependence upon investment by European and American TNCs. With a few exceptions, the larger industrial enterprises are generally "affiliates of foreign corporations that own the bulk of the capital" ranging between 60 and 100 percent.[3] The character of the industrialization that has taken place in West Africa, then, reflected the international strategy of transnational manufacturing firms. Such an industrialization process predominantly managed by TNCs, to quote Lynn Mytelka,

> does not promote development where development is conceptualized as a process of structural change and capital accumulation that moves a society closer to conditions in which the basic needs of people (shelter, food, clothing, etc.) are met, full employment prevails, and socio-economic equality increases. Rather, as in much of Latin America, it produced underdevelopment, that is, a process of structural change and capital accumulation that moves a society in a direction that makes it more difficult to achieve these conditions--a process marked by segmentation and disarticulation of Latin American political economies. . . .[4]

Given this assessment, and particularly the pervasiveness of neo-colonial structures in Africa and the nature of external and internal linkages between the elites of the continent and their international and domestic constituencies, there's one question that should be asked: Would trade liberalization and industrialization in ECOWAS actually lead to the lessening of the high degree of external dependence as the crucial first step toward achieving basic structural development goals or to the perpetuation of neo-colonialism and underdevelopment? Who appropriates the benefits of the ECOWAS trade liberalization and industrialization programs: a large proportion of the West African population or the comprador bourgeoisie, the metropolitan powers or the transnational companies? In other words, would ECOWAS lead, in terms of production, toward national and regional development, or would it imply a process of denationalization in favor of non-member countries and foreign interests? What steps should be taken toward realizing the goal of autonomous industrialization?

This chapter attempts to analyze some of these all-engaging issues. The main thrust, however, is to examine the extent to which ECOWAS as an economic integration scheme is sufficiently equipped in terms of resources and power to tackle the disturbing problems posed by the question of dependency or neo-colonial mesh. Briefly, the chapter is focused on the extent to which the ECOWAS institutions could be used actively, even aggressively, to redress the existing asymmetry in power, status, and wealth between the peripheral West African sub-region and the dynamic, hegemonic centers of the world.

THE PROBLEM OF EXTERNAL PENETRATION

Joseph Nye has observed that academic theorists of regional integration, especially of neo-functional persuasion, initially paid insufficient attention to the "external causes and effects" and only belatedly have incorporated them within their analytical frameworks.[5] It is now widely recognized that regional change processes are not autonomous or self-generated, but rather they are responsive to a context of global interdependence and interaction. For, as Schmitter has put it, "No matter what their original intentions, it should prove difficult to isolate regional deliberations from their context of global economic and political dependence."[6] By their very nature, regional integration schemes "are discriminatory." And, as they seek to establish differential inducements for "insiders," it is to be anticipated that "outsiders," especially hegemonic ones with superior resources, will attempt to reduce the severity if not eliminate such differentials. Thus a regional integration process would seem to pose a challenge between those forces outside the region which seek to control and subordinate the integration process to extraregional purposes and those forces within the region which seek to use it to gain greater autonomy and bargaining power vis-à-vis hegemonic outsiders.

The actions of external actors, or what Schmitter has termed, "external penetration," can have a profound effect on the direction of an integrative undertaking. For example, in both the Central American and the European common markets foreign investment has played a key role, even though in neither instance was that the original plan.[7] Similarly in the Caribbean, TNCs became a powerful force encouraging the creation of a "laissez-faire integrative system"--that is one which does not include mechanisms for regional industrial planning[8]--which would benefit them as they alone were sufficiently integrated to take advantage of the enlarged market. They strongly opposed any attempt to initiate an effective integrative system in which a fundamentally laissez-faire system can be modified to include elements of compensation through planning.[9]

In the specific case of Africa, there is ample empirical evidence to indicate that African countries experience serious problems of guaranteeing sovereignty over wealth and natural resources within the context of an integration framework.[10] The major problem is that rather than strengthening sovereignty, the present patterns of economic cooperation tend to have the opposite effect due to interventions by TNCs. To this may be added the analysis by Langdon and Mytelka of UDEAC which provides an excellent case study of the way in which TNCs "derive benefits from regional integration."[11] By making use of the transnational linkages established between foreign capital and local political and economic elites, TNCs thereby weakened the effectiveness of mechanisms designed to correct the inequitable distribution of integration costs and benefits, thus leading to Chad's withdrawal from UDEAC. Similarly in East Africa, despite the Kampala Agreement of April 1964, a TNC went on to establish a tire factory in Kenya (and not in Tanzania according to the agreement) thus frustrating the implementation of the agreement.[12] TNCs thus play a role of distortion of the costs and benefits analysis in an integrated framework and may interfere with efforts by an African integration group to allocate industries to different members of the system.

Recent studies have stressed the serious impact of TNCs on Africa's two major regional groupings--the UDEAC and the East African Community. A 1981 ECA report has, for instance, severely criticized the segmentation of the UDEAC market by TNCs and condemned their activities as "unconstructive and as constituting a disintegrative, rather than an integrative force in the regional economy." The report discusses how TNCs have thwarted efforts at regional industrial planning.[13] Mamdani has in a recent study similarly highlighted the impact of TNCs and the local comprador forces on the East African Community that greatly contributed to the wrecking of the Community.[14] In these two regional groupings, as in others, TNCs seek to structure not only national but also regional markets.

This brief review of the role of TNCs in the present stage of regional groupings in Africa cannot do full justice to the complexity of the problems posed by external penetration in integration processes. It does, however, make evidently clear that TNCs are not neutral vis-à-vis the processes of economic integration. Rather, they should be considered as one of the strongest actors in regional cooperation. They can influence policies, participate in or even dominate their implementation, and become critical integrating or disintegrating forces in the pursuit of their corporate objectives. Their participation in a regional economic scheme, as variously stressed in Constantine Vaitso's special documentary report to UNCTAD, involves the use of their economic and non-economic power to mold the conception and structure of integration according to their interests, to directly or indirectly participate in the intergovernmental negotiations on the instruments of integration and their content, and to control the actual execution of implementation of regional cooperation.[15] Thus unless adequate measures are adopted, a situation could be created whereby the advantages from regional economic cooperation are primarily realized by transnationals that undertake the production, marketing, and distribution of commodities produced from integrated industries. ECOWAS will therefore be confronted with the problem of how to control external actors in the economic activity of the subregion, for these private external interests may seek to get inside the boundaries of the emerging regional system. By so doing, they might completely nullify any hoped for effect on the Community's trade liberalization scheme on intragroup trade as well as on the process of industrialization.

Given this background, it is easy to envisage the kind of problems likely to confront ECOWAS in the area of external penetration. There is, for example, the problem of initiating measures effective enough to combat attempts by extraregional powers to take advantage of the newly created regional opportunities and thus derive more benefit from integration than would the intraregional participants. Or, put specifically, there is the problem of extricating the member states of ECOWAS from the existing dependency relationships with the metropolitan powers and of using national and regional institutions to bring about greater local control over resources. For the term integration implies the replacement of the existing ties with the metropolitan centers by a new pattern of economic and political interaction within the region. Given the complexity of this problem, the question that arises, then, is: How adequate are the provisions made in the ECOWAS Treaty to confront the issues posed by dependency relationships? What institutions under the treaty have been specifically charged with what Schmitter has termed "policy externalization?"[16] To what extent can TNCs be prevented from getting the lion's share of the benefits accruing to ECOWAS integration processes while at best making rather limited contributions to the development of the West African countries and at worst preventing development?

Even before the establishment of ECOWAS, the increasing penetration of the West African sub-region by TNCs, as in other parts of Africa, had raised the question of how one could deal with their impact. Could it be done satisfactorily through minor reforms in tax structures, in transfer pricing mechanisms, or in programs to employ local staff? Or could foreign investment change occur through cancellation of contracts or concessions, limitation on profit repatriation, requirement of local equity participation, or formal expropriation or nationalization? In response to such questions, and as an effort to control the key sectors of the economy, many West African countries had by the late 1960s enacted new foreign investment regulations, adopted new economic policies regarding foreign investment, and created new laws and policies. The new measures ranged from acquisition of majority interest in the equity or assets of the local subsidiaries of TNCs, joint ventures, indigenization, to outright expropriation or nationalization. The goals of these new attempts at management have been to control foreign investment--to decrease their overall participation in the local economy, to increase government control, and to increase the host country's share of the economic rewards--while at the same time attracting foreign capital, technology, and skills for national development.

Attempts to manage the TNC through any of these new laws and policies have varied from country to country and within countries from industry to industry. Variations in some cases depend on the specific characteristics of internal policies: past history of foreign investment behavior, prevailing ideologies, and the extent of mobilization among certain groups. In some cases, the government has sought to establish control over the operations of TNCs by acquiring a majority interest in the equity or assets of local subsidiaries. In other instances, the government goes further beyond joint-venture agreements by nationalizing foreign mining interests. Thus while Ghana has acquired 55 percent of all previously foreign-owned mining and timber concessions, Sierra Leone acquired 51 percent of the diamond mines (the Sierra Leone Selection Trust), and Liberia 50 percent of the equity in Lamco, an iron-mining company. In Guinea the government holds 49 percent in a joint venture with an international consortium of companies exploiting bauxite in the Boke project,[17] while Nigeria first acquired 55 percent of all the petroleum concerns operating in the country and, later in 1979, nationalized the British Petroleum interests. By 1975 Togo and Mauritania had also taken majority stakes in the mining company operations in their countries. Besides the extractive industries, West African governments either nationalized or took majority shares in services and manufacturing sectors. Among the common targets here are petroleum distribution, branch banks, and insurance operations belonging to large foreign companies.

The question poses itself whether the desired results have been achieved in the face of the broad allocative power of TNCs and their prevalence in all national and international affairs. Have these arrangements put effective control of TNCs in the hands of West African states? To what extent have these mechanisms really curbed exploitation by transnationals and therefore created an effective base for an independent national economy in West Africa? And is this the road toward the "death" of dependency relationships? To what extent is economic power slipping gradually from the grasp of the giant TNCs operating in the sub-region?

While the new policies and investment laws are necessary as a logical step toward the achievement of the "economic kingdom" by an emergent West African state, both to fulfill its aspirations and to attempt to satisfy the masses through welfarism, they are not sufficient indicators of increased African control. Important constraints on the actual ability of these countries to manage TNCs remain. Almost all the measures indicated above require a relatively sophisticated apparatus capable of formulating, implementing, and overseeing an intricate array of criteria, rules, and provisions--all this vis-à-vis organizations with access to worldwide resources and talent. It is exactly this capability and level of control that the West African countries do not possess. An ECA-sponsored mission to 16 African states (including 5 ECOWAS countries--Ivory Coast, Liberia, Niger, Nigeria, and Sierra Leone) in early 1977 to survey the activities of TNCs in specified sectors, found that legislative and institutional measures adopted to control TNCs "have largely been ineffective."[18] There are instances where, in spite of the proclaimed nationalization, there have been in fact, no significant "takings," mainly because the management has been left to the same foreign firms who have been able to retain their original benefits. Hamid has noted, for example, the case of Mauritania which nationalized its iron resources--Societe Anonyme des Mines de Fer de Mauritanie (MIFERMA)--in 1974 but the management still remains in the hands of the French company.[19] Other notable examples of the continued flourishing of privately-owned enterprises include the case of Guinea, where the Halco and Fria bauxite operations continue to be privately controlled. Similarly, Nigeria's massive nationalization of British Petroleum interests in 1979 and its comprehensive indigenization of lesser enterprises in the 1970s have not had any real impact, for there are still scores of foreign-owned construction and manufacturing corporations that, as Leslie Rood puts it, "are doing a handsome business."[20] This, in brief, was the nature of the challenges posed by TNCs to the West African sub-region when ECOWAS was created. The external dependence thus constitutes one of the main obstacles to the creation of a West African regional economy through an integration process that involves the operation of effective corrective measures.[21]

ECOWAS AND THE ISSUE OF "POLICY EXTERNALIZATION"

To fulfil their integration process, ECOWAS countries would need considerable foreign capital. The main attraction of a TNC's direct investment is supposed to be its transfer of finance capital and provision of access to technology, foreign markets, and managerial and technical skills. Given the low organizational and technical level of the ECOWAS countries, these may indeed be indispensable elements in their development process and may only be obtainable through some form of arrangement with the TNC. For, since emphasis is placed on "production deepening," involving many completely new activities, the existing technological infrastructure of many member states of the Community is quite inadequate to meet the requirements of integration. Colman and Nixson have emphasized that, in many cases, it is only TNCs that have "the financial resources and technical expertise to develop new and better products" which may be essential for agricultural development, exploit mineral resources, and undertake large-scale construction projects.[22] Precisely put, sizeable injections of foreign capital, especially direct investment, which brings with it technology and management, will be needed to put the large pools of unemployed labor and natural resources in the sub-region to work. However, direct foreign investment can be an important stimulus to economic growth and social development in the sub-region so long as the interests of the foreign investor and host government are congruent. Thus, the fundamental dilemma facing the West African countries in their integration process concerns the reconciliation of their acknowledged need for foreign capital and technology and the evolution (or survival) of their own autonomous entrepreneurial class as well as the process of local private capital accumulation. The debate, therefore, is not on whether foreign firms will participate in the ECOWAS integration process or not; but rather on how, under what conditions and in what mix: foreign direct investments in wholly-owned subsidiaries, joint ventures, licensing agreements, or management contracts?

ECOWAS protocol on the rules of origin anticipated the problems posed by external linkages and accepts that "the promotion of trade in goods originating in member states as well as the collective economic development of the Community requires indigenous ownership and participation."[23] Conditions which goods must satisfy to qualify as "goods originating in the Community" are specified. While these ensure a reasonable measure of participation of local factor endowments it is clear that a lot of room is left for foreign participation and for the utilization of foreign resources and capital.[24] Two provisions, however, allow for the alteration of the basis of determining origin. The Trade Commission is empowered by Article 11(2) to make proposals, on the basis of appropriate statistics, to the Council of Ministers to review periodically any conditions of acceptance of goods originating in member states for Community trade. These provisions could be used to ensure that a foreign firm does not establish in a member state simply to exploit the enlarged market. They could encourage greater involvement by Community members in their own process of economic development.

At the summit meeting at Lome in May 1980, the Community took advantage of these two provisions (Article 11 paragraphs 2 and 3) and made some amendments to the protocol on the rules of origin. Furthermore, as already stated in the previous chapter, the Authority at its May 1983 meeting fixed the desirable level of national participation in the equity capital of industrial enterprises whose products should benefit from the preferential duty arrangements resulting from the trade liberalization program.

Although the objective is to ensure that governments or nationals of Community origin hold a reasonable percentage of equity capital, the amended provision may not effectively tackle the problem of foreign ownership and participation. For a long time to come most industrial enterprises in the sub-region will continue to have foreign majority ownership. In the case of Ivory Coast and Senegal, for example, where local equity participation in local TNC affiliates "is still, as a matter of policy, on a limited scale," the ownership level requirements approved by the Conakry summit "could currently be met only for a limited number of the largest industrial establishments."[25] Even the 51 percent indigenous ownership and participation, which will take effect throughout ECOWAS countries as from 28 May 1989, merely gives a false sense of satisfaction because in practice, the management will probably still lie in the hands of the TNCs who can continue to manipulate economic decisions in their favor.

A major area of development policy that must be stressed here relates to the whole problem of ownership and control of resources and the resulting relationship between host countries and transnationals. The main question of significance includes how to exercise effective control over the activities of TNCs and how to ensure an optimal degree of their integration into the local economy. What needs to be emphasized is that, although ownership is one way of acquiring control, it is not the only one and sometimes not the most effective. If local ownership is dispersed, control can be exercised even through minority positions. Briefly stated, a mere acquisition of ownership does not necessarily imply effective control. For ownership, wholly or in part, is not a sufficient condition to assure control of a foreign enterprise. To put a different slant on the same thing, the transfer of a majority equity interest in foreign-owned enterprises to the citizens of the host country does not necessarily guarantee a change of control that involves, among other things, "the exercise of decision-making powers" in such vital operational and managerial matters as budget, expansion, and development programs, appointment of top management, borrowing, reorganization and the integration of the undertaking with the developmental objectives of the host country. Thus, unless this transfer of ownership is matched by a meaningful transfer of crucial managerial powers and the acquisition and mobilization of technical expertise for the purposes of effective management, the control, especially of the extractive sector, by a developing country "will prove largely illusory."[26]

Similarly, the attempt by some West African countries to exercise control over the technology component of a foreign project through joint-venture schemes, including majority ownership of equity, misses a central issue. Control over a foreign company can be exercised much more effectively through technology than through equity participation. Majority equity ownership, as a recent ECA report has concluded, "will neither reduce the technological dependence of the host country nor ensure a genuine transfer and diffusion of the imported technology."[27] This partly explains the failure of the various Nigerian Enterprises Promotion Decrees of the 1970s to make any appreciable progress toward

economic independence. The decrees were in fact not an answer
to the problem of dependence. For, as Ake rightly puts it:

> Achieving majority Nigerian equity participation in the
> petroleum industry does not say much about progress
> towards economic independence, for those who own the
> technology in fact control the crucial means of production.
> If the technology is withheld then Nigeria's oil wealth, for
> all practical purposes, ceases to exist.[28]

Hence, on the whole, the ability to ensure real transfer of decision
making from the transnational to the host West African states or
their nationals remains problematic.

Briefly, then, ownership and participation, as provided in the
ECOWAS protocol, by themselves do not necessarily ensure effective local control especially when it is seen that great reliance is to
be placed on foreign technology and know-how. Although it is
intended that this reliance on external resources should be minimized by pulling their sub-regional resources together, the tendency of the Community technocrats to look outside for sources of
development may tend to lead to greater dependence, making the
possibility of achieving self-reliance even more difficult. Thus,
unless the role that foreign partners are allowed to play within the
Community market is carefully circumscribed and progressively
minimized, they may become a dominant force within the Community. If this happens then we would have created opportunity
for undermining sustained economic development in the sub-
region.

And moreover, although Article 30 of the ECOWAS Treaty
calls upon the member states of the Community to "harmonize
their industrial policies so as to ensure a similarity of industrial
climates" and to exchange certain types of industrial information,
"no institution or body of ECOWAS is given the power to allocate
industries, or to ensure that industrial policies are indeed har-
monised." The Council of Ministers of the Community has the
power under the treaty to make recommendations in this regard
but unless the recommendations "are accepted" by the Authority of
Heads of State and Government, they would not in any way be
binding. Of considerable significance is the fact that although
"policy externalization" can be initiated under Article 32 which
calls upon the Council of Ministers to "take steps to reduce gradually the Community's economic dependence on the outside world
and strengthen economic relations among themselves," there is no
institution or machinery in ECOWAS that is "empowered" to enter

into negotiation with external actors on behalf of the Community. Similarly, the Community has no institution that would be responsible for controlling the importation of technology.[29] Neither has the treaty any specific provisions for a common regime on foreign investment and divestment beyond harmonization of industrial policies in the fields of industrial incentives, company taxation, and Africanization. Specifically, no agreed upon modalities of collective response to the fully anticipated (and desired) increase in external penetration have been suggested under the treaty.

Thus, the redefinition of ECOWAS' economic relationships with the outside world, which are "crucial if the reduction of dependence is a goal," are largely ignored by the Lagos Treaty. Yet for economic integration to be meaningful and lead to collective self-reliance, very advanced forms of integration, such as control of new technology transfers and industrial location, are required.[30] Besides, ECOWAS can only play a meaningful role in the economic development process of the integration countries if it is accompanied by a simultaneous change in the latter's production and ownership structures. Without such measures, the degree of success of West African economic integration will be sharply limited. For example, without joint regulation of technology and capital imports, it would be unlikely that ECOWAS' policy of industrial allocation among its economically disparate member states would succeed, as the experience of UDEAC, East African, and Central American integration has illustrated. I agree, therefore, with Langdon and Mytelka that in order to transform integration into an instrument of autonomous development, regional policies that regulate external linkages in the interest of domestic development must be enacted. In their view, the cornerstone of such an approach "would be a set of measures through which direct foreign investment and technology transfer are collectively regulated."[31] The following section, therefore, outlines briefly measures which may be adopted in order to reinforce the ECOWAS provisions aimed at reducing dependency relationships.

THE POLITICAL ECONOMY OF REGULATION

Rothchild and Curry have observed that if governments in Africa harmonize some of their policies, they can present a "unified front" to a multinational company that is deciding in which country to invest.[32] Harmonization may reduce the alternatives from which TNCs are free to choose. For as a result of the commonly agreed upon rules and regulations for foreign investment adopted by members of a regional grouping, their coordinated efforts tend to overcome to some degree the advantages of mobility and flexibility enjoyed by the TNCs. Where regional cooperation enlarges the market to which the TNC gains access, the inducement to invest is enhanced. In order to gain access to large regional markets, TNCs have been willing to accept terms and conditions that they would reject from (individual) small countries. Under such conditions the ECOWAS countries not only secure the cooperation of the transnational companies on better terms but can also benefit from the economies of scale. Hence, measures taken at the regional level may have the potential for influencing, if not channeling, the activities of TNCs in desired directions; they may increase the share of host countries in the benefits associated with these activities. Thus, a country's participation in an integration scheme not only increases its bargaining power by expanding its markets, but also facilitates--where regional investment plans are involved--the conclusion of agreements between a group of nations and the TNCs interested in operating in a specific sector.

Policy measures at this level at controlling TNCs may include --alongside the goals of industrial development and equitable distribution of costs and benefits--those that aim at reducing dependence on metropolitan powers. Consequently, the distinguishing characteristic of this type of integration scheme is the inclusion of measures designed to overcome or reduce the pattern of dependence on metropolitan countries that "constitutes a major limiting force on the operation of the other integration measures."[33] Thus, for an integration scheme to enjoy a reasonable likelihood of achieving success it must include measures aimed at reducing the problems posed by dependence. This type of integrative system, which may be distinguished from what Mytelka has termed "a laissez faire" integrative scheme, is represented thus far only by the Andean Group.[34]

The regional integration experiment of the Andean Community is a unique one. For the first time, governments in developing countries combined forces not merely to encourage mutual trade but also to attack the problems of foreign investment and technology dependence through regional regulation and planning.[35] To ensure that foreign direct investment has, in fact, "developmental emancipatory effect," and that the immediate benefits accruing to the host economy are as favorable as possible, complete control over the activities of foreign affiliates was thought to be necessary. With these objectives in mind, the basic assumption of Decision 24, the Andean Foreign Investment code, is that, first, foreign capital and technology have to be acquired selectively;

second, these inputs only become fully effective if they are eventually controlled domestically; and third, considerable information is required on the one hand, to make proper choices regarding what, when, and under what conditions foreign direct investment is to be admitted and, on the other hand, to avoid irregularities by existing foreign affiliates. A number of provisions of the code are designed to implement these objectives.

Although the progress of the efforts by the Andean Group at controlling TNCs is still very limited,[36] the Andean Code as a whole, despite its modification, has substantially effected a shift in the pattern of direct foreign investment in the region. It has demonstrated that progress in this area is possible, but that effective implementation of common rules is very difficult. In its comprehensiveness, detail, and relevance the code, as Dale Furnish has remarked, "may represent the most concrete resolution of the foreign investment problem possible in Latin America today, and perhaps even the truest consensus of the entire Third World."[37] The orientation, criteria, and specific policy provisions (which were developed in the Andean Pact in the early 1970s) have become model cases followed in many developing countries. They have also influenced official positions taken in the activities of the United Nations family and the Group of Non-aligned countries. It is no wonder, then, that over 20 countries have already accredited observers to the Andean Group.[38]

The position of ECOWAS with regard to the adoption of measures at the regional level designed to reduce dependence on the metropolitan countries is not yet crystallized. In recent years, however, ECOWAS has shown signs of wishing to develop a positive approach toward foreign investment. I have already referred to the first major initiative in this area taken in 1980 and reinforced in 1983 relating to local participation provision in the rules of origin. Added to this, the Community decided to commission a study during the 1982/83 fiscal year to deal with existing regulations relating to foreign investment in member states and subgroupings, the objective being to provide policy options in relation to harmonization and rationalization of foreign investment regulations. The industrial program of the Community drawn up in 1981 also includes the establishment of "portfolios of investment proposals" so as to facilitate investment follow-up actions, and preparation of investment policy and guidelines, that is to say, a code of conduct for foreign investors.[39] As an important aspect of the effort aimed at reducing dependence, the Community has taken a bold decision to create a special regional framework for corporate activities to which reference has already been made.

Regional companies designed to promote "authentically regional enterprises" are to be established to safeguard indigenous development of industry, and to provide an attractive method for the channeling of funds into the sub-region from outside of West Africa. The protocol covers such important areas as industrial legislation, investment incentives and regulations relating to foreign investment, and all the other legal issues that affect regional industrial cooperation.

Although the regional company concept has the potential for offering access to the West African sub-region for foreign capital, which is likely to be encouraged by the fact that 16 states are backing the regional investment, it is certainly not one that primarily is designed for the facilitation of foreign corporate activities in the sub-region. The ECOWAS company concept is fundamentally African; it will be African owned, African controlled, and above all, it will be a citizen of West Africa. If it is able to attract funds that would not otherwise have been available, and if it uses its resources judiciously to promote distributional goals as well as growth, the ECOWAS enterprises could play a significant role in the integration process. It is too early to know whether this is likely to happen.

However, for the general effectiveness of these measures, and particularly for the Community to achieve a better bargaining position with foreign investors, avoid distortions or inequities in the integration process, and accelerate the process of economic integration, ECOWAS may have to learn from the experience of the Andean Group and adopt a common set of more or less restrictive conditions for the entry of foreign capital into the sub-region. In sum, the main objective of the ECOWAS investment code should be geared toward keeping TNCs at arm's length and to offer sub-regional entrepreneurs--whether private, state, or cooperative--a significant amount of protection against their ubiquitous transnational competitors that mere tariff barriers have failed to give in the past. The message of the code should reflect the general concern for evolution of the countries' capitalization, the promotion of authentically national enterprises, and the development of local technological and productive capabilities. If the code meets these objectives, it can offer an alternative to economic domination by foreign capital in the form of a sharing of investments and more domestic participation in, and control over, all facets of West African economies. Together with the regime for Community enterprise, the code can at least create the bases for autonomous industrialization by establishing ECOWAS' intention to diminish the

roles of market forces, the international economy, and outside
capital in their respective processes of development. Initially,
however, as in the case of the Andean Pact, ECOWAS' efforts in
this direction may confront a number of complex problems.

THE POTENTIAL THREATS TO ECOWAS' MEASURES

In considering these "radical" proposals for the Community in
the light of the Andean experience, full account must be taken of
the "social forces and vested interests," both internal and external,
that are opposed to what would seem to them to be somewhat
revolutionary programs because of attendant political and economic sacrifices. In these circumstances, it may be not only naive
but dangerous to believe that the implementation of regional
measures aimed at regulating external linkages in the interest of
domestic development "can be effected by goodwill" expressed by
the variety of actors in the West African integrative process.[40]
Would the former metropolitan countries, for instance, support
measures designed to reduce their control over the economies of
their ex-colonies? Also, would the emergent bourgeoisie in the
West African countries abandon the symbiosis with international
capital which has provided them so handsomely with the means
for their own embourgeoisement, and do so in the interest of
promoting collective self-reliance, especially in regard to production? The rest of this section attempts to analyze some of these
questions. The objective here is to consider whether ECOWAS as
an institution is in a position to withstand the negative reaction of
the various groups most likely to take positions on measures
regulating direct foreign investment and technology transfer.

Perhaps the first major threat to the Community's measures
would emanate from the metropolitan powers. For it is unlikely
that former colonialists would easily allow their areas of influence
and their sources of raw materials to slip from their grasp. To
continue to maintain age-old dependency relationships, these powers may apply several adaptive strategies. They may use openly
obstructive measures, such as, for example, refusing to recognize
the authority of regionally elaborated decisions, seeking to invoke
global or universalistic international norms, making separate and
differential appeals in individual members of the Community, or
threatening reprisals. Should these measures fail to achieve their
objectives, these powers may, by aiding, advising, subsidizing,
cajoling, or flattering sub-regional and national actors in West
Africa, seek to influence the course of collaborative efforts and

thereby to protect their essential interests. There is, also, a tendency that these metropolitan countries will unite and through such kinds of summit meetings, as for example, the annual conferences of France and the French-speaking African Heads of State and Government, or the biannual meetings of the Commonwealth countries or the Lome Conventions, may gradually and systematically undermine the Community's policies directed toward disengagement from the international political and economic system.

Besides, within the Community itself the more developed member countries will probably be more willing than the less developed states to support measures to restrict investment and technology transfer. The former countries, as "poles of growth," will be more likely to have sources of local capital or to be confident of attracting foreign investment even under more restrictive conditions than the latter countries. On the other hand, the less developed member states of the Community, "with much less productive capacity to marshal in the effort to develop and with a desire to attract investment under almost any conditions," will be quite reluctant to support any measures that might constitute the slightest deterrent to foreign investment.[41]

The major hurdle, however, relates to the extent to which the new social and political forces at the center of economic and political decision making in the West African countries will be favorable to such a "nationalistic" approach to industrialization. The most important of these new social and political forces in this context, Mytelka has stressed, is the "national bourgeoisie," consisting of indigenous entrepreneurs, owners of capital, and investors in national production, principally in industry and commerce.[42] Hence one condition for the adoption of measures calculated to reduce dependence "is the extent to which there is an emerging, albeit very weak, national bourgeoisie" that is large enough to be in competition with the transnational sector, enlist the help of the government in its effort, and has "reached a critical mass."

This type of national bourgeoisie does not as yet appear to be apparent in West Africa. For the penetration of the domestic economies of the sub-region by foreign interests has prevented the emergence of a social group that places priority on national ownership and control to achieve national developmental objectives. The bourgeoisie in the various West African countries, since it is in a position to benefit immediately and directly from the expanded markets resulting from the freeing of trade, has become the advocates of measures to establish a free trade area. However, this group is not likely to support higher levels of integration, involving a common investment policy. For, as Axline has remarked, the commitment of the national bourgeoisie "to principles of laissez-faire capitalism" makes this class likely "to oppose distributive policies, particularly corrective measures which require a large degree of state involvement. . . ."[43] More significantly, since there are close ties between the section of the bourgeoisie in control of the state and the transnational sector, this dominant group will find its position influenced by its identification with the position of the external actor with which it is affiliated. Hence Sunkel refers to this class as "private transnational technocracies and bureaucracies"[44]--that is, a class whose interests are tied to, and dependent on, the transnational company. In the circumstances, it is difficult for one to make a clear distinction between the national bourgeoisie and the comprador bourgeoisie since the bourgeoisie in Africa is "essentially a comprador class," who cannot disengage on the massive scale necessary to substantially reduce the exploitative relations without endangering its material base.[45] Thus, the structural integration of the West African economies and the national bourgeoisie into the international capitalist order has constituted, as Segun Osoba has observed in the case of Nigeria, "a major constraint on the ability of the bourgeoisie, even if it were willing, to change radically this structure of dependency."[46]

To this point in the analysis, it has become quite obvious that the ability of ECOWAS to control the West African regional economy in the interests of autonomously generated development remains limited. It may perhaps be pertinent at this stage to conclude this section by recalling Streeten's three crucial questions relating to the issues confronting developing countries in their efforts at adopting measures designed to regulate direct foreign investment and technology transfer:

1. Even if the will and the political power exist, do LDC governments have the ability to control TNCs to the extent that they consider desirable?
2. Even if they have the political power, do they have the will?
3. Even if they have the will and the ability, do they have the political power?[47]

Given the entrenchment of neo-colonialism in West Africa and the extent of diversification of markets and sources of investment and technology among different metropolitan countries, or the multilateralisation of foreign exploitation, involving the alignment of different interests in various ways with the TNC, Streeten's searching questions cannot readily be answered in the affirmative.

EEC AND ECOWAS STRATEGY OF COLLECTIVE SELF-RELIANCE

The pattern of structural imbalance and dependence of the West African sub-region on the metropolitan countries has been reinforced by the relationship of ECOWAS countries to the European Community through the Lome Conventions since February 1975.[48] The significance of the 16 ECOWAS countries within the group of 64 ACP states lies in the fact that, in terms of population, ECOWAS claims over three-fifths of the entirety of the ACP; in terms of trade, exports, and imports, it claims almost five-sevenths of the totality of trade between the ACP and EEC.[49] Not surprisingly, therefore, under the Lome system the EEC has given a variety of assistance to the Community such as, for example, its sponsoring of the ECOWAS Customs and the Statistical Nomenclatures Harmonisation Project as well as its agreement in principle to contribute to the implementation of the Community Tele-communications Programme to the tune of about $50 million.[50] Besides, the direct EEC financial assistance to the ECOWAS institutions since 1977 amounts to 312,275 ECU or $341,620, excluding technical assistance to both the ECOWAS Secretariat and the Fund.[51] Furthermore, the EEC is a major source of a variety of assistance to the ECOWAS member states themselves. Table 6-1 indicates that by September 1982, the EEC's total financial assistance to ECOWAS member states (under both Lome I and Lome II) amounted to 1,255 million ECU. Out of this amount 791 million ECU or 63 percent was disbursed. EEC's total commitments to ECOWAS member states during the first three quarters of 1982, as shown in Table 6-2, amounted to 327 million ECU out of which only 96 million ECU or about 29 percent had been utilized. The low level of disbursement in 1982 may be due to the low capacity of ECOWAS member states to utilize the facilities or the stringent conditions attached to the loans.[52]

The EEC's variety of technical and financial assistance to both the ECOWAS institutions and the member states of the organization would seem, on the face of it, to support the view that the Lome scheme is compatible with the move toward regional economic grouping in West Africa. Closely studied, however, the implementation of some key provisions of the Lome system would seem to constitute one of the most important constraints, at least in the long run, on the degree of economic cooperation attainable within ECOWAS, whose treaty in effect "suggests 'unlimited' goals or perhaps eventual economic and political union." The ECOWAS-EEC linkage raises some fundamental questions. For example, to what extent does this relationship facilitate the realization of the objectives of ECOWAS' strategy of self-reliance or its goal to function as an independent autonomous unit? Can it be said that the genuine transformation of ECOWAS would not be constrained in the long run by the logic of its continued dependent relationship with the EEC? How does the EEC-ECOWAS linkage tend to perpetuate (or de-emphasize) the client status of the West African countries as a consequence of their integration into the international (Western) economic system?

TABLE 6-1. EEC's Assistance to ECOWAS Member States: From Lome I, 1975 to Lome II, September 1982

Country	Commitment	('000 ECU)* Disbursement
Benin	62,438	43,689
Cape Verde	14,043	8,265
The Gambia	36,098	23,498
Ghana	79,833	32,524
Guinea	73,355	45,940
Guinea-Bissau	44,331	27,091
Burkina Faso	118,179	56,683
Liberia	35,211	21,429
Ivory Coast	104,775	63,866
Mali	125,895	83,766
Mauritania	98,430	67,156
Niger	134,338	87,237
Nigeria	20,459	13,138
Senegal	212,561	158,488
Sierra Leone	41,531	21,002
Togo	53,583	37,572
Total	1,255,060	791,344

*1 ECU=US $1.016 as of November 1982.
Source: EEC Office, Lome.

TABLE 6-2.   EEC's Assistance to ECOWAS Member States: From Jan.-Sept. 1982

Country	Commitment	('000 ECU)* Disbursement
Benin	6,085	130
Cape Verde	3,939	699
Ivory Coast	42,096	19,195
The Gambia	13,405	8,201
Ghana	19,274	273
Guinea	5,766	1,054
Guinea-Bissau	12,920	1,819
Burkina Faso	35,913	2,664
Liberia	1,156	700
Mali	36,798	6,168
Mauritania	21,835	519
Niger	32,454	5,060
Nigeria	1,308	250
Senegal	74,450	45,292
Sierra Leone	9,927	1,253
Togo	8,842	2,360
Total	326,888	95,637

*1 ECU=US $1.016 as of November 1982.
Source: EEC Office, Lome.

Together with other African states, the ECOWAS countries negotiated with the EEC in the hope of achieving a superior rate of development, or at least of reducing the level of underdevelopment. The aim was to seek "enhanced opportunity and equity to meet basic human needs." In general, Africa's main interest was first to "guarantee the traditional markets in Europe" and, second, to "restructure its exports" to include more processed and manufactured goods. On the other hand, the main interest of Europe in negotiating the Lome system was to ensure "a reliable flow of cheap primary products" and to retain her already established markets in Africa for manufactured and capital goods.[53]

Given this background, it would appear readily apparent that the interests of the EEC are basically incompatible with the major objectives of the ECOWAS strategy of self-reliance. For Lome is a scheme to consolidate and maintain the status quo of the old order whereby the supplies of badly needed raw materials to the EEC countries would be guaranteed, and the ECOWAS and the other ACP countries, "who by specialisation would remain primary producers, would also be able to provide ready markets for the manufactured products of the industrialised EEC countries."[54] Hence the Lome agreement is a means to preserve certain elements of the existing international division of labor. Such a division of labor will ensure underdevelopment for the ECOWAS members and their continued dependence on the EEC.

This becomes quite evident when it is realized that the implementation of the key provisions of the Lome scheme would have the effect of strengthening those aspects of economic transaction between Europe and West Africa which would eventually frustrate the kind of regional economic grouping being envisaged in the sub-region. In the area of trade cooperation, for example, whereas, as evidenced in the ECOWAS trade liberalization scheme, the Community aims at encouraging the growth of horizontal economic transactions among its member states, the Lome arrangement is geared toward intensification or reinforcement of the existing pattern of vertical trade links between Europe and West Africa. And, as these latter links increase, "horizontal links among the West African states themselves will either correspondingly decrease or grow at a much slower rate."[55] The trend in the pattern of trade relations is reinforced by the impact of the Lome aid provisions. The tying of aid to procurement in the EEC countries encourages increased economic transaction between Europe and West Africa, a system that runs counter to the development of cooperation between the ECOWAS members themselves or the developing countries--a priority goal of the ACPs which is enshrined in Article 91 of Lome II. In this regard, the EEC aid procurement terms under Lome have not improved much over those of the neo-colonial Yaounde scheme. They generally reinforce the unilateral dependence and underdevelopment of the ECOWAS and the ACP countries.[56]

Second, the interests of the EEC would tend to constitute an impediment to West African efforts to industrialize and achieve the much needed diversification of their economies. This is most readily apparent from the Stabex scheme, one of the most notable innovations in the Lome regime, designed to compensate ACP states for losses of export earnings due to fluctuations in certain eligible commodity prices. A point worth stressing here is that only unprocessed commodities on the Stabex list qualify for financial transfer. Thus the scheme is biased against the development of processing for exports, since it applies to raw materials only. And because processed raw materials are not included in the overall calculations, related domestic industry is not encouraged, nor is domestic consumption. In this regard, the scheme is not only a disincentive to industrialization in ECOWAS but also geared toward perpetuation of inherited one-sided market structure. It is a scheme for short-term compensation rather than necessary long-term change and diversification. It does not interfere with the functioning of the international market mechanism governing trade in the products in question. There is thus a large measure of truth in the assertion of Langdon and Mytelka that Stabex is at one and the same time "an incentive to maintain the present levels of production" in the specified commodities listed under the scheme, and "a disincentive" to diversify commercial agricultural production, process raw materials locally, or develop domestic food production--all activities that would promote domestic linkages and bring the structures of demand and production more into line.[57] Thus Stabex looks like "stabilizing poverty."

Third, the problem posed by Stabex in relation to the realization of ECOWAS objectives is compounded by the failure of the Lome Conventions to explicitly recognize or sufficiently encourage the full permanent sovereignty of ECOWAS and other ACP countries over their own economic activities and natural resources, a subject that has found concrete expression in the deliberations on the establishment of a New International Economic Order and given a new lease of life with the publication of the two Brandt Commission Reports in 1980 and 1983, respectively.[58] Hence, despite the multifaceted role being played by the European TNCs in the ECOWAS countries, provisions do not exist within the Lome scheme for controlling the negative effects of their activities. Moreover, as stipulated in Title 5, Chapter 2 of the Lome I Convention, the European corporations operating in ECOWAS or ACP countries are not prevented from repatriating their profits, while the governments of these countries are to refrain from making any attempt to regulate direct foreign investment and technology transfer. In this regard, the EEC has sought to protect and encourage the expansion of European multinational firms into the African states that are restricted by the Convention in making independent decisions. Thus as a regional grouping, ECOWAS cannot learn from the experience of the Andean Common Market, and initiate regional policies that regulate external linkages in the interest of domestic development. Worrisome, also, is the arrangement under Lome I by which industries and firms in the ECOWAS and other ACP countries will be tied to EEC firms (Title 3, Article 26b). As Ake has rightly observed, such an arrangement "can only extend and tighten the vertical integration of the ACP economies to those of the EEC," and it is bound to increase the role and the power of TNCs in the economies of the ACP countries.[59]

All this would seem to constitute a limitation upon the justified and necessary striving for an internally located and relatively autonomous process of growth, diversification, and integration by the ECOWAS members in response to the regional self-reliance objectives of the *Lagos Plan of Action*. Thus, although greater economic self-reliance is a necessity for ECOWAS as a regional economic integration scheme, since it enables it to escape from the historic dependency on the industrial centers and facilitates its development, the successful implementation of this strategy within the EEC-ECOWAS framework remains problematic. What is more disturbing is that this pattern will have the effect of "tightening vertical relations" between West Africa and Europe far more effectively and far more extensively than in the past and create enclaves that may well have the result of strengthening the pattern of foreign transnationals in the economies of the countries of the sub-region.[60] To a great extent, therefore, Lome is not a progressive document that may constitute "an inching towards interdependence." It is, in many respects, the EEC's brand of neo-colonialism. For the whole system tends to generate further inequalities rather than development, and the EEC's vision of interdependence looks suspiciously like the partnership between horse and rider.

This chapter has focused attention on the external linkages of ECOWAS, in particular on the extent to which these relations constitute an impediment to the realization of the Community's regional self-reliance objective. It has been emphasized that the activities of such external actors as the TNC or EEC constitute an obstacle to the transformation of the West African economies from a dependent structure responsive to the external demands of the world market to an integrated economy responsive to domestic needs and resources. Given the degree and nature of dependence on Western Europe arising from the structures of trade and technological relations inherited from the pre-emptive colonial intrusion into the West African body politic, it is not surprising that the EEC-ECOWAS linkage, together with the activities of TNCs in the sub-region, would tend to delay and prevent indigenous industrialization and perpetuate unequal exchange. Thus instead of the ECOWAS countries moving toward greater autonomy, toward national and collective self-reliance, and toward orienting economic decisions around their national and regional political constituencies, the locus of decision-making of these countries tends to gravitate toward the private and public sectors of the EEC. Thus to pin much hope on the Lome regime is to follow a recipe for perpetual underdevelopment.

The conclusion toward which this chapter tends is that ECOWAS in its present stage of development is not sufficiently equipped in terms of resources and power to bring into reality a process of autonomous, self-sustaining growth. Neo-colonialism has become so entrenched, exhibiting so many facets and imping-ing on so many aspects of life in most West African countries that a narrow focus may be chasing its shadows rather than its sub-stance. Its forces can only be eliminated through a systematic restructuring of the existing mode of production. Since ECOWAS is at present not adequately equipped to bring this about, the only alternative open to the Community is to pursue objectives capable of more or less immediate realization. In this regard, it will be necessary for the Community to promote industrialization, increase the ratio of sub-regional to external trade, diversify its economic relations, shift exports toward the manufacturing sectors, and increase the bargaining power of the sub-region. Taking together these efforts, perhaps, will reduce somewhat the continued vulnerability of the sub-region to outside forces.

NOTES

1. M. Berger, *Industrialisation Policies in Nigeria* (Munich: Afrika Studies, no. 88, Institut fur Wirtschaftsforschung, 1975), pp. 161-63. Cited in Steven Langdon and Lynn K. Mytelka, "Africa in the Changing World Economy," in *Africa in the 1980s: A Continent in Crisis*, ed. Colin Legum et al. (New York: McGraw Hill, 1979), p. 168.
2. For details, see Rita Cruise O'Brien, "Factors of Dependence" in *Decolonisation and After: The British and French Expe-rience*, ed. W. H. Morris-Jones and Georges Fischer (London: Frank Case, 1980), pp. 283-309.
3. Peter Robson, *Integration, Development and Equity* (London: George Allen and Unwin, 1983), p. 41.
4. Lynn K. Mytelka, *Regional Development in a Global Econo-my: The Multinational Corporation, Technology, and Andean Integration* (New Haven and London: Yale University Press, 1979), p. xiv.
5. Joseph S. Nye, Jr., "Comparing Common Markets," *Inter-national Organization*, vol. 24, no. 4 (Autumn 1968):811.
6. Philippe C. Schmitter, *Autonomy or Dependence as Regional Integration Outcomes: Central America* (Berkeley: Research

Series no. 17, Institute of International Studies, University of California, 1972), p. 8.

7. Raymond Vernon, "The Role of U.S. Enterprises Abroad," *Daedalus,* vol. 98, no. 3 (Winter 1969):123. Also Constantine Vaitsos, *The Role of Transnational Enterprises in Latin American Economic Integration Efforts: Who Integrates and with Whom, How and for Whose Benefit?* UNCTAD, TAD/E1/SEM./52, Lima, Peru, (1978).

8. Lynn Mytelka has distinguished 3 models of integration system in the Third World. The first model (type 1) is a "laissez faire integration system" in which trade liberalization leads to asymmetrical patterns of exchange, to polarization, and to increased dependence, as typified by LAFTA. Type 2, a hybrid, in which a fundamentally laissez-faire system has been modified to include elements of compensation through planning, for example, CACM, UDEAC, or EAC. The third (type 3) links planning to regulation within a regional context, for example, The Andean Group. See Mytelka, *Regional Development,* p. 10.

9. Ibid., p. 18.

10. See Jack N. Behrman, "Multinational Corporations, Transnational Interests and National Sovereignty," *Columbia Journal of World Business,* vol. 4, no. 2 (March-April 1969):15-21.

11. Langdon and Mytelka, "Africa in the Changing World Economy," p. 179.

12. See *A Methodology for the Study of the Role of Transnational Corporations in the present stage of African Regional Cooperation,* Joint ECA/CTNC Unit on Transnational Corporations, Working Paper no. 12, 7 December 1979.

13. ECA, *Report of the ECA Mission on the Evaluation of UDEAC* (Libreville, Gabon:1981). Cited in Robson, *Integration, Development and Equity,* p. 54.

14. See Mahmood Mamdani, "The Breakup of the East African Community: Some Lessons" (Paper presented at the fifth biannual conference of the African Association of Political Science, Dakar, Senegal, June 1983).

15. Vaitsos, *Role of Transnational Enterprises.*

16. The concept of "policy externalization" refers to the process whereby integration units jointly elaborate a common position in negotiations with outsiders. Schmitter, *Autonomy or Dependence,* p. 1.

17. S. K. B. Asante, "Restructuring Transnational Mineral Agreements," *The American Journal of International Law,* vol. 73, no. 3 (July 1979):340-41. This other Dr. Asante is

currently deputy executive director of the United Nations Center on Transnational Corporations, New York.

18. ECA, *Transnational Corporations in Africa: Some Major Issues* Doc. E/CN. 14/703, Part 2 (16 March 1979), pp. 1-4.

19. G. M. Hamid, "The Lagos Plan of Action and the Development of Mineral Resources in Africa," *Africa Development*, vol. 7, nos. 1, 2 (1982):157.

20. Leslie L. Rood, "Nationalisation and Indigenisation in Africa," *Journal of Modern Africa Studies*, vol. 14, no. 3 (1976):435. See also Chibuzo S. A. Ogbuagu, "The Nigerian Indigenisation Policy: Nationalism or Pragmatism?," *African Affairs*, vol. 82, no. 237 (April 1983):241-66; Thomas J. Biersteker, "Indigenization in Nigeria: Renationalization or Denationalization?" in *The Political Economy of Nigeria*, ed. I. William Zartman (New York: Praeger, 1983), pp. 185-206.

21. For further details see S. K. B. Asante, "Expectations and Reality: Transnational Corporations and Regional Self-reliance Objectives of the Lagos Plan of Action" (Paper presented at an international conference on "ECA/OAU Lagos Plan of Action, and the Future of Africa," University of Ife, Nigeria, March 1984).

22. David Colman and Frederick Nixson, *Economics of Change in Less Developed Countries* (Oxford: Philip Allan, 1978), p. 238.

23. *Protocol Relating to the Definition of Concept of Products Originating from Member States of the Economic Community of West African States*, 5 November 1976, Articles II, IV and V.

24. Osita C. Eze, "ECOWAS: Hopes and Illusion" (Paper presented at the conference of African Association of Political Science, Rabat, Morocco, 1977).

25. Robson, *Integration, Development and Equity*, p. 118.

26. Asante, "Restructuring Transnational Mineral Agreements," pp. 352, 369.

27. *Transnational Corporations in Africa: Some Major Issues* (A note by ECA Secretariat), Doc. E/ECA/UNCTC/21, January 1983.

28. Claude Ake, *A Political Economy of Africa* (London: Longman, 1981), p. 115.

29. John P. Renninger, *Multinational Cooperation for Development in West Africa* (New York: Pergamon Press, 1979), p. 64.

30. Ibid., p. 65.

31. Langdon and Mytelka, "Africa in the Changing World Economy," p. 189.

32. Donald Rothchild and R. L. Curry, Jr., *Scarcity, Choice, and Public Policy in Middle Africa* (Berkeley: University of California Press, 1975), pp. 173-74.
33. Andrew W. Axline, "Underdevelopment, Dependence, and Integration," *International Organization*, vol. 31, no. 1 (Winter 1977):88.
34. Mytelka, *Regional Development in a Global Economy*, p. 10.
35. For a recent discussion of this subject see Rachelle L. Cherol and Jose Nunez del Arco, "Andean Multinational Enterprises: A New Approach to Multinational Investment in the Andean Group," *Journal of Common Market Studies*, vol. 21, no. 4 (June 1983):409-28.
36. David E. Hojman, "The Andean Pact: Failure of a Model of Economic Integration," *Journal of Common Market Studies*, vol. 20, no. 2 (December 1981):139-60.
37. Dale B. Furnish, "The Andean Common Market's Common Regime for Foreign Investment," *Vanderbilt Journal of Transnational Law* 5 (Spring 1972):3.
38. R. French Davis, "The Andean Pact: A Model of Economic Integration for Developing Countries," *World Development* 5 (1977).
39. Details are provided in *ECOWAS Work Programme, 1981-1986*, ECOWAS Doc., ECW/WORK/P/8186.
40. P. E. Ollawa, "On a Dynamic Model for Rural Development in Africa," *Journal of Modern African Studies*, vol. 15, no. 3 (1977):422.
41. Axline, *Caribbean Integration* (London: Frances Pinter, 1979), pp. 48-49.
42. Mytelka, *Regional Development in a Global Economy*, p. 22 and note 54.
43. Axline, "Underdevelopment, Dependence and Integration," p. 99.
44. Osvaldo Sunkel, "The Pattern of Latin American Dependence," in *Latin America in the International Economy*, ed. V. Urguidi and R. Thorp (London: Macmillan, 1973), p. 22.
45. Claude Ake, "Explanatory Notes on the Political Economy of Africa," *Journal of Modern African Studies*, vol. 4, no. 1 (1976):22. See also Gavin Williams, "Nigeria: The Neo-colonial Political Economy," in *Political Economy of Africa: Selected Readings*, ed. Dennis Cohen and John Daniel (London: Longman, 1981), pp. 45-66.
46. Segun Osoba, "The Deepening Crisis of Nigerian National Bourgeoisie," *Review of African Political Economy* 13 (May-August 1978):69.

47. Paul Streeten, "Costs and Benefits of Multinational Enterprises in Less Developed Countries," in *The Multinational Enterprise*, ed. J. H. Dunning (London: George Allen and Unwin, 1972), p. 242.
48. For an extended discussion see S. K. B. Asante, "ECOWAS, the EEC, and the Lome Convention," *African Regional Organisations*, ed. D. Mazzeo (Cambridge: Cambridge University Press, 1984), pp. 171-95; also S. K. B. Asante, "The Experience of the EEC: Relevant or Impediment to ECOWAS Regional Self-Reliance Objective?" *Afrika Spectrum* 17(1982/3): 307-22; S. K. B. Asante, "The Lome Convention: Towards Perpetuation of Dependence or Promotion of Interdependence?" *Third World Quarterly*, vol. 3, no. 4 (October 1981):658-72.
49. *The Courier* 77 (January-February 1983):10.
50. *Report of the Executive Secretary to the Council of Ministers meeting, Lome, May 1980*, ECOWAS Doc., ECW/CM/vii/2. The European Investment Bank has recently announced a loan of about ECU 10 million under the Second Lome Convention to the ECOWAS Fund toward the inter-regional telecommunications project in West Africa. See *The Courier* 84 (March-April 1984), yellow p. 8.
51. Robert C. Tubman, "Co-operation between the European Economic Community (EEC) and the Economic Community of West African States (ECOWAS) Fund" (Paper presented at an international colloquium on Relations Between Europe and Africa in the Framework of the North-South Dialogue, Lome, March 22-26, 1982).
52. Robert C. Tubman, "ECOWAS as a Sub-regional Institution and Its Relations with the EEC" (Paper presented at an international colloquium on the Lome Conventions: "Underlying principles, practical applications and prospects," Lome, November 15-19, 1982).
53. Timothy M. Shaw, "EEC-ACP Interactions and Images as Redefinitions of Euro-Africa: Exemplary, Exclusive and/or Exploitative?," *Journal of Common Market Studies*, vol. 18, no. 2 (December 1979):142.
54. Sam Olofin, "ECOWAS and the Lome Convention," *Journal of Common Market Studies*, vol. 16, no. 1 (September 1977):67.
55. H. Assisi Asobie, "Nigeria and the European Economic Community, 1970-1980: An Analysis of the Processes and Implications of Nigeria's Association with the EEC under the First Lome Convention," *Africa Development*, vol. 7, no. 4 (1982):54.

56. For further details, see S. K. B. Asante, "International Assistance and International Capitalism: Supportive or Counter-Productive?" in *African Independence: The First Twenty-Five Years*, ed. Gwen M. Carter and P. O'Meara (Bloomington: Indiana University Press, 1985).

57. Langdon and Mytelka, "Africa in the Changing World Economy," pp. 197-98.

58. North-South: A Programme for Survival. Report of the Independent Commission on International Development Issues (Brandt Commission) (London: Pan, 1980), pp. 187-200; *Common Crisis, North-South: Co-operation for World Recovery* (London: Pan, 1983), pp. 82-83.

59. Ake, *Political Economy of Africa*, p. 166.

60. See UN Doc. E/CN.14/ECO/90/Rev. 3, June 1976. For my latest analysis of this subject see S. K. B. Asante, "Lome III: The Crucial Issues Ahead," *West Africa* (16 and 23 January 1984). Also, Chief Peter Afolabi, "Lome Shows 'Signs of Cracks and Asymmetry,'" *The Courier* 82 (November-December 1983), yellow pp. 15-17.

7

NATIONAL BULLS IN THE COMMUNITY CHINA SHOP

In the previous chapter, attention was focused primarily on extraregional forces and their potential for constituting themselves as an impediment to the realization of ECOWAS' regional self-reliance objective. Specifically, the chapter was concerned with the asymmetrical interdependence that characterizes economic relations between the member states of ECOWAS and the rest of the world. By contrast, the present chapter is devoted to analysis of the complexity of problems posed by (internal) political factors. These are, indeed, highly critical elements of any effective integrative schemes. They have been the major cause of the collapse of many a Third World integration process. Discussion of these internal factors, which are highly politically impregnated, is focused on five principal areas.[2] First, the politics of regional integration generally; second, the political implications of the ECOWAS Treaty; third, the role and leadership of Nigeria as strong "core" state in the sub-region; fourth, the social and political problems posed by free mobility of labor, and fifth, the disturbing issues raised by the co-existence of ECOWAS and CEAO.

THE POLITICS OF REGIONAL INTEGRATION

Joan Spero has recalled that "The interaction of politics and economics is an old theme in the study of international relations."[3] This assertion is even more true today in the study of contemporary world system. For in the present system, politics cannot be so easily dissociated from economics: the two are interwoven strands in the fabric of world order. Political and economic factors are frequently so closely intertwined that they cannot be disentangled. Even at the systematic level, scholars like Bergsten, Keohane, and Nye[4] see politics and economics almost inevitably linked: "An international economic system is affected by the international political system existing at the time, and vice versa."

This linkage would seem to be ignored by the neo-functionalist school of regional integration theorists who are broadly apolitical in their analysis--a fault that "encompasses a multiplicity of deficiencies." The neo-functionalists generally do not concentrate on the possibility that political leaders will indeed see beyond day to day decisions to grasp the essence of the integration process in which they are engaged. In view of their major concern with empirical problems of potential economic unions, they have tended to focus upon nonpolitical variables in their formulations. The contention of this group of theorists is based on the principle that what occurs in regional integration is a "process by which a series of essentially functional economic and non-political decisions are made incrementally." The result, in their opinion, is an almost inadvertent process of political integration. Thus purposeful behavior tends to be ignored in this approach. However, while politics might be disguised in the European context, in a Third World-- and especially African--context possessing less economic fat, "the sinews of power become bare." This is symbolized in the theme of what has been termed "the primacy of politics."

In relation to our subject matter, a few general questions may be asked. What, for instance, is the relationship between economics and politics in integrative systems? Is it possible to establish regional economic integration without some degree of political coordination? In other words, to what extent is economic cooperation directly or indirectly related to political harmony?

Although in theory, economics and politics ought to be distinguished as separate disciplines, in practice, however, they cannot be kept separate in any economic integration movement on account of the complex ramifications of individual and state activities involved. To a great extent, integration is political as well as economic in both its objectives and procedures. On the other hand, economic changes made to satisfy the requirements of an extended market can create a need for political union, although they cannot of themselves effect such a union. Haas contends that "The decision to proceed with integration or to oppose it rests on the part of existing political actors."[5] On the other hand, many economic problems involved in integration can be solved only through political measures. The development and orientation of regional trade; the maintenance of full employment; the regulation of cartels and monopolies; the prevention of depression and inflation; and the coordination of regional economic plans--all this necessarily requires legal provisions, executive decisions, and administrative harmony which fall within the responsibility of the highest spheres of government. As Felippe Herrera warned a few years ago:

> We have a long way to travel and all the longer, the more we delay in recognising that economic integration cannot be attained exclusively through strictly economic measures, that economic integration is not in itself enough to assure the progress and welfare of nations, and that every development progress entails simultaneous struggle on the fronts of technology, law, education, institutions, and fundamentally politics.[6]

To sum up, all of the regional organizations--regardless of whether their purpose is promotion of security, promotion of economic well-being, or promotion of human welfare--are political in nature. Not only do political objectives motivate the establishment of these organizations: political actions also bring them into being, and it is politics that characterizes their functioning, too. As ongoing entities, Cochrane has stated that these organizations are marked by conflict among participant-actors over goals and over the distribution of costs and benefits just as is politics at the national level. "It is not going too far, then, to say that regional organizations are in reality political systems."[7]

Thus, whether one follows Lasswell to define politics as the study of "who gets what, when and how," or Easton, to define it as the process of making authoritative allocation of values (authoritative in the sense of being binding on the members of the particular community) it follows that insofar as economic integrations set up institutions, or arrangements that are meant to either render a service or create rules or norms of behavior, or adjudicate, conciliate or in any way settle disputes, one cannot avoid talking about politics. As Rothchild notes, organizations that are predominantly economic have significant political dimensions if anything, for the simple reason that "international organisations are political in their inception, termination, and basic arrangements even if the conflict factor is minimized in their daily operations."[8]

The involvement of politics in integrative schemes is more pervasive and more divisive in the case of Africa. It has been

aptly said that economic integration in Africa "must be sufficiently elastic to accommodate political aspirations" and that it is
important to "marry the economic propositions with political
dogma."[9] This is essential because it is often difficult in Africa
today to consider economic development problems without considering political realities. Experience has shown how in Africa
political problems have obstructed implementation of joint development proposals, no matter how plausible.[10] Thus, economic decisions and intraregional bargaining which in more developed
countries would be left to a much greater extent to technocrats
become of major political consequence. For economics in Africa
"is indeed high politics." In such circumstances the ability of the
technocrat, in whom neo-functionalist theorists of integration
placed greater hope, to act independently in the interest of regional cooperation, is severely limited. Economic issues become
prematurely politicized.

The main reason for this is that in Africa economic policy is
not simply a political concern but a central one, usually second
only in priority to internal and external security, and often oc-
cupying far more time, resources, and effort than decisions directly connected with security. The process of nation-building and
the desire to channel the factors of production into the most advantageous uses have forced many African governments to take
control of the machinery for planning for economic development
in order to ensure that the "benefits of industrial progress, economic advancement, and indeed the fruits of independence" are
evenly distributed among all the inhabitants of the country.[11]
Thus, while the concept of integration may everywhere be the
same, the problems of integration are qualitatively different in the
African setting.

Against this background of our analysis of the close relationship that exists between politics and economic integration, it is
quite evident that, even though perhaps to avoid emotional national conflict, none of the 64 articles of the ECOWAS Treaty
makes any explicit mention of political considerations, the political
implications of the scheme cannot be denied. Indeed, the very
decision to establish the Community and the framework within
which its activities will be performed are the consequences of political bargaining. James Nti of the ECOWAS Secretariat drove
this point home when he told some newly recruited foreign service
officers at Lagos: "The very decision of sovereign countries to
come together to integrate their economies is very much a political
matter; one does not need to read about political union before one
realises the political significance of economic integration."[12] In

the same vein, it was quite evident at the time that the 1967 Treaty of East African Cooperation was being negotiated that the decision process was inherently political, not only during the process of founding the Community but also in the way that partner states coped with subsequent crises. This much is apparent in the observation of James Gichuru, Kenya's minister of finance: "We were selfish to the extent that we had to safeguard our own country--as did the Ministers from the other two countries. It was quite a tug-of-war."[13]

Almost every detail and degree of West African economic integration envisaged in the Lagos Treaty requires a bold political decision and the coordination of economic and political policies. In West Africa, perhaps more than anywhere else, economic integration means more than merely refurbishing an old house; it means jointly building a new and larger house for millions of West Africans. Such a larger regional house can only be raised by the cooperation and sacrifices of all participating governments. Indeed, all structural and regional levels required for its growth will, in the final analysis, take place only through the decisions and actions of governments.

PROBLEMS OF POLITICAL INSTABILITY

This situation would in the first place demand a long-term and steadily increasing commitment to cooperation from each member state of the Community and second, necessarily require political stability to enable the ECOWAS members to withstand the pressures generated by the necessary reforms envisaged in the Lagos Treaty. Even the ability to plan both at the national and at regional levels would require some elements of political stability. As Waterston has emphasized:

> Experience demonstrates that when a country's leaders in a stable government are strongly devoted to development, inadequacies of the particular form of planning used--or even the lack of any formal planning--will not seriously impede the country's development. Conversely, in the absence of political commitment or stability, the most advanced form of planning will not make a significant contribution towards a country's development.[14]

Political instability should therefore be stressed as one of the major problems that might militate against the effective implementation of the provisions of the ECOWAS Treaty. For in pursuit of the objectives of the treaty, important interests would be hurt as tariffs are reduced and taxes raised. While many industries will want to expand, the government will have to channel investment funds to those select industries that national and regional planning studies indicate can produce goods at a regionally competitive price within a reasonable time and that regional market studies show have the greatest possibility for an expanding market. In the circumstances, governments fearful of being overthrown will probably not be able to endure the growing wrath of frustrated vested interests; they will be inclined toward providing their constituents with immediate benefits even if they be ephemeral and harmful to the long-term development of the nation. Consequently, governments in West Africa that suffer from chronic instability will probably have great difficulty in pursuing the strategy of economic development espoused in the Lagos Treaty.

It is common knowledge that the West African sub-region ranks high in political instability and perhaps ideological differences. The internal insecurity of many member states of ECOWAS has been reinforced by the epidemic of military coups, countercoups, and threats of coup. Since the early 1960s there have been more than a dozen coups and countercoups in the sub-region. Nigeria, the most populous and economically viable country of the Community, had its government under Shehu Shagari changed in a bloodless coup in late December 1983. And on 3 April 1984 the Guinean armed forces announced that they had seized power, only three days after the burial of President Sekou Toure, the then ECOWAS chairman. It is significant to note that out of the 16 member states of ECOWAS, no less than 11 were under military rule as of May 1985. And even more significantly, this number constituted more than one-half of the military regimes of the whole of Africa. The result is that in this kaleidoscopic atmosphere, West African heads of state and government, whether military or civilian, progressive or conservative, all feel unsafe.

One very notable feature to note is that, unlike Europe where public opinion plays a crucial role in determining the pace and scope of European integration, in the Third World, especially Africa, integration systems tend to be highly vulnerable to regime changes, mainly because integration efforts are generally sustained by the actions of political elites. Thus whenever coups d'etat or "revolutions" topple the governments of countries belonging to an integration scheme, the scheme's future may be jeopardized, as evidenced by the impact of the 1971 Ugandan coup on the East African Community.[15] Military takeovers tend to reinforce the feeling of insecurity of political leaders and make them more inward-looking and less likely to regard any increased integration with favor, despite their rhetoric to the contrary. A case in point was Liberia's long delay in ratifying the ECOWAS protocol on free movement of persons (signed by the ECOWAS heads of state and government in Dakar in May 1979),[16] in view of that country's feeling of insecurity, following the bloody overthrow of President Tolbert in April 1980, a popular leader in West Africa and at the time of his death chairman of the Organization of African Unity. It was this same feeling of insecurity that more than anything else constrained the Ghana government in September 1982 to capriciously close the country's borders with its neighbors for almost one year after the December 1981 coup d'etat, an action that was in flagrant breach of the spirit and letter of the ECOWAS idea. The same can be said about the continued closure of Nigeria's borders by the military powers that overthrew the civilian administration in December 1983.

Second, overthrow of a government belonging to a regional grouping may cause one or more of other member states to treat the new regime as a pariah, especially in a situation where close personal links had been maintained with the former leader. The Liberian coup, for example, precipitated a series of events that not only estranged Liberia from ECOWAS but also strained the relations between that country and other ECOWAS members. Treating the new regime as a pariah, the ECOWAS heads of state and government summarily excluded the new Liberian leader, Samuel Doe, from their summit meeting at Lome in May 1980, even though he was already in the Togolese capital. In retaliation, Doe announced the suspension of Liberia's membership in ECOWAS, as he interpreted the measures against him as "an unfriendly act, detrimental to the goals of the Community. . . ." In a series of actions that stopped just short of a diplomatic hiatus, the Liberian leader recalled the country's envoys to Nigeria, Senegal, and Sierra Leone.[17] Thus, a change of regime in Liberia, which is not an irregular occurrence in the West African sub-region, effected a not insignificant jolt to the solidarity of the ECOWAS member states.

The Liberian coup also had a serious impact on the Mano River Union, whose members are also signatories to the ECOWAS Treaty. Ever since the Liberian coup, the very existence of the Union has been threatened by the political apathy of its member states. The coup effectively rocked the very foundations of the Union, which is now "balancing on a political knife edge." The

Heads of State summit of the Union, scheduled for January 1981, failed to meet until January 1983, despite the frantic efforts by the late President Sekou Toure of Guinea. Described by many as a failure, the 1983 summit only succeeded in driving a larger wedge between President Stevens of Sierra Leone and Doe.[18] Given the absence of effective insulation of African regional integration schemes from national politics, regime change may generally preclude even limited interstate cooperation on narrow functional matters of mutual concern.

Third, this feeling of political insecurity has greatly reinforced a jealous attachment to notions of sovereignty in the sub-region resulting in a resort to tactics of border closures, such as, for example, the Togo-Benin border that was closed from late 1975 to March 1977. The border crisis between Sierra Leone and Liberia in March 1983 almost developed into war between the two "founding fathers" of the Mano River Union. These episodes make a mockery of West African unity and are in conflict with the spirit of the sub-region's integration efforts.

This issue of national sovereignty is put in an even sharper focus in the case of an economic integration that involves some degree of coordination of the economic and social policies of member countries. Countries will not be able to continue managing their instruments of economic policy as they did before integration. And to lose control over instruments of economic policy is to lose sovereignty. This requirement of policy coordination raises difficult problems for less developed countries, especially if they have become independent in recent years. For integration would mean losing something of what they have just obtained after waiting for many years.

And since the demand for political independence was based on the right of each country to govern itself, there is a legitimate desire on the part of many West African states to find their own salvation in economic as well as other fields. Besides, many of them are still in the first stages of building a pluralistic society and, under these circumstances, governments want to have as much control as possible over economic policy. The demonstrations of their sovereignty have led to adopting national currencies, national central banks, national airways, national shipping lines, and the like. As noted above, some have even passed indigenization decrees to protect the economic interests of their nationals. Insofar as these are thought to be outward manifestations for nationhood and sovereignty, they have become symbols of attachment eliciting loyalties that cannot transcend the national borders. While this does not rule out joint endeavor in a form of an economic grouping such as ECOWAS, it does suggest the existence of very real limits on the extent to which these countries are willing to part with or pool their sovereignty.

Green and Krishna have thus concluded that in the African context, even if economic integration "holds out the promise of improving the viability and performance of each territorial economy the problem exists of reconciling itself to economic (real or apparent) sacrifice of part or all of its sovereignty, so soon after independence."[19] It will always be difficult for political leadership groups in West Africa to surrender some measure of their sovereignty when they do not feel secure and they see the basis of their claim to national leadership threatened by an increasing need for institutional cooperation when the exclusive use of nationally available development-aid ties seems to be in jeopardy. The executive secretary of the Community painfully referred to this problem when he remarked in his annual report of May 1982:

> There are important and crucial variables such as national interest and ceding of some aspect of national sovereignty which are not normally given the weight they deserve in the analysis but which are crucial for the success of any integration among developing countries. As the work of the Community is based on consensus, our activities are sometimes bogged down because member states are unwilling to part with some aspect of national interest for the greater benefit of the Community.[20]

Dr. Ouattara, therefore, urged the necessity of a review of the mechanisms for formulating plans and programs "if the Community is to have the necessary impact on the lives of the people of the sub-region." Evidently, the member states of the Community are not yet prepared to welcome the unpleasant fact that in the emerging world economy and with the expanding operations of transnational enterprises, there is, in practice, no such thing as absolute national sovereignty.

NIGERIA: THE ELEPHANT IN THE GRASS

The jealous attachment of the West African leaders to notions of sovereignty has led to the fear that the potential politico-economic weight of Nigeria within ECOWAS would enable that country to eventually dominate the Community. Some observers of the West African scene would even see ECOWAS as "greater Nigeria."[21] Since in a recent extended study, Olatunde Ojo has covered much of the role of Nigeria as "leader in the process of forming ECOWAS,"[22] I intend only to highlight briefly a few salient aspects of this subject that do not appear to have received adequate attention from scholars.

Generally, regional integration may occur among relatively equal states or exist largely as a "sphere of influence" for a dominant country. In the latter case, there is, for example, the Council of Mutual Economic Assistance (COMECON) in Eastern Europe which is dominated by the economic and foreign policy interests of the Soviet Union. Similarly France and West Germany both employ Western European regionalism as an economic and diplomatic base. On the basis of this trend, can it be said that ECOWAS also exists as a "sphere of influence" for Nigeria?

Nigeria's physical size, demographic weight, and enormous wealth makes it--albeit involuntarily--something of a bull in a regional china shop. In 1980 its GNP accounted for no less than 75 percent of the sub-region's total; and it has the largest and most diversified industrial sector, at least in absolute terms. The country is liberally endowed with a wide range of natural and mineral resources, including petroleum, iron ore, tin, coal, and limestone. All this received a tremendous boost from the history-making commissioning of the iron and steel industry on 29 January 1982.[23] With this establishment, Nigeria entered the "steel age" and took the first major stride in creating a sound, technological industrial base. Admittedly, therefore, ECOWAS presents another glaring case of a partnership of unequal partners. Given the tendency of industries within the integrated area to cluster in a few industrial growth points, there is some apprehension that--unless a satisfactory distributive mechanism is instituted --the ECOWAS might widen rather than narrow the "economic gap" between its members.

I have already noted the experiences of the partnership of unequal partners having widened rather than narrowed the "economic gap" between states of a regional grouping, and have cited the case of the defunct East African Community as a typical example in Africa. In certain respects, within the erstwhile Latin American Free Trade Association (LAFTA), Argentina, Brazil, and Mexico occupied an analogous position. These three countries were able to increase their intraregional trade at a faster rate than most of the lesser developed members. Even in Central America, where differences in levels of development are somewhat less pronounced than they are in South America, new industry has tended to gravitate to the relatively more advanced centers in El Salvador, Costa

Rica, and Guatemala, by-passing the two less developed countries, Honduras and Nicaragua.

It is thus argued that, in view of Nigeria's comparative advantage, it will be the most tempted to pursue inward-directed (nationalistic) policies of development. Since Nigeria is in the position to attract large sums of domestic and foreign capital, it will be better enabled to develop industries with the best capabilities of taking advantage of the sub-regional market. In the circumstances, Nigeria will accelerate its own national development at the expense of especially the small and weak member states of the Community. Although member states in this category will need the sub-regional market more, they will be the most sensitive to any "exploitation" by Nigeria.

The fear of Nigeria dominating the grouping was made apparent during the annual summit meeting of the Heads of State and Government of ECOWAS held in Lome in November 1976. At this meeting oil-rich Nigeria insisted on having more votes for a bigger say on how the Community's budget should be operated and managed. This demand would have meant that voting power would be tied to contributions, but other states argued that voting was a question of sovereignty. This issue was forcefully driven home by the late President Tolbert of Liberia who warned the summit that the founding of the Community must not be used to undermine the sovereignty of member states: "Rich or poor, large or small, young or old," he declared, "we are sovereign states and equal partners. This is the only way to journey together into a prosperous future."[24] The enthusiastic cheers that greeted this statement is a clear indication that national sovereignty would play a significant role in the working of the Community. It is, also, a clear warning that all states, but in particular Nigeria, would have to tread warily in order that the jealousies which have troubled similar communities elsewhere should not impede the working of the group.

Indications of the danger of such jealousies and fears were again quite evident during the protracted debate over the choice of Lagos, the Nigerian capital, as the headquarters of the Community. In view of Nigeria's already commanding position vis-à-vis other member states of the Community, and its ability, should it so desire, to dominate the grouping, President Senghor opposed the choice of Lagos and suggested that the headquarters be located in the capital of a smaller country. The Senegalese leader had for long persisted in the view that membership of ECOWAS be expanded to include "all states on the Western side of Africa facing the Atlantic such as Cameroon, Equatorial Guinea, Gabon, Zaire and Congo Brazzaville," apparently to dilute Nigeria's status in ECOWAS.[25] Senegal's argument against the siting of the Community's headquarters in Lagos is supported not only by the experience of the EEC but also by that of many regional economic groupings in developing areas. In LAFTA, for instance, the headquarters were established in one of the smaller countries. Both the Standing Executive Committee and the Executive Secretariat were installed at Montevideo. Similarly, there is a concentration of UDEAC institutions at Bangui, the capital of the least developed country in the Union, which has been chosen as the headquarters of the common institutions.

As for the fear of Nigeria being "an elephant who has to be watched" lest it should trample upon the weaker members of the Community, it is no one but Nigeria itself that can dispel it. If Nigeria offers creative leadership to the new Community, a leadership aimed at maintaining the integrity of the union, guiding its goals, enabling it to adapt new and changing needs and circumstances, then the others will become almost unconsciously endeared to it.[26] To this extent, Nigeria's role in ECOWAS, like that of the United States in the contemporary Western world, may probably be aptly described as one of leadership without dominance. This leadership has recently been seriously tested, inter alia, by the Community's ratification of the protocol on free movement of persons.

REGIONAL MOBILITY WITHIN ECOWAS

Labor mobility in West Africa has a long and varied history. Even before the European colonization, West Africa, like the rest of the continent, was the scene of mass movements. Mabogunje has noted that during the precolonial period, people were "moving across ethnic boundaries" and, in the process, social norms were developed with "respect to the position of such strangers in different societies," and various institutions were established to cope with their needs and problems.[27] Colonialism did not appreciably alter this trend. Rather, it re-created the conditions for the free movements of people and stimulated such movements through improvement in transportation by rail, road, sea, and air. This practice has remained up to the modern period.

Traditionally, the entry (and exit) of the alien is the jealously guarded preserve of the state. Under general international law, a state may be under an obligation to admit its own nationals, but the admission of aliens is traditionally the exclusive preserve of the national authorities. Hence the alien may be refused admission or once admitted, deported in the exercise of discretion of national authorities, though this is subject if at all only to limited review by the court. Although bilateral agreements on free movement, such as that between Ghana and Togo or the exchange of notes between Nigeria and Ivory Coast in November 1964 on visa abolition, have from time to time imposed obligations on these states in respect of each other's nationals, these obligations have been subject to far-reaching exceptions and have often been enforceable only as between states.

This traditional picture has been modified by the ECOWAS protocol on free movement of persons signed in May 1979.[28] As far as ECOWAS is concerned, the movement of labor is part of the philosophy of its founders and it is written into the Lagos Treaty establishing the Community. The basic principle of the Community is that the economic process must not be distorted, and if goods, capital, and services are to be permitted free movement then it would represent a distortion if labor were not. The ECOWAS accord therefore provides for free movement of goods and citizens within the Community. And, like the EEC, ECOWAS' free movement means the right to accept offers of employment actually made and to move freely for this purpose within the territory of member states, to stay there in order to carry on employment, and to live there after having been employed there. This includes the abolition of visas and the right to reside anywhere in the West African sub-region. This right to enter, reside, and establish business in any ECOWAS territory is to be accomplished in three stages, all taking a minimum transitional period of 15 years from the definitive entry into force of the protocol.

The first stage, which took immediate effect, is the right of entry without visa. The second stage is the right of residence, while the third and last stage is the right of a citizen of one country to establish business in another country. Under the first stage, a citizen of the Community has the right to visit any member state other than his own for a period not exceeding 90 days without visa requirements. He shall, however, be required to possess valid travel documents. These should include international health certificates in the case of all visiting ECOWAS visitors, and valid driving license, document or ownership, insurance policy, and international customs carnet recognized within the Community in the case of persons driving vehicles into another partner state. Visiting ECOWAS expatriates can, however, upon application be granted extension of their time to stay. Notwithstanding these provisions clearly stipulate under Article 3 of the protocol, member states of the Community "shall reserve the right to refuse admission into their territory . . . any citizen who comes within the category of inadmissible immigrants under their laws." However, the provisions of the protocol should not operate to the prejudice of citizens of the Community who are already in residence and established in a member state provided they comply with the law in general and in particular the immigration laws of the member state.

The protocol is unique in the sense that it is more comprehensive and more clearly spelled out than similar provisions of UDEAC (Article 63) and CEAO (Article 14), although the objectives and intentions of these provisions are the same as those of ECOWAS. On the other hand, the 1967 treaty of the defunct East African Community made no such provision for the free movement of labor or capital within the region. This somewhat constitutional defect of the treaty proved to be damaging to the Community. For in 1970 a new labor policy in Uganda reserved employment exclusively for its own citizens, a move that threw 20,000 Kenyan migrants out of work.[29]

Similarly, further afield in Latin America, the general treaty establishing the CACM committed the five member states to the free movement of goods and services but not of persons. In a region characterized by the frequent overthrow of governments, it was felt that free movement of persons was a political and security issue and not, like free trade, a strictly economic matter falling under the jurisdiction of the Ministries of Economy. In spite of these considerations, the free movement of persons became so pressing a controversial issue in the 1960s that it led to a series of crises resulting in an outbreak of war between two partners of CACM--Honduras and El Salvador--in July 1969.[30]

These selective cases would tend to emphasize the significance of the elaboration of the ECOWAS free movement of persons provision. Closely studied, however, the ECOWAS protocol provided for only a fragmentary freedom. For whereas in the case of the EEC, for example, the free movement of persons provision confers rights upon individuals justifiable before the national courts, either of their own state or of another member state, the ECOWAS protocol confers no such rights. In the circumstances, a Community citizen who is faced with a deportation order in an ECOWAS member state has no implied legal rights to any hearing. Although the Lagos Treaty provides for the establishment of a tribunal to adjudicate in matters regarding the interpretation or application of the treaty provisions, its jurisdiction is clearly limited to disputes between member states. Individuals cannot initiate action before such a tribunal. Thus although the ECOWAS protocol on free movement of persons appears to be the only provision of the Lagos Treaty that attempts to involve the man in the street, the involvement becomes illusory without the means of enforcing such involvement. Briefly then, the doctrine of "primacy" of Community law has not been acceptable to the national courts of the ECOWAS member states. The absence of such regulations of the EEC-type in the ECOWAS Treaty is one of the fundamental differences between the legal structure of ECOWAS and EEC. It identifies ECOWAS as less of a supranational organization.

Second, the ECOWAS protocol on free mobility of persons does not appear to include the abolition of any discrimination based on nationality as regards employment, remuneration, and other working conditions. And third, the protocol does not make provision for third countries. No doubt the growth effect of economic integration will generate an increase in employment opportunities within the integrated area and will act as an additional force of attraction of labor from third countries. In other words, labor will tend to move from non-ECOWAS countries (characterized by the persistence of chronic unemployment) into the Community in response to changes in employment opportunities.

Despite these inadequacies, the importance of this provision for the promotion of the ECOWAS idea cannot be overstated. For many ECOWAS citizens this is the greatest gift the Community can bestow on them. The Community citizens would be able for the first time to travel freely across national boundaries to seek to improve their vocation, or in some cases to find employment where the opportunities at home were few and far between. Unlike the pre-ECOWAS era, this freedom of movement is now fully backed by a Community law. Consequently, this is an operational feature with which trade unions at national level should be particularly concerned.

Undoubtedly, the mutual economic benefit that the member states of ECOWAS could reap from the free movement of labor across their international boundaries would be immense. For, as Cukwurah has correctly stressed, this is a vital way of ensuring the rational use of the Community's human resources, which involves equating labor supply with demand without seriously endangering standards of living and levels of employment or, indeed, national security in member countries.[31] Furthermore, free movement can contribute to improvements in the conditions of employment, by raising expectations, by facilitating comparisons, and by

increasing contacts. It can also of course contribute to West
African integration and to promoting the feelings of a genuine
Community. Taken in its entirety, this provision appears to be
the first real effort at African unity. It is a solid foundation upon
which all political, social, and economic programs of Africa
should be based. The slogan of African unity at present begins
and ends at OAU conferences, whereas Africans are treated as
strangers from a different world if they venture to travel from
their homes to other African nations.

THE CRUCIAL POLICY ISSUES AHEAD

While the free movement of persons or labor of various categories as well as entrepreneurship within the Community is welcome, it cannot be denied that this is one of the most elusive and
difficult objectives for the Community to attain, for the simple
reason that the path to this objective is strewn with countless
problems of state security, politics, and economics. Political,
social, and cultural friction is likely since the unemployed and the
underemployed conceivably would tend to migrate to the prosperous areas of the sub-region where job opportunities are available.
This would particularly be the case in an area like West Africa
where unemployment and shortage of capital are among the acute
problems facing the governments. In the circumstances the self-
employed, such as craftsmen, traders, and businessmen may see
their markets as being curtailed in the light of the keen competition that is likely to ensue.

As a corollary of this, while free mobility within a grouping
ensures more efficient use of resources it can provoke the hostility
of citizens of host countries. Migration of workers from one nation to another is always a sensitive issue, even in advanced countries with better job prospects. There is the possibility of job discrimination against visitors in order to preserve these jobs for indigenes. On the other hand, there is the possibility of generous
job offers to visitors to display unity spirit but to the anger and
displeasure of the indigenes. This is what happened in 1965 when
President Houphouet-Boigny attempted to introduce dual citizen-
ship within the Conseil de l'Entente. The proposal, intended to
give non-Ivorian workers in the Ivory Coast that country's citizen-
ship while retaining their own nationalities was bitterly opposed
by the Ivorians, especially the white-collar workers, on the ground
that it constituted a threat to their employment.[32]

Also, in situations where aliens are allowed entry into an ECOWAS member state with a view to participating in the development of the economy of that country, they are very often confronted with such existing national investment legislations as, for example, the Ghanaian Business Promotion Act No. 334 of 1 August 1970, Ghana's Investment Decree of 1975, and the Nigerian Enterprises Promotions Decree of 1972, each of which reserved certain sectors of the economy and categories of enterprises for its citizens. While it is true that such legislative measures constitute an integral part of the long process of political consolidation whereby the new African states endeavor to take their economic destiny in their own hands, their adverse effects on cooperative development schemes as envisaged in the ECOWAS Treaty cannot be overemphasized. The hard fact is that member states of ECOWAS cannot pursue such measures and expect at the same time to accomplish the objectives of the Lagos Treaty, which are to compromise some aspects of their jealously guarded national sovereignty.

It is against this broad background that one should appreciate the political, economic, social, and even cultural implications of the free movement provision enshrined in the ECOWAS Treaty. For its implementation would seem to pose a number of disturbing questions. For example, to what extent have the citizens of West Africa been prepared to accept their new role of being their brother's keeper? Have the landlords in West Africa been told to start now to condition their minds to accepting tenants from other West African countries who may turn up to work or trade? Are the traders in West Africa aware that they have to make room for one another irrespective of country of origin but certainly in the spirit of ECOWAS? Furthermore, as James Nti has much more significantly put it in a recent address:

Are there enough job openings for all those who seek jobs in host country bearing in mind the level of their qualifications and skills? . . . Are their qualifications acceptable to employers in the host country? If they are, are such employers prepared to place them correctly at the level to which they rightly belong or are the employers prone to take advantage of the fact that such job-seekers are desperate and are prepared to take any job and any salary in an attempt to keep body and soul together in a place far away from home? Are employers prepared to give them the same conditions of service as they give to the indigenes of the country? Are they magnanimous enough to consider the special needs of migrant workers such as adjustment problems, housing problems, problems related to social security and pensions schemes, and problems related to training on the job or in-house or out-side the job to assimilate them into the society in which they find themselves and make them more competent and more productive?[33]

These are some of the crucial problems that relate to migrant labor and which will become more acute as the other two phases of the protocol on free mobility of labor become operational. Even now, in the course of operation of the first phase of the protocol, some of these problems have aroused a great deal of apprehension in some ECOWAS member states. This is particularly sharp and penetrating in Nigeria, where a substantial number of ECOWAS citizens have flocked in recent years in search of profitable economic opportunities. Indeed, the implementation of this first phase of the protocol has generated such an apprehension and aroused so great an indignation that it prompted the Nigerian government to expel the illegal ECOWAS immigrants from that country in January 1983 and April 1985 respectively.

THE NIGERIA EXPULSION ORDERS OF 1983 AND 1985

Under the section of the protocol currently in force, ECOWAS citizens are not allowed to accept employment without permit. Nevertheless, through various means, the ECOWAS citizens as well as persons from non-ECOWAS neighboring countries have taken employment in Nigeria without the necessary papers contrary to the Nigerian Immigration Laws. These constitute the very large volume of cheap labor in construction and service industries. A disturbing aspect of this is that this group is not so easy to monitor and thus constitutes added problems to the Nigerian Ministry of Internal Affairs. In addition to this, the growing bulk of ECOWAS expatriates in the cheap labor market "has negative effect on the cohesive action of the Labour Unionism" in Nigeria because these "guest-workers," as they are called in the European Community, "are not only ready to accept inferior condition of service but are also readily available to replace their Nigerian counterparts."[34]

Generally, Nigerian public reaction to this situation, as well as to other developments in the country following the influx of ECOWAS citizens, may be conveniently grouped into three main categories. First is the "negative employment effects" of the ECOWAS protocol that have provoked criticism and disgust among some labor organizations, the press, and individuals. The Gongola State branch of National Union of Construction and Civil Engineering Workers, for example, vehemently condemned ECOWAS for having made it possible for contractors in the state to indulge in employing "cheap labor" from ECOWAS and non-ECOWAS neighboring countries "while Nigerians roam about without jobs." Such indiscriminate recruitment, according to the Union, is "a calculated attempt to undermine the Union's organisation."[35] Indeed, for private entrepreneurs in Nigeria bent on maximizing profits, the presence of this "exploitable labour force . . . is godsent." Thus, for the unskilled Nigerian worker, who has been "outmaneuvred and undercut," the ECOWAS citizen is a threat and a rival. Besides, the preference for this "exploitable" group of ECOWAS citizens as well as ECOWAS expatriate professionals to indigenous Nigerians has a wider implication for the Nigerian economy. For it undermines the Nigerian Indigenisation Decrees of 1972 and 1977 which reserve certain employments for Nigerians.

The second category of criticism of ECOWAS is based on social and health grounds. It is argued that the ECOWAS immigrants "perpetuate illegal syndicate activities," including smuggling of goods across the national borders, and commitment of such crimes as prostitution, destitution, and vagrancy. It is also alleged that this uncontrolled influx of ECOWAS citizens brings along all types of disease to Nigeria. And since Nigeria has no valid proof to ascertain the aliens' health status, it is "dangerous to allow them to mix freely with indigenous Nigerians." The third and final body of criticism of ECOWAS relates to the question of law and order and, in particular, security. This situation has been exacerbated in the last few years by the protracted Chadian civil war, the Kano riot of December 1980, and the Nigerian-Cameroon border dispute of 1981. Although there has been no evidence of involvement of ECOWAS expatriates in any of these crises, ECOWAS as an institution was blamed for what had happened.

All three categories of criticism have almost invariably called for a review of ECOWAS agreement as the very first step toward mitigation of its impact on Nigeria, since after all, ECOWAS, as a correspondent overstated it, is an institution that exists "at the expense of Nigeria and yet one hardly finds a Nigerian in any responsible position in that organisation."[36] No less a politician than the Senate leader of the Nigerian People's Party, Senator Obi Wali, called for reassessment of Nigerian's commitments to ECOWAS because "the question of security has not been properly assessed in terms of individual state."[37] To many Nigerians, the excessive number of illegal immigrants was one of the remote causes of Nigeria's social problems. They traced the recent Kano, Maiduguri, and Kaduna disturbances to this influx of ECOWAS citizens. All this, together with the pressure on the government to find jobs for the Nigerian unemployed, culminated in the federal government's expulsion of illegal immigrants in January 1983.

For by the end of 1982, the presence of illegal immigrants working in Nigeria in contravention of the Nigerian Immigration Act of 1963 and the ECOWAS protocol on free movement of persons was becoming increasingly intolerable to the Nigerian government. This was accentuated by the changing conditions and climate of economic boom of the early 1970s, while the country was approaching a crucial general election year and, therefore, becoming seriously concerned about matters of security. To enforce Nigeria's immigration laws, therefore, the government announced on 17 January 1983 the expulsion within the following two weeks of all unskilled foreigners residing and working illegally in the country.[38] The federal government later reviewed the order to allow for: an extension of four weeks that terminated on 28 February 1983 was granted to all those employed in skilled work; regularization of the stay in Nigeria of the professional and technical grades provided their employers were able to make adequate representations for Expatriate Quota slots to be granted for the posts they occupy; all citizens of ECOWAS member states, Cameroon, and Chad who had been living in the country prior to the coming into force of the 1963 Immigration Act to remain in Nigeria irrespective of what they do; and confirmation of the fact that by virtue of section 8, subsection 1(a) of the Immigration Act, 1963, the order did not affect aliens employed by federal and state governments.[39]

Two years later in 1985, the expulsion exercise was repeated when the recently established federal military government of Nigeria declared on 15 April that all illegal aliens were to leave the country by 10 May. While the 1983 expulsion order affected an estimated 2 million illegal immigrants, the 1985 illegal aliens numbered about 700,000. This second order was issued for much the same reasons as in 1983: the immigrants' abuse of the ECOWAS protocol on free movement of persons and second, the involvement of these immigrants in crimes. The fundamental reason for the order was, however, economic: a troubled economy that continued to be badly hurt by depressed crude-oil prices. At a time when jobs were scarce and prices for basic goods were high, there was a tendency to regard the aliens in the midst of Nigeria's over 84 million people as an unacceptable strain on the country's limited resources.

While it is conceded that technically, Nigeria has not breached any part of the ECOWAS protocol on free movement of persons by its expulsion of illegal immigrants, it would seem, however, that this action by the government of Nigeria does strike a blow not only at the spirit of ECOWAS but also the whole concept of West African unity which, as already discussed in this study, has since the mid-nineteenth century been the mainspring behind any effort at establishing a community in the sub-region. Throughout the colonial period, no West African was considered an alien by any West African country, especially the four former British colonies of the Gambia, Ghana, Nigeria, and Sierra Leone which formed the National Congress of British West Africa in March 1920. An important resolution of the Congress at its inaugural meeting in Accra (from 11-20 March 1920) specifically declared, among other things, that "the Aboriginal inhabitants of the several colonies of British West Africa are not Aliens or Foreigners to one another"; and advocated "the avoidance of all discriminatory Ordinances in that relation." So far as the Congress was concerned, the only aliens in West Africa described as "undesirable," and for whom immigration laws should be introduced throughout the sub-region so as to keep them out, were the Syrians, because they were "a menace to the good government of the land."[40]

Although admittedly, this concept of West African unity would seem to have been modified by the attainment of independence by these countries and by the subsequent establishment of separate national institutions and currencies, it is still an important concept that continues to draw West African countries together. ECOWAS, is therefore, the only all-embracing institutional expression of this old concept to which all stalwart West African nationalists since the last century--from Africanus Beale Horton of Sierra Leone through Casely Hayford of Ghana (the architect of the National Congress of British West African movement), to the modern nationalists like Kwame Nkrumah and Nnamdi Azikiwe--have made due reference. It has been a "symbol" of West African nationalism and an inspiration to pan-West African thought and activity. And although with the formation of ECOWAS, this concept has been "transformed" into practical reality and that a living thing is born, it is still a jealously guarded concept that draws West African countries together. Any serious disregard of this concept is likely to strike a deep blow at the very foundations of ECOWAS itself. And it is the aspirations associated with this age-old concept that the Nigerian quit orders would seem to have effectively disturbed. Besides, even technically, taking the ECOWAS Treaty itself, the Nigerian action is strikingly not in consonance with the general undertaking by the member states of ECOWAS to "make every effort to *plan and direct their policies with a view to creating favourable conditions for the achievement of the aims of the Community. . . .*" (emphasis added, Chap. 1, Article 3, of the ECOWAS Treaty).[41] Furthermore, the April 1985 expulsion order, and the way it was applied, not only ran counter to the spirit and ideals of pan-West African solidarity; it was also a flagrant breach of Nigeria's commitments under Article 14, clause 2, of the December 1984 regional security agreement signed in Lagos between Benin, Ghana, Nigeria, and Togo, which required a member country to protect other members' citizens in its territory.

Although Nigeria's expulsion orders have struck a blow at the spirit of ECOWAS as well as the long historical associations and the ethnic affinities that exist among West African countries, they have at the same time given the member states of the Community the unique opportunity to reassess the full implications of this popular protocol on free movement of persons with a view to strengthening it by initiating some complementary measures. And one important lesson to be learned from the Nigerian experience is that there is the need for a conscious and systematic public education of the wider implications of ECOWAS, its aims and objectives, the benefits to be derived from it as well as the costs involved in the implementation of its provisions. Second, that the social, economic, and human problems that arise from the phenomenon of labor migration constitute a challenge to member states of the Community. Third, and as a corollary of this, that labor movements in the absence of any protective measures can lead to various social evils such as crime among migrant workers, unsatisfactory conditions of employment, and damage to the economy and development of the migrants' own country as well as that of the receiving country. And finally, that labor movements have implications for labor and social policies in such areas as harmonization of national labor legislation of member states, conditions of work, and the role of employment exchanges in the machinery for facilitating the geographical mobility of workers.

Generally, the freeing of labor movement within the West African sub-region could create as many problems as it solved if certain other complementary measures and social cushioning measures are not introduced as well, such as the right of free establishment for the self-employed, social security for migrants, social services and housing for migrants, and possible vocational training provisions. In West Africa, as in the European Economic Community, the exchange of labor among the various national markets cannot rely exclusively on the blind forces of supply and demand, for this could lead to results that would be prejudicial to the subregional economy and to the migrants themselves--particularly so if there were a lack of knowledge about prevailing conditions in the countries of destination.[42] In this respect, intergovernmental agreements and legislation ought to lend themselves to organizing systematic forms of more permanent cooperation among national employment services in order to make adequate provisions for maintaining a balance between labor supply and demand, based on a standard classification of skills and jobs. In this regard, ECOWAS can learn from the experience of the European Co-ordinating Office (European Office for the Co-ordination and Balancing of Employment Supply and Demand) and establish an agency like an "ECOWAS Citizens Bureau" to act as an intraregional labor clearing house capable of meeting effectively the need of industry, agriculture, and public services. It should also be capable of serving the interests and aspirations of the working classes by preventing any migration that would result in unemployment in the country receiving immigrants and a shortage of labor in the country from which they migrate.

There is one other serious barrier to the free movement of labor that the West African governments will have to deal with and for which no provision is made in the ECOWAS protocol under discussion. Migrants will lose the social security rights they have already acquired or are in the process of acquiring in the country where they have been residing, and will not be able to easily obtain similar protection in their adopted country. In other words, lack of provision for social security for migrant workers or insufficient arrangements which mean that rights acquired in different member countries are lost will tend to reduce intra-union labor mobility. Perverse movements may also be generated if the purchasing power of social security contributions differs from country to country.

To avoid undesirable repercussions on both the strength and the direction of labor movements, it would be necessary for ECOWAS to establish social security rights based upon the many precedents in international welfare law--such as, International Labour Convention No. 48 and the vast array of bilateral agreements on reciprocity in this field--set during the past 50 years, and upon the example of their application within the European Community.[43] An agency similar to the EEC's Administrative Commission for the Social Security of Migrant Workers could perhaps be formed to specify the ways of assessing compensation between social security institutions of different member countries of ECOWAS and administer and interpret regulations governing this exercise. This agency could, inter alia, ensure that there is equal treatment of all workers irrespective of nationality; be responsible for the totalization of insurance periods so that periods completed under the legislation of different ECOWAS member states are added up; and establish close cooperation between the social security institutions of ECOWAS countries. The application of the principle of the totalization of insurance periods will also ensure that the pension rights of migrant workers are not lost.

There are also such other social policy measures as establishment of vocational training institutions for training migrant community workers or the setting up of a social fund like the European Social Fund designed to complement the free movement of labor protocol.[44] However, such measures may well seem at the moment to lie beyond the capability and resources of the fledgling ECOWAS. Yet they are necessary as a first step toward giving the Community "a human face."

ECOWAS-CEAO: CONFLICT OR COOPERATION?

Another politically sensitive issue likely to confront the Community is the parallel existence of ECOWAS and the six-nation Francophone CEAO, and the resulting interlocking relationships as member states of the CEAO are also signatories to ECOWAS. This has been a subject of continuing debate in recent years among observers of the West African scene.[45] Generally, the debate is centered on the extent to which the two organizations are compatible, particularly in the area of trade liberalization now being implemented by both groupings. It is predicted that as the two schemes reach an advanced stage in their respective developments, a degree of incompatibility would be a potential source of conflict.

The origins and the establishment of CEAO, its aims and objects, as well as its institutional structure have already been discussed in this study. Basically, one does not see much difference between ECOWAS and CEAO in terms of their broad objectives, although, to some extent, their specific approaches tend to differ. It is, however, important to make some brief observations. First, the participation of the "regional superpower" Nigeria in ECOWAS as well as the fact that the former colonial powers did not initiate cooperation but had to react to it distinguishes ECOWAS from

CEAO. Nigeria is no doubt one of the foremost of the new "middle powers" that are assuming an increasing importance in world affairs. Many scholars of regional integration schemes have stressed the importance of the emergence of one country, or a group of countries, as "the prime movers of the integrated efforts." As Abangwu has, for instance, underlined: "There must emerge a dynamic centre of gravity within the prospective integrating area: a country or group of countries willing to bell the cat as leaders in the process of integration."[46] In neo-functional terms, Nigeria is playing the role of a strong core state. Second, whereas ECOWAS was inspired solely by African political leaders and is being administered by African technocrats and bureaucrats, one has to take note of the overpowering influence of Jacques David, a former French customs official in the colonial administration, in the establishment of CEAO.[47] The CEAO states, like those of UDEAC, are harnessed to the French system to a degree that makes them collectively dependent on France, and hence deserving of the latter's support.

Third, and closely related to this, CEAO, like such other African regional groupings as UDEAO, UDEAC, and even the EAC, has its origins in the colonial period. ECOWAS is unique in the sense that first, it does not have its origins from the colonial period and, second, it extends beyond the geographic framework set up by the colonial powers. This should not suggest, however, that ECOWAS would be any less susceptible to external (or ex-colonial power) interests; rather, it does suggest that ECOWAS would seem to possess a larger potential and opportunity than the CEAO for breaking out of the ex-colonial enclave. And fourth, it has been asserted that there is greater solidarity of CEAO than ECOWAS because the former organization has fewer members, common language and currency, as well as common administrative or colonial background. This is largely true. The member states of CEAO have had much experience of cooperation amongst themselves since the colonial era.

The implications of these observations may not constitute an obstacle to cooperation between ECOWAS and CEAO. Since ECOWAS became operational in 1977, the Secretariat in Lagos has been working consistently toward the creation of "an efficient cooperation framework" for all the economic cooperation institutions operating within West Africa, in particular the Francophone CEAO. The rationale behind this effort is that if the policies and programs of the intergovernmental organizations in the sub-region are not coordinated, it would lead to duplication, unnecessary competition among them and, above all, dissipation of the meager resources of the sub-region. This consideration led to a convening of the first meeting of heads of intergovernmental organizations in West Africa held in Monrovia on 17 and 18 January 1979. At this meeting "the modus operandi" was agreed upon.[48] A program for cooperation between ECOWAS and other intergovernmental schemes in West Africa was prepared.

ELEMENTS OF POTENTIAL CONFLICT

These efforts notwithstanding, the cooperation between ECOWAS and CEAO is not likely to continue undisturbed, particularly as the two organizations attain a stage of maturity. There are some elements that seem to contain the seeds of future conflict, as briefly noted in a special report by the United Nations Development Programme (UNDP) and the UNCTAD.[49] The report stressed some important differences between the compensation and revenue loss provisions of the treaties of CEAO and ECOWAS that might be a source of potential difficulty. For instance, the two treaties differ in respect of the basis on which member states are to make contributions in respect of revenue losses. In the CEAO, contributions are based on a member's share of manufactured exports to the Community. In ECOWAS, a member country's contribution is specifically related to the margins of preference accorded to its own exports, thus linking costs and benefits more closely. Also, the share of revenue losses to be compensated for is not specified in the ECOWAS Treaty and the provision of compensation is not necessarily automatic and uniform as it is under the CEAO Treaty, "but is to be related to budgetary needs." Finally, while compensation is payable under the CEAO Treaty only in respect of manufactured exports of Community origin, the relevant coverage is not specified in the ECOWAS Treaty.

A second area which might be a source of conflict relates to the creation of customs union in the future. It is envisaged that the CEAO would mature into a customs union by 1986 while the 15 years teething period envisaged for ECOWAS places its maturity into a customs union at 1990. Thus the CEAO as a customs union would precede the ECOWAS as one. There appears, therefore, to be room for a conflict of loyalty between the two in those countries (Francophone) that belong to the two bodies. One is left wondering how such conflict could be resolved. Would the six Francophone countries, for example, continue to support ECOWAS and remain loyal to it after their international trade and economic development interests have come to be catered for by CEAO?

The third major problem confronting ECOWAS is the evident incompatibility of some of the provisions of both the Community and CEAO treaties, particularly in the area of trade liberalization. The relatively advanced stage of CEAO trade liberalization scheme would seem to pose some crucial problems for the development of ECOWAS. For instance, though the CEAO's ultimate goal is the establishment of a customs union with a common external tariff over a period of 12 years, it does not envisage a general free trade area within the customs union as is the case for ECOWAS. The CEAO trade liberalization scheme calls for a preferential trading area through the use of the Taxe de Cooperation Regionale (TCR). A free trade area will exist only for goods "which are raw produce," that is, unprocessed, unworked, and entirely local.

The implication of the coexistence of the two liberalization schemes of ECOWAS and CEAO becomes evident in practical terms after the two customs unions (ECOWAS' and CEAO's) have been established. The same product, for example, canned beer, would be traded within CEAO countries under the TCR preferential treatment, and be subjected to the agreed TCR import duty rate, while in ECOWAS, it would carry no import charges as long as it meets the ECOWAS origin requirement.This would no doubt result in an unsatisfactory situation within ECOWAS.

Closely related to this is yet another contradiction between the CEAO and ECOWAS Treaties. Under the ECOWAS scheme, the rights and obligations of members deriving from previously signed contracts (which includes the CEAO Treaty) are not affected. On the other hand, ECOWAS members (including the CEAO members) are obliged to remove all provisions (discriminations) from prior treaties that are not compatible with the provisions of the ECOWAS Treaty, and not to enact new ones. This in turn means that according to the ECOWAS Treaty (reciprocal grant of most favored status) CEAO members would be obligated to extend all preferences granted to each other to all of ECOWAS. In other words, the customs union of CEAO logically has to cease to exist at some time in the future and to merge with ECOWAS.

This complicated issue has not in the least disturbed the CEAO which has been making a persistent request to ECOWAS for a "derogation from Article 20 of the ECOWAS Treaty" which requires that "Member States shall accord to one another in relation to trade between them the most favoured nation treatment." The request for "derogation" would allow the CEAO member states to keep among themselves the preferential treatment afforded by their respective liberalization programs. Thus, it was a welcome development that at the May 1983 Conakry meeting of the ECOWAS leaders a decision was finally adopted for the implementation of a single trade liberalization scheme for industrial products originating from member states of the Community with effect from 30 May 1983.[50] By this decision, the Council reaffirmed the determination of all ECOWAS member states to work toward a customs union and appealed to the CEAO to merge its aims and aspirations with those of ECOWAS so as to avoid duplication of efforts and facilitate total solidarity toward the creation of a single customs union and economic integration under the ECOWAS Treaty. This was reinforced by the decision of the ECOWAS Heads of State summit of November 1984 at Lome relating to the implementation of the Conakry decision on the adoption of a single trade liberalization scheme. The Lome meeting also requested an in-depth analysis of the studies on rationalization of cooperation efforts within the West African sub-region.[51]

At the present state of regional cooperation no final judgment can be passed as yet on the prospects for ECOWAS and CEAO. However, the urge to contemplate the future relationship between the two organizations is compelling. It would seem that, to some extent, the routes to effective cooperation between them are littered with some discouraging factors. And if I may engage in dreams for a while, I can see the immediate future punctuated by a series of misunderstandings and even tensions. CEAO activities since the creation of ECOWAS reflect the view consistently put forward by President Houphouet-Boigny, and later advocated by President Senghor, that unity among Francophone states would be the first major step toward a wider West African unity. The CEAO members need to be convinced of the greater potentials of ECOWAS and, by implication, of the redundancy of the continued operation of their organization. The success of such efforts would depend on their regard for ECOWAS as a body for solving economic problems associated with CEAO.

This last point is extremely important particularly when it is realized that CEAO is now an operational grouping with its members enjoying free trade with one another, finance certain projects jointly, and have a common regional development tax on imports. By the end of 1976, for example, interstate trade in industrial products had expanded considerably with Ivory Coast and Senegal accounting for about 20 billion francs CFA out of a total of 20.8 billion francs CFA. Significantly, too, by December 1978, some 618 industrial products that were subject to TCR were produced by 175 enterprises or companies. Besides, both the CEAO fund and the recently created "Solidarity Fund" of the Community in June 1977 have been growing progressively. While the ECOWAS fund is still at its rudimentary stage of development, the resources of the CEAO fund had grown from 1,047 million francs CFA in 1975 to 2,280 million in 1976. By 1980 this had increased to 6,760.0 million francs CFA. The resources of the fund had been utilized partly to compensate those states that had lost customs revenue as a result of the introduction of the TCR and partly to carry out feasibility studies of possible Community projects.[52] Against this background, it would clearly be unrealistic to expect the member states of the CEAO to give up these benefits at a time when the future of ECOWAS is still uncertain. This was clearly the fundamental message of Senegalese President Abdou Diouf's recent statement:

> It is in everybody's interest that if ECOWAS reaches its cruising speed, the CEAO should normally melt into the structures of ECOWAS. We are convinced that the future is with ECOWAS; if ECOWAS reaches its cruising speed, and overcomes its present difficulties. What we do not want, we members of CEAO, is to be asked to eliminate something that works well, that produces brilliant results-CEAO, while ECOWAS has not reached cruising speed.[53]

This chapter has in a nutshell attempted to highlight the major internal political factors that are likely to disturb the smooth running of ECOWAS as a sub-regional economic grouping. It has stressed, among other things, the "primacy of politics," particularly in integrative schemes among developing countries. Given the emphasis placed on newly won sovereignty and the sensitive nature of economic issues, African governments have been unwilling to delegate authority to regional institutions. It must be emphasized, also, that the political volatility endemic to West Africa in particular is not only a consequence of the personalization of political power, it is also of the vaunting ambitions of military establishments in the sub-region to take over civilian administration at will and, on occasion to attempt to implement their own pet dreams of a phony revolution. Such an unconstitutional change of regime seriously affects the continued stability of a regional economic cooperation scheme. Strained relations among member states of the grouping have been the characteristic concomitants of such political upheavals. Also analyzed in this chapter are the political, economic, and social implications of the ECOWAS free mobility of labor provisions, and the challenge that this has posed to the strength and diplomacy of Nigeria in recent years. Finally, the critical problems posed by the coexistence of CEAO and ECOWAS, particularly the incompatibility aspects of the two treaties, have been briefly examined. It is argued that effective cooperation between the two organizations in the future remains problematic.

NOTES

1. This title is adopted from the topic of Helen Wallace's contribution in Helen Wallace, William Wallace, and Carole Webb, *Policy-Making in the European Community* (New York: John Wiley and Sons, 1978), p. 33.
2. Note that the other major internal factor--unequal distribution of costs and benefits--has already been discussed in Chapter 5.
3. Joan E. Spero, *The Politics of International Economic Relations* (London: George Allen and Unwin, 1977), p. 1.
4. C. Fred Bergsten, Robert O. Keohane, and Joseph S. Nye, Jr., "International Economics and International Politics: A Framework for Analysis," *International Organization*, vol. 29, no. 1 (Winter 1975):3.
5. E. B. Haas, *The Unity of Europe: Political, Social and Economic Forces 1950-57* (Stanford: Stanford University Press, 1958), p. 13.
6. Felippe Herrera, "Economic Integration and Political Reintegration," in *Latin America: Evolution or Explosion?*, ed. Mildred Adams (New York: Dodd, Mead, 1963), p. 99.
7. James D. Cochrane, *The Politics of Regional Integration: The Central American Case* (New Orleans: Tulane University Press, 1969), preface.
8. Donald Rothchild, "The Political Implications of the Treaty," *East African Economic Review*, vol. 3, no. 2, New Series (December 1967):14.
9. Bingu Mutharika, *Toward Multinational Economic Cooperation in Africa* (New York: Praeger, 1972), p. 15.
10. A notable example was the 1964 projected West African free trade area involving Liberia, Guinea, Ivory Coast, and Sierra Leone which became a victim of political conflict between Ivory Coast and Guinea. See Amadu Sesay, "Conflict and Collaboration: Sierra Leone and Her West African Neighbours, 1961-80," *Africa Spectrum* 2 (1980):163-80.

11. Mutharika, *Toward Multinational Economic Cooperation*, p. 16.
12. James Nti, "ECOWAS: An Approach to Regional Economic Co-operation" (A talk at the 18th Induction Course for newly recruited Foreign Service Officers, Lagos, July 1980).
13. *Daily Nation* (Nairobi), 28 June 1967, p. 18.
14. Albert Waterston, *Development Planning: Lessons of Experience* (Baltimore: The John Hopkins Press, 1965), p. 4.
15. Thomas S. Cox, "Northern Actors in a South-South Setting: External Aid and East African Integration," *Journal of Common Market Studies* vol. 21, no. 3 (March 1983):291.
16. *West Africa*, 1 June 1981.
17. *Africa* 107 (July 1980), p. 36.
18. *Africa Now*, 30 (October 1983), pp. 23-25.
19. R. H. Green and K. G. Krishna, *Economic Cooperation in Africa: Retrospect and Prospect* (Nairobi: OUP., 1967), pp. 53-54.
20. ECOWAS Doc., ECW/CM/xi/2, *Annual Report of the Executive Secretary, 1981-1982*, (May 1982).
21. This view was variously expressed at a seminar on ECOWAS held at the Institut fur Afrika-Kunde, Hamburg, (West Germany), August 1976.
22. Olatunde Ojo, "Nigeria and the Formation of ECOWAS," *International Organization*, vol. 34, no. 3 (Autumn 1980):571-604.
23. *West Africa*, 8 February 1982. For details about Nigeria as a market, its development, and oil production, see "Nigeria Special Report," *South* (February 1982):41-78.
24. Cited in *Africa*, 64 (December 1976).
25. *West Africa*, 26 May 1975.
26. Okon Udokang, "Nigeria and ECOWAS: Economic and Political Implications of Regional Integration" (Paper presented at the conference on Nigeria and the World, Lagos, January 1976).
27. Akin L. Mabogunje, *Regional Mobility and Resource Development in West Africa* (Montreal: McGill University Press, 1972), pp. 3-6. An extended and interesting discussion of problems of labor movements in West Africa is provided in A. Oye Cukwurah, "ECOWAS: Obstacles to Labour Migration and Residence" (Paper presented at the conference on ECOWAS, Lagos, August 1976).
28. ECOWAS Doc., A/P 1/5/79, *Protocol Relating to Free Movement of Persons, Residence and Establishment, Official Journal* 1 (June 1979).

29. John Ravenhill, "Regional Integration and Development in Africa: Lessons from the East African Community," *Journal of Commonwealth and Comparative Politics*, vol. 17, no. 3 (1979):238.

30. Stuart I. Fagan, *Central American Economic Interpretation* (Berkeley: University of California, 1970), pp. 70-72.

31. Oye Cukwurah, "ECOWAS: Obstacles to Labour Migration and Residence."

32. *West Africa*, 20 September 1976.

33. James Nti, "Economic Co-operation of West African States" (Address given at the Inter-territorial Conference of Employers Organisation in English-speaking West Africa, 17 September 1980).

34. R. I. Onwuka, "The ECOWAS Protocol on the Free Movement of Persons: A Threat to Nigerian Security?" *African Affairs*, vol. 81, no. 323 (April 1982):199-200.

35. *National Concord* (Lagos), 27 February 1981.

36. Eugene Onwumere, "Nigeria and ECOWAS," *Daily Times*, 20 February 1980.

37. *Nigerian Tribune*, 26 February 1981.

38. *West Africa*, 31 January 1983.

39. Chief Adejoju Adeyemi, "The Nigerian Expulsion Order of Illegal Immigrants" (Address by the Nigerian High Commissioner to Ghana at a symposium organized by the Political Science Students Association of the University of Ghana, Legon, Ghana, 25 February 1983).

40. Colonial Office (Public Record Office, London) 5543/54/2760, Resolutions of the Congress of British West Africa, Accra, Gold Coast, 11-29 March 1920.

41. For an expanded discussion of the Nigerian expulsion order of 1983, see my two-part article, S. K. B. Asante, "ECOWAS and the Nigerian Expulsion Order of January 1983," *West Africa*, April 11 and 18, 1983.

42. For details see S. K. B. Asante, "ECOWAS and Freedom of Movement," *West Africa*, 3 July 1978.

43. See Estanislau Fischlowitz, "A Labour Common Market," *Americas*, vol. 14, no. 8 (August 1962):17-19.

44. Roger Lawson and Bruce Reed, *Social Security in the European Community* (London: Chatham House, PEP, 1975), pp. 46-47; also Colin R. Beever, *Trade Unions And Free Labour Movement in the EEC* (London: Chatham House, PEP, 1969), pp. 25-47.

45. See for example, Rainer Kuehn and Frank Seelow, "ECOWAS and CEAO: Regional Cooperation in West Africa", *Develop-*

ment and Cooperation 3 (May/June 1980):11-13. For a detailed discussion of this subject see S. K. B. Asante, "CEAO-ECOWAS: Conflict and Cooperation in West Africa", in *The Future of Regionalism in Africa*, ed. R. I. Onwuka and A. Sesay (London: Macmillan, 1984).

46. George C. Abangwu, "Systems Approach to Regional Integration in West Africa," *Journal of Common Market Studies*, vol. 13, nos. 1, 2 (1975):131.

47. Makhtar Diouf, "Approaches to Economic Integration in Black Africa: Assessment and Suggestions" (Paper presented at an international seminar on Planning Economic Integration: Experiences, Policies, and Models, West Berlin, November 1979).

48. ECOWAS Doc., ECW/CM/VI/2, *Report of the Executive Secretary to Council of Ministers*, Dakar (November 1979).

49. *Preliminary Study on Approaches to Fiscal Co-operation and Harmonisation in ECOWAS*, report prepared for ECOWAS by the UNDP/UNCTAD, Lagos (1980) ECW/FISC/1, p. 17.

50. ECOWAS Doc., ECW/HSG. VI/4/Rev. 1, *Final Communique*, Conakry (May 28-30, 1983); also Decision A/DEC/1/5/83.

51. ECOWAS Doc., ECW/HSG/VII/6/Rev. 1, *Final Communique*, Lome, (November 22-23, 1984). Note that the ECOWAS May 1983 summit at Conakry called upon the ECA to undertake analysis of the activities, plans, programs of West African Intergovernmental Organizations with a view to rationalizing their activities. Accordingly, the ECA has submitted for study and necessary action a 99-page report of 460 paragraphs entitled *Proposals for Strengthening Economic Integration in West Africa*. For the reaction of the ECOWAS Executive Secretariat to this report see *Comments on the ECA Study Report "Proposals for Strengthening Economic Integration In West Africa*," ECOWAS Doc., ECW/1GO/1/5, Lagos (March 1984).

52. W. A. Ndongko, "Regional Economic Integration of French-Speaking Countries in Africa: The Case of the West African Economic Community (CEAO)" (Paper presented at the International Conference on Law and Economy in Africa, University of Ife, Ife, Nigeria, February 1982).

53. "Senegal and Africa," *West Africa*, 31 October 1983.

8

ECOWAS:
A LOOK AHEAD

The July 1985 Lome summit marks the tenth anniversary of the founding of ECOWAS. In operational terms, this meeting is officially described as the eighth annual session of the Community since the organization was formally established in March 1977. Since that date, ECOWAS has been moving, though rather imperceptibly, toward the avowed and overall objective of making the West African sub-region one indivisible economic whole eliminating any distinction or discrimination on national basis in respect of any economic policy, strategy, or activity. Admittedly, the road toward the present stage of the Community's development has been rough and bumpy: implementation of resolutions has been tardy and sometimes unimpressive. But this is not surprising considering, in particular, the immense diversity of the sub-region, the nature of the underdeveloped economics, the lack of basic infrastructure, and the countless other obstacles that are awesome impediments to West African unity. And, moreover, ECOWAS is involved in physical integration of the sub-region as well as the development of the production base of the economies of its member states. There are also many related issues that have to be attended to together, if the Community is to fulfill its mandate of ensuring the accelerated and balanced development of West Africa. Given the limitations imposed by some vital resources and the need to ensure that some countries are not dragged along at a forced pace, the gradualist approach has been adopted in each sector as the general cooperation program has been expanding in coverage.

This chapter attempts a brief review of the evolution of the Community over a decade of its existence. In reflecting over the record of performance of this first great West African experiment at regional cooperation and integration, I have sought to highlight whenever possible the critical issues and challenges ahead. Second, an attempt is made to see ECOWAS in the context of the wider world: its responses to the demands and principles of the New International Economic Order as well as the OAU's *Lagos Plan of Action* and the Africa report of the World Bank, *An Agenda for Action* or the *Berg Report*. While throughout no substantial policy prescriptions are intended, the chapter somewhat attempts to make some specific observations toward this end.

HASTENING SLOWLY: A DECADE OF ECOWAS

By May 1980, when the third summit of the Authority was held at Lome, the "conceptualisation phase" and the establishment of the functional structures of the institutions of the Community had been completed. The Community was preoccupied during the early years with staffing as well as complex administrative problems. To make ECOWAS institutionally operational, efforts were directed during this period to establish an effective administration, to improve and to complement basic documentation, to collect basic information upon which technical work of the Community was to be built, and to formulate regional policies and programs. The Lome summit made some far-reaching decisions that marked the end of the period of formulating the major Community policies and measures that were required to "give practical form to the framework for co-operation" as defined by the ECOWAS Treaty. By May 1985, the Community has been able to make some appreciable inroads into some of its top priority areas such as trade development and expansion, immigration and related matters, and had adopted a range of important protocols needed to give effect to treaty provisions.

Trade Liberalization

I have noted the Community's adoption of a comprehensive trade liberalization scheme, which is in the process of implementation. The significance of this ambitious scheme for the growth and development of the Community as a whole has already been highlighted. Suffice it to say that by opening up a larger West African market through trade liberalization, economies of scale and more broadly based specialization can be more efficiently developed than otherwise would be the case. I have also indicated that the extent of the benefits to be derived from the trade liberalization program is likely to depend significantly on the extent to which it is linked with cooperation in other sectors of the West African economy. Consequently, parallel measures to expand industrial production and to improve distribution through improved communications and transport arrangements have been undertaken. With the adoption of these necessary parallel measures, including also monetary and financial cooperation, the Community trade liberalization can be expected to afford considerable developmental benefits.

It has been observed also that the implementation of the trade liberalization scheme has not been expeditious, as there has been a certain lack of the necessary enthusiasm on the part of many member states to support and institute measures required of them. The coming period will thus call for an effective monitoring system to ascertain compliance with the program and ensure success of the use of the harmonized documents. In this regard, it has become necessary to have a well-established ECOWAS machinery in each member state to coordinate and monitor the implementation of Community decisions and programs within the country. Such a national secretariat would be responsible not only for preparing country positions on Community issues; it would also serve as an effective link between the member state and the institutions of the Community. In addition to the national secretariats, the Conakry summit adopted a proposal to establish a special unit within the ECOWAS Executive Secretariat to monitor the implementation of Community acts and decisions.

Undoubtedly, however, an effective implementation of the ECOWAS trade liberalization program is likely to pose a number of delicate problems. For while seeking to maximize overall benefits, the scheme must ensure a fair distribution of benefits and costs, aim to reduce developmental disparities, offer payments support where necessary, ensure adequate fiscal compensation, take into consideration disparities in import and export regimes, and keep in mind direct trading requirements. Besides, the work on a common external tariff to create a customs union would need to be commenced although the treaty does not envisage such a tariff to be established until five years after the creation of a free trade zone. On the other hand, the operation of the compensation scheme would demand an improvement in quality of trade and fiscal data from member states. To meet the demands, the introduction of a modern computerized data system with a national component like the one completed and launched in Bamako in January 1985 is a welcome development.

Free Mobility of Persons

One other major undertaking by the Community during the period under review is the application of the first phase of the protocol relating to free mobility of persons, right of residence, and establishment. This protocol has had the greatest impact on the working life of trade unions, the various labor groups and organizations, traders, and market women. Its implementation has generated a continuing debate and criticism. The problems or the uneasiness that the implementation of this protocol has created are not entirely unexpected, especially during this early stage of application. It is the first sub-regional decision the member countries have had to implement and it is also the first that affects the ordinary citizen.

To strengthen the protocol and to make it easier to implement, measures should be taken, for example, to promote local tourism and particularly to reduce the cost of traveling. Among other things, difficulties are likely to arise in connection with different national standards and educational qualifications. Such problems would be compounded when the protocol is fully applied. In the circumstances, it would be necessary for the Community to promote the easy and correct placement of professionals by preparing a directory of authorized training institutions in member states. Diplomas awarded by these institutions should then be evaluated, together with preparation of a manual giving the equivalences of these diplomas. This would ensure the recognition by each member state of the diplomas or degrees granted in other states. It may also be necessary for nationals of member states to register (where necessary) with professional bodies like medical councils or bar associations.

Furthermore, ECOWAS members should agree upon the need to promote improved standards of living for workers, so as to make possible their harmonization while the improvement is being maintained. Rules may be established whereby machinery for clearing job vacancies on a Community basis is set up and cooperation and common action about information on labor mobility problems is provided for. As additional incentives, Community workers should have preference over workers from third countries in filling job vacancies and workers should have the right to be joined by their families. Besides, the Community should set up a machinery designed to identify the types of jobs that are sought after, and the quality of the job-seekers, as well as the cost of labor in member states and study trade union organizations in member countries and their attitudes toward the reception of job-seeking immigrants.

As discussed in the previous chapter, the Community's policy of free movement of labor has brought social problems with it, as any radical change must do. It would, therefore, be a step in the right direction if the Community should take some complementary measures. For example, free movement of labor gives the opportunity of putting men in the places where the work is available, but if the men are not trained for the available work the benefits are nullified. Hence the need for initiating in the future a vocational training policy at Community level. Besides, even if the legal provisions for nationals and those from other ECOWAS member countries are identical, the latter are nevertheless at a disadvantage in a number of ways because of practical difficulties experienced as regards differences of language, religion, customs, occupational or administrative practices. The only thing that can be done about this is the provision of special voluntary or public services to help the workers in new countries to adapt and assimilate. In this case, the authorities in the country of origin and the host country should cooperate with each other in promoting such services, with trained staff, to assist migrants before they leave and on their arrival in the host country. All these should be geared toward the aim of preventing or, at least, reducing to a minimum, economic, social, or political frictions and conflicts that are likely to attend the full application of this popular protocol.

Ahead perhaps lie wider horizons: the free movement of persons in ECOWAS is still only a fragmentary freedom. It should be reinforced in the future by a common ECOWAS passport, a passport union, and the abolition of all controls on the movement of persons between member states. These measures may ultimately require the adoption of common immigration laws and policies on persons from outside the Community, on the analogy of the common customs tariff and the common commercial policy for goods from outside the sub-region. The extension of the civic rights of nationals resident in other member states is a further step: from free movement ECOWAS nationals suffer the penalty of disfranchisement. As a first stage, it should not be beyond the wit of man to enable ECOWAS immigrants to enjoy equal voting rights with nationals in ordinary elections for say shop stewards or their equivalent, and for representation to joint worker-management committees. Until these developments are realized, the nationals of other member states will continue to be aliens, albeit privileged aliens, rather than ECOWAS citizens.

Of some significance for the effective implementation of the free movement of persons protocol is the need to integrate the varying legal systems among ECOWAS states. In a sub-region in which the member states are divided between the two main systems of law--the common law and the civil law--the Community citizens will constantly be moving from one legal zone into the other. This, therefore, calls for a study of the legal implications of free movement so as to bring some uniformity in legal protection of Community citizens and also uniform definition of their legal rights and duties wherever they may be within the Community.

Law indeed has a major role to play in the functioning of an economic integration scheme like ECOWAS. This is an element often overlooked by the specialists in the field. Yet it must be emphasized, even ad nauseum, that the way in which community law and national law operates determines to a great extent the progress, problems, and degree of efficiency of an economic integration system. Vargas-Hidalgo has reminded us that it is not enough to agree upon a decision that is "based on serious economic analysis and which is the product of difficult political negotiations if there is no legal structure capable of implementing the decision and giving practical content to it."[1] In the case of the Andean Common Market, for example, the member states have been employing "a mix of solutions" for the legal problems posed by economic integration, sometimes relying on the principles of community law but often utilizing international law methods despite the large differences that exist between the two systems of law. By way of contrast, the EEC has been able to cope with many critical situations through a more developed community system, to whose growth the European Court has greatly contributed.

On the other hand, the Treaty of ECOWAS has created a Community whose "legal regime is distinct from those of its constituents." While the ECOWAS leaders affirm as the ultimate objective of their efforts "accelerated and sustained economic development" of their states and the creation of a homogeneous society, leading to the unity of the countries of the sub-region, the diverse legal systems of these states are likely to constitute an obstacle to the harmonization of policies and the promotion of Community interests.[2] The prevailing plural legal systems of the member states of ECOWAS are based on those of the former metropolitan powers of Britain, France, and Portugal. Not surprisingly, the English- and French-speaking ECOWAS members sometimes differ in their conception and interpretation of certain provisions of the Lagos Treaty.

In this regard, the Community should consider the idea of integrating the legal systems of all ECOWAS member states in the future. Such a move would in the first place help to remove the prevailing discrepancies in company, taxation, transport, and immigration laws. It would also contribute significantly to the early implementation of ECOWAS decisions and directives. However, implementation of such a measure may not be immediate; it may probably be spread over a long period of time. What is perhaps practicable, therefore, is a program of law harmonization to be drawn up by an appropriate commission of the Community. In this connection, the establishment of some machinery such as, for example, a "West African Centre for Law Harmonisation," is a necessary step toward this direction. This center would then study the attendant problems with a view to an eventual integration of the legal systems.

The ECOWAS Fund

It is not only the Secretariat in Lagos that has begun to take off, but also the ECOWAS Fund based in Lome, which has been in effective operation since 1979. Acting as the catalyst and sponsor for projects in member states, the Fund has been established with an authorized capital of $500 million and called-up capital of $50 million. By 18 October 1983, contributions to the Fund's called-up capital totaled $44,550,242.66 out of $50m. So far as meeting obligations are concerned, the ECOWAS members would appear to be more favorably disposed toward the Fund than to the Secretariat. By the end of 1981, the Fund had been able to finalize the policy measures that are vital to its smooth operation. Consequently, basic instruments relating to the conditions applicable to loans, guarantee, counter-guarantee, backing, and subsidies have been introduced. This would facilitate the operations of the Fund in relation to its co-contracting parties, especially in relation to the financing of Community-based projects.

Perhaps the most ambitious project undertaken so far by the Fund is the setting up of a special fund for the modernization and development of telecommunications under the Fund's own management. In May 1982, the board of directors of the Fund approved a financial package of $12.5m for the partial financing of the telecommunications program in seven member states. The telecommunications program is the first Community project to be funded with Community special funds. The investment in the telecommunications project is in itself important as it will not only test the capacity of the member states to invest in joint projects, but also the suitability of the procedures, loan conditions, and guarantee mechanism devised by the Fund. This is indeed a challenge to the political will and the extent of commitment of member states of the Community to ECOWAS, as the implementation of the project will involve extensive cooperation among the ECOWAS countries that would be required to coordinate the various national telecommunications networks.

In November 1983, the board of directors authorized a loan of $986,118 to the telecommunications, transport, and energy sectors; $53,640 to support the immigration and money program; and $214,535 for agriculture and natural resources. The Fund also intervened in the field of transport through the co-financing with other international financial institutions of a loan of $3,745,000 granted to the government of Benin for the construction of two bridges on the Mono and the Sazue rivers which service a highway of community interest.[3]

Although the decision of the Fund to issue special "ECOWAS Gold Coins" for the purpose of raising funds was rejected at the May 1979 Dakar summit, the Fund's proposal on issuance of ECOWAS postage stamps in the member states to commemorate ECOWAS Day was approved by the Authority. And, in order to keep its shareholders and the general public informed of its activities, the Fund launched in March 1982 a quarterly newsletter, like the *ECOWAS News* of the Secretariat in Lagos, which focuses attention also on developmental potentials in member states.

The Need for Political Stability

This study has also sought to argue that the likelihood of establishing a viable integration scheme in the West African subregion will depend, among other things, on the political conditions within the countries involved. Factors such as nationalism, attachment to notions of national sovereignty, political instability, and even the nature of leadership will directly affect the cooperation of governments on a regional level. Thus, unless regional integration in West Africa is firmly based on a new kind of political commitment to greater self-reliance, it may not be a very substantial vehicle for economic development. There is always the need, particularly in the special case of West Africa, for far-reaching political decisions that will endow the institutions of the Community with the efficacy needed to withstand elements of possible stagnation in the near future. In this regard, some degree of shared political commitment would be necessary before economic development in West Africa would be a joint cooperative enterprise. For some form of sub-regional political and economic institutions and policies could gradually eliminate the real or apparent reasons for coups or pseudo-revolutions that West Africa has been experiencing since the early 1960s.

That coups have upset cooperative regional linkages there can be no doubt. As stated previously, the Ugandan coup of 1971 greatly contributed to the dissolution of the East African Community, once regarded as a model for African regional cooperation. Similarly, the CACM was almost brought to a halt when the Honduran coup d'etat in 1963 ousted the Liberal government of that country which had been favorable to the common market. In contrast to the Liberals, the post-1963 Honduran military government had no definite position on the common market. The result was a chain of events culminating in an outbreak of war in July 1969 between Honduras and El Salvador that brought CACM to a verge of collapse. It is in light of such discouraging experiences that the idea of shared political commitment among ECOWAS members as some measure of guarantee against political instability in the sub-region is worth serious consideration.

Defense and Non-Aggression Pacts

To this extent, the adoption of the Non-Aggression Pact in April 1978 and the protocol relating to Mutual Assistance in Matters of Defence in June 1981 by the Community is a welcome development. This would certainly add an important dimension to West African solidarity and open a new form of cooperation among the ECOWAS members. It is a move toward the much needed political stability of the sub-region. More important is the fact that this is the first purely political decision of the Community. Although there had been obviously strong political overtones in other measures--such as, for instance, the lowering of tariffs, or the eventual unification of currencies, or the free mobility of people between countries--it can be argued that these involve basically economic decisions. On the other hand, making war can only be a political decision. Significantly, too, the sovereignty of the individual member state has been restricted in a new era. This is not necessarily a bad thing; the whole idea of establishing the Community implied the surrender of a degree of sovereignty by the members, and this has been made clear from the start, although this is certainly a delicate area. While it might be argued by some that a non-aggression pact is always of doubtful value--when one recalls, for example, the cynical use by Hitler's Germany of the Soviet-Nazi pact of August 1939--there is no doubt that the ECOWAS non-aggression agreement does have a value as a statement of intent and a demonstration of the good will that exists in the sub-region.

In a similar vein, the significance of the defense protocol cannot be overemphasized, particularly at a time when almost every African state is becoming more and more vulnerable to external aggression. Thus to set up a joint defense force for the West African sub-region is indeed a major breakthrough. It is an implied criticism of the OAU which, though assumed under Article 11 of its charter responsibility to defend the sovereignty, territorial integrity, and independence of its member states, has so far not been able to work out a formula for the defense of the continent. To some extent, however, the ECOWAS defense idea would appear to be a revival of a regional defense system recommended by the OAU Defence Commission in December 1971 following the attempted Portuguese-led mercenaries' invasion of Guinea in November 1970. The defense protocol will allow an ECOWAS allied defense force to be called into existence to meet any aggression against an ECOWAS member state. The importance of this protocol lies in the fact that there cannot be any meaningful development without peace and adequate security.

One should not, however, underestimate the difficulties involved in organizing a joint defense structure. Various crucial issues may be raised, foremost of which is the question of diversity: language barriers; ideological differences; diversity in military traditions, including variations in training, mode of deployment, as well as the types and resources of equipment used by the various armies without more continuous training than seems envisaged. There is also the lack of technical know-how, poor communication infrastructure, as well as the lack of a well-developed transport command within the various armed forces. Besides, as the London-based weekly *West Africa* pertinently asked in its columns: How many states in West Africa will really want an army of foreigners operating within their borders at a critical time? If a Bokasa should emerge in the sub-region and French forces be used to overthrow him, would the ECOWAS allied force go to his rescue? If President Jawara of the Gambia should again feel threatened by Libya, would it be practical for him, instead of merely calling for Senegal's assistance, to activate the complicated business of calling out the ECOWAS force?[4] And this involves, according to Article 16 of the defense pact protocol, a "written request for assistance to the current chairman of the Authority of

ECOWAS" and a meeting of the heads of state and government of the Community.

Besides, there is the question of unanimity rule which would prove to be a serious handicap to Community action in some special circumstances. As stated above, both the Authority and Council of Ministers of ECOWAS are governed by the unanimity rule. Since no exception is made to this rule under the defense pact, it would mean that should any ECOWAS member state take up arms against a partner state, nothing can be done by the Community (as stipulated in Article 17 of the defense protocol) except with consent of the aggressor member state. In other words, ECOWAS can take no action to preserve the territorial integrity of any of its member states except with the agreement of the member who is engaged in violating it. Thus the existence of the unanimity rule is a proof that the mutual defense pact has not provided a complete guarantee against war. In the circumstance, the term "collective defence" as the basic principle on which the ECOWAS protocol on mutual assistance on defense is based would cease to have any meaning. For it is not impossible that an ECOWAS member can take up arms against a partner state. Apart from the experience of faraway El Salvador and Honduras stated above, there was an occasion nearer home in Africa when a few years ago Tanzania moved troops to Uganda to drive away Idi Amin, then head of state of Uganda, into exile, although it can be said that the East African Community, to which the two countries belonged, had then almost ceased to function.

The myriad of problems indicated above are not strictly peculiar to West Africa. They are a kind of problem that any group of nations trying to organize a collective defense system is bound to be confronted with. Perhaps the creation of a common defense structure, as envisaged by the ECOWAS defense pact protocol, will provide the necessary remedy or incentive for tackling the constraints to military cooperation. The bond of alliance would help to reduce gradually mutual suspicion and make the rationale for "sharing military secrets more meaningful than it is the case outside an alliance system." To this extent, the adoption of the non-aggression pact and the defense protocol in West Africa has a good deal of merit, particularly when viewed in light of its implied degree of some measure of political commitment. This may be buttressed by the creation of an intelligence service for exchange of information on the movement of each other's "subversives."

Furthermore, the degree of political commitment implied in the establishment of a common defense force would save or divert millions of dollars now squandered on fanciful military needs to fend off hypothetical incursions. The armed forces of 14 members of the Community (excluding Guinea-Bissau and Cape Verde) had approximately 211,000 men in 1970, apart from the police and gendarmes. Of these, Nigeria alone had 163,000. Excluding Nigeria, the ratio of total men in the armed forces to the combined population of the remaining ECOWAS member states was 1 to 900 in 1970; that of France was 1 to 780; of the People's Republic of China 1 to 260; and of the United States, 1 to 65.[5] In 1969, West Africa as a whole spent $203.8 million on defense. Almost a decade after, in 1978, all the 16 ECOWAS countries had a total of 315,000 men in their armed forces and spent $2.1 billion on military expenditures (the figures for Nigeria alone were 204,000 men and $1.8 billion, respectively).[6]

Separately, few of the governments in West Africa will be willing to reduce their armed forces to any appreciable extent. Only the collective disarmament of these countries and a coordinated approach to the task of regional defense, as envisaged in the ECOWAS defense protocol, will perhaps make it possible to overcome many persistent factors of tension and will produce a substantial saving in resources that can be usefully applied to accelerate the economic development in West Africa. An inter-West African state army for national and regional needs could do much to assuage bursts of nationalism and could help to unite the governments and the governed for the common task of progress. If regional cooperation means anything at all, should not every West African state be its brother's keeper? The mutual defense pact that Guinea signed with Sierra Leone in March 1971 enabled Guinean troops to intervene in Sierra Leone to protect the Sierra Leone government against another attempt at a military takeover.[7] This is a type of coup insurance that the ECOWAS defense pact should seek to make West African-wide in order to create political stability for the progress of the Community.

ECOWAS AND THE WIDER WORLD

It has been argued that there is clear and impressive evidence that regional integration has generally stimulated efforts at penetration by public and private external agents, and that this has created pressures upon regional actors to respond collectively. Thus ECOWAS will not be operating free from public and private external impact. An attempt is made in this section, therefore, to review briefly ECOWAS' relations with external forces, emphasizing also the extent to which the Community has attempted to implement the main objectives of both the *Lagos Plan of Action* (LPA) and the New International Economic Order (NIEO) in the sub-region.

The Dependency Issue Revisited

Throughout this study, special attention has been focused on the dependency of the West African sub-region on external forces and the extent to which this continues to generate underdevelopment. It has been argued that the size and dependent nature of the national economies of the West African countries means that external factors, which have largely been ignored in the study of European integration, will constitute extremely important influences in the integration process. These external forces, of which foreign governments, particularly former metropolitan powers, and TNCs are two main examples, can directly affect the opportunity costs of participation in the West African integration scheme. The high dependence on external factor inputs has reduced the capacity of the ECOWAS members to establish sovereignty over natural resources and control over domestic development policies. The various strategies of indigenization, partial nationalization, and sometimes outright expropriation that have been adopted and implemented in recent years have had only a marginal impact on the development prospects of the sub-region. There is a lack of impact because underdevelopment is so deep and pervasive; the international economic system, including the operation of TNCs, is highly adaptive; and the new class in West Africa--both the nationalist bourgeoisie and comprador--would not be prepared to extricate itself from its links with international interests. However, ECOWAS is not entirely helpless in face of the complex problems posed by dependency and neo-colonial mesh.

For if non-dependence through the adoption of measures regulating direct foreign investment and technology transfer is not achievable at least for the immediate future, does it follow that the ECOWAS countries must resign themselves to the inevitability of dependence and limited development? Since adoption of measures aimed at a very greatly diminished reliance on economic relationships with the rest of the world is at present out of the question for the small and poor West African countries, it may be necessary for the Community to adopt, in addition to measures already outlined in this study, a pragmatic and flexible approach toward the problem of dependency and neo-colonial mesh; that is a pursuit of objectives capable of early realization.

In this regard, one salient possibility worth reconsidering is the Community's attitude toward foreign direct investment. A question worth asking here is this: would it not be possible for recipient ECOWAS countries to benefit from foreign investment (even when investment leads to a capital outflow) through the acquisition of technology? Through foreign investment, the ECOWAS countries might acquire vital technology which would otherwise be more costly or might be unobtainable altogether. One is tempted to accept, therefore, the premise of Gerald Helleiner that "turning inward" or "reducing dependence" *need* not mean diminishing external relationships so much as consciously *employing* them as one of several instruments for the pursuit of a truly *independent strategy*.[8] It is not, however, suggested here that foreign investment is completely or invariably beneficial to the West African sub-region.

One other factor of considerable significance that requires stressing is that TNCs, which are the major agents of dependency in the sub-region, often thrive upon the ignorance of the governments of ECOWAS countries on matters such as technology, natural resources, investment financing, and the world financial, monetary, and market conditions. This situation can partly be explained by the absence, in most of these countries, of the requisite machinery to study, monitor, and evaluate, on a continuing basis, the role and impact of the activities of TNCs on the development process. There is also the fact that most of the member states of the Community are too small or too inequitably endowed with financial and human resources, capital, skills, and technology to enable them to negotiate effectively with, or exert significant bargaining power over, the highly sophisticated representatives of TNCs, whose power lies in their technical knowledge, knowledge of markets and finance, as well as managerial skills. The only counter is for the local personnel in West Africa to acquire knowledge and hence control of the foreign company. There is therefore the need for the Community to mobilize resources at the regional level in order to give greater opportunities for effective control. ECOWAS can establish the necessary technical resources as a special unit at the Secretariat in Lagos staffed with an interdisciplinary team composed of development economists, engineers, sociologists, and environmentalists, and corporate legal experts, who would be capable of negotiating effectively on behalf of the Community and/or its individual member state with the TNCs-- either to negotiate an agreement on establishment of a new subsidiary or to set up effective mechanisms to control TNC behavior that would not kill the "golden goose." The regional unit may also be charged with the collection, analysis, and dissemination of information on TNC operations in the member states, including the extent of compliance with the provisions of any future investment code and other closely related policies.

Besides coordinating the Community's policies on TNCs, the regional unit may also act as the focal point of contact with the United Nations agencies, other international organizations, and African development and research institutions dealing with TNC issues of interest to the West African sub-region. Harmonization of codes of investment, fiscal concessions, enterprise behavior, and possibly ownership under the direction of the special ECOWAS technical regional unit would furthermore have the potential for gradually rendering ineffectual the deleterious impact of the "symbiotic TNC-state" relationship on measures designed to control TNCs or perhaps making such "unholy alliance" much more difficult to develop. But it must be stressed that the prospects for harmonization of foreign investment law in ECOWAS depend on finding solutions to the technical problems involved in implementation.

Indeed, the major challenge in the implementation of the program for self-reliance envisaged under the *Lagos Plan of Action* implies the planned development of local capacities, domestic resource-based industries, local technologies, and financial institutions, as a basis for negotiations with foreign-owned TNCs, at national, sub-regional, and regional levels.[9] Thus, collective self-reliance through regional cooperation espoused in the *Plan* cannot be achieved in a vacuum nor can technology be acquired or accumulated if there is no local expertise to receive it. Therefore, in order to change the ownership and control patterns in the West African sub-region, the development of local technical and managerial capabilities is an integral part of the development strategy. Without local skills and technological management capabilities, the objective of autonomous, self-reliant development can hardly be achieved. The limited success of the Andean Foreign Investment Code of December 1970 can partly be explained by the lack of managerial capabilities and trained personnel, of evaluation criteria, and of institutional capacities to handle the code's application, particularly in the area of technology imports.[10] Thus the economic prosperity of the ECOWAS countries in the 1980s and beyond would depend, to a considerable extent, on their ability, particularly at the regional level to accurately interpret the legal, social, economic and political implications of the international economic situations, especially the activities of TNCs and to restructure the domestic production and distribution through a definite shift in the patterns of ownership and distribution of the major means of production.

Another option still available for ECOWAS in the effort to tackle the problem of dependency, especially on the former metropolitan countries of Western Europe, is the diversification of the Community's external economic relations--trading partners and sources of technology and capital--to include countries like the United States, Australia, Canada, or Japan. This approach has the potential for strengthening the bargaining position of the governments of the sub-region by enabling them "to play off" one developed economy against another. Potentially more serious is the almost total lack of ECOWAS countries' exports to Japan, despite the increasing importation of Japanese manufactures by these countries. Still as a counterstrategy to the exclusive dependence on Western Europe, the ECOWAS members may also develop closer economic relations with the industrialized countries of the socialist community such as members of the Council for Mutual Economic Assistance (CMEA) or COMECON, the Eastern European common market.

Diversification, not elimination, of dependencies in the initial stages of regional adventure would seem to be almost a *sine qua non* for regionalism in Africa today. A more diversified structure of dependencies will, nevertheless, improve the maneuverability of ECOWAS which, in a longer term perspective, bodes well for a collective self-reliance and genuine reduction of dependence. Ali Mazrui stressed in his recent Reith Lectures that:

> there are occasions when freedom begins with the multiplication of one's masters. If one is owned and controlled by only one power, freedom is often particularly restrictive. But if an African society cultivates the skills to have more than one hegemonic power competing for it, this has possibilities for liberation. To be dependent on two giants, especially when the giants have rivalries between them, is sometimes an opportunity to play one against the other-- and maximize one's own options.[11]

Added to this, the Community may develop some preferential economic links with other African regional groupings like the Preferential Trade Area for Eastern and Southern African States (PTA) and regional economic cooperation schemes in the developing countries of Asia (for example, ASEAN), or Latin American (for example, the Andean Group). Considerable new markets could be established through establishment of economic links with these various groupings. Joint action by the developing countries, at the regional or interregional level, can be crucial in enabling them to defend the prices of their exports of raw materials and to protect their sovereignty over their natural resources. It can also encourage the "growth of indigenous capacities in science and technology," facilitate the marketing of their products, help to increase their industrial capability and, above all, strengthen their decision-making power in multilateral institutions.

All of these contacts would seem to represent the ECOWAS members' desire to blunt the impact of their continuing dependence on the industrialized nations by diversifying that relationship beyond exclusive reliance on Western Europe. It is an effort to improve their position in the world political and economic system and to make their strategy of autonomous development more successful.

As for the ECOWAS-EEC linkage, the fear is that the Lome system, if prolonged unduly, will constitute the West African subregion--indeed the whole of Africa--into a "permanent appendage of Europe." Considered in light of our previous discussion, therefore, it would be necessary for the ECOWAS members to move toward greater autonomy and individual and collective self-reliance and orient economic decisions around their national and regional political constituency rather than allow the locus of decision making to gravitate toward the private and public sectors in the EEC countries. And it is only through a restructuring of the subregional economies that ECOWAS can install the long expected new economic order.

ECOWAS and the NIEO

It has already been indicated that the establishment of ECOWAS is in many respects in respond to the trends in the international relations as embodied in the NIEO, its Programme of Action, and the charter of Economic Rights and Duties of the States. It has been noted earlier, also, that the United Nations has, in its declaration of a NIEO, recognized that collective self-reliance and effective cooperation among developing countries would further strengthen their role in global economic activities. The ECOWAS objective of promoting cooperation and development in all fields of economic activity is thus in keeping with the proposals enunciated in the NIEO. Briefly, the Lagos Treaty aims at achieving two of the basic principles behind the concept of the NIEO: the marshaling of the resources of the developing countries for developmental purposes and encouraging these countries to practice collective self-reliance in order to accelerate the pace of their economic development. To this extent, the objectives of ECOWAS are complementary to those of the NIEO. For while ECOWAS has the broad objective of enhancing economic development and well-being of the people of West Africa, the NIEO has the same objective for the people of the developing world as a whole.

The relationship between the NIEO and ECOWAS as a scheme for regional economic cooperation and development comes into sharp focus when looked against the issue of the exercise of permanent sovereignty over natural resources. In order to attain an effective degree of self-reliance, a framework needs to be created to enable indigenous enterprises to gradually assume control of some of the important stages in the production and manufacturing processes. The degree of regional development is conditioned by the ability to control development resources. It has been argued that ECOWAS is not at present equipped in terms of resources and power to exercise such a control, although the protocol relating to Community enterprises is geared toward this direction.

While much has been said and written about the NIEO in recent years, comparatively very little attention has been focused on the extent to which the realisation of the aims and objectives of the NIEO would benefit particularly the poor, underdeveloped countries in Africa, of which the ECOWAS members constitute a substantial proportion. To what extent are the West African countries in a position to derive some benefits from the NIEO proposals, in view of their present state of underdevelopment?

Although, no doubt, the NIEO is of much importance to the ECOWAS members, as well as the other African states, these countries would not appear to be in the position to derive any real immediate benefits from the various NIEO measures proposed for industrialization, for example, because of their "dependence on agriculture and lack of adequate market size."[12] According to the World Bank classification, a country is non-industrial if manufacturing contributes less than 20 percent of the value added to the commodity-producing sectors. By this definition, 26 out of 42 ECA members are non-industrial, and this includes a majority of the member states of ECOWAS.[13] In the circumstances, developing countries who would benefit from the NIEO industrialization measures for at least the short- and middle-range time frame would be those with very much larger and more industrial bases: the Latin American countries, Taiwan, or Hong Kong. Thus, for the present, ECOWAS members generally would not appear ready to take advantage of the NIEO proposed industrial measures.

For the same reason, the NIEO tariff removal measures and elimination of non-tariff barriers from developing countries would be of little benefit to most African states mainly because these countries manufacture so little for export. The same can be said of the NIEO measures regarding transfer of technology, as few or none of the ECOWAS countries have reached the level of sophistication that would enable them to benefit from the proposals. Hugh Arnold has thus concluded that many of the "cornerstone measures" of NIEO are of only marginal relevance to the development prospects of Africa as a whole in the next few decades.[14]

It is not implied here, however, that NIEO proposals which, as indicated above, conform to many of the objectives of ECOWAS, are of no benefit to the countries of West Africa and, therefore, should be disregarded. No doubt the NIEO measures are relevant to the conditions of the sub-region but this is *only* in the long run. For just as OPEC moves and high oil prices have enriched only a few states, so the NIEO measures are likely to markedly advance only the already superior growth potential of a few developing countries. On the whole, except in few cases, the degree of benefits that ECOWAS can derive from the NIEO measures would depend upon the extent to which the Community realizes the aims and objectives of the Lagos Treaty.

ECOWAS, the *Lagos Plan of Action*, and the Berg Report

It has been stated earlier in this study that the goals, objectives, and characteristics of the strategies of the *Lagos Plan of Action* (LPA) are in close conformity with those of ECOWAS. In fact, the *LPA*, which contains the fundamental ideas and sentiments concerning the future economic development of Africa, as perceived by Africans, is "a natural extension" of the main themes of ECOWAS reviewed in this study. For it is the basic realization of Africa's poor economic performance, both at the national, regional, continental, and international levels, coupled with the dismal developmental prospects for Africa in the 1980s, that nourished the adoption of the *LPA*, and to a large extent the creation of ECOWAS. The *LPA* therefore sets out to encourage national and sub-regional action in improving the performance of several sectors of the African economy, especially in the top-priority areas of food and agriculture, industrialization, trade, transport, and communications. Significantly, the ECOWAS programs examined here are fully in line with these continental goals of the *LPA*.

On the other hand, the development objectives and the characteristics of the strategy of both ECOWAS and the *LPA* are out of step with the World Bank Report, or the Berg Report, *An Agenda for Action*, which advocates a strategy that may be described as outward looking, or externally oriented, or export-led approach. Unlike ECOWAS or the *LPA*, the *Agenda* gives a peripheral attention to such important sectors of development as industrialization, the role, use, and control of mineral resources, and the question of inter-African economic cooperation. It may be pertinent to highlight briefly here the major priority areas of the *LPA* that are compatible with the key provisions of ECOWAS but divergent from the views of the *Agenda*.

One such key sector of the economy that is given high priority in the *LPA* is the commitment of the African leaders to "achieve self-sufficiency in food production and supply." Faced with a thoroughly disturbing rapidly increasing dependence of Africa on food imports "over the past two decades," the *LPA* recommends a five-year crash program (1980-85) aimed at bringing about immediate improvement in the food situation and laying the foundations for the achievement of self-sufficiency in cereals and in livestock and fish products. With regard to food production, African countries are urged to implement the Regional Food Plan for Africa (AFPLAN) that was adopted by the African ministers of Agriculture in Arusha, Tanzania, in 1978. On regional basis, the *Plan* recommends the establishment of an African Food Relief Support with a view to assisting member countries in time of food emergency.

It comes as no surprise that one of the top priorities of the *LPA* is the achievement of African self-sufficiency in food, for unless steps are taken in the 1980s to solve the food production problems many African states "may end up in the 1990s as permanent food aid clients" of the industrialized world. It can hardly be disputed that food has in the last decade or so acquired a new dimension. Besides subsistence, food has gained international recognition as an instrument for political strategy. Countries such as the United States view their "food power" as one more weapon in their diplomatic arsenal--a principal tool in the negotiating kit. Hence the problem of food is more than a question of sustenance. It is intimately tied with economic development as well as social and political stability and more so, for national security and pride. A people who cannot feed themselves is a people who are not in control of their destiny.

This is particularly serious in the case of the ECOWAS countries where food crisis has, in the first place, occasionally culminated in a violent change of political regimes. It was, for example, the serious rice riots in Monrovia in April 1979 that subsequently contributed to the ousting of the Tolbert regime in Liberia in April 1980. In Guinea-Bissau, the coup that overthrew the administration of Louis Cabral in April 1981 was generally regarded as a rice coup. Second, the sub-region's food import bill has particularly been on the increase over the last decade, as analyzed in a recent joint ECA/FAO special report prepared for ECOWAS.[15] It is evident from this special study that the future of West Africa will initially be determined largely by the ability and competence of its people and governments to attain self-sufficiency in food through self-reliant efforts at improving their overall agricultural productivity with due emphasis and full commitment to increased and accelerated food production, as recommended in the *LPA*. This objective is enshrined in the Lome Declaration on Economic Recovery in West Africa adopted at the November 1984 ECOWAS summit.

In response to the target of self-sufficiency in food production contained in the *LPA*, the Community in May 1980 adopted the ECOWAS Agricultural Programme comprising four sectors in order of priority: food crops, livestock, fisheries, and forestry. The main objective of the program is to fight against the serious food problem of the sub-region, the improvement in rural incomes and living conditions as well as the provision of the necessary inputs for the Community's industrial program. The 1982 Colonou summit reinforced this program by adopting the ECOWAS Agricultural Development Strategy, a blueprint for agricultural development in the sub-region. The summit urged member states to aim at sub-regional food self-sufficiency at a faster rate than has been adopted in the *LPA*: a Community "target of self-sufficiency in food production within the next five years" was agreed upon. This was given a further impetus by the May 1983 Conakry summit which gave top priority to those industries that would contribute to the development of the rural sector in order to achieve self-sufficiency in food and raise the standard of living of the rural population.

Thus both the ECOWAS and the *LPA* recognize or sharply perceive the imperative for food policy reform and the need for widespread adoption of food strategies. On the other hand, as a necessary corollary to the external integration prescriptions it advocates, the *Agenda* calls for reduced emphasis on self-sufficiency, apparently in food and certainly in manufactures. It advocates increased rural production for export and not just for local consumption, that is, an outward-looking growth based on agricultural export with minimal regional cooperation. While it does not entirely underrate the importance of food production, it clearly advocates the "even if export crop output were to grow at the expense of food crop production, it is not necessarily bad." This emphasis on production for export at the expense of food production is certainly a recipe for the perpetuation of the situation in which African countries will continue to depend on food aid or food imports. This is in sharp contrast to the strategies of both ECOWAS and the *LPA* whose leitmotif is the nationalistic assertion of the need to alter the colonial patterns of Africa's position in the international division of labor.[16]

Higher priority in the *LPA* is also accorded to industrialization, trade, transport, and communications. The *Plan* recognizes industrialization as the *sine qua non* of development--hence the designation of the years 1980-90 as "Industrial Development Decade in Africa." Almost in the same vein, the harmonious development of the industrial sector of the economies of the West African sub-region is one of the primary objectives of ECOWAS to which this study has focused attention. In conformity with the industrial development approaches of the *LPA*, the ECOWAS industrial program includes the establishment of Community industrial enterprises whose viability depends on markets larger than the small markets that individual member states presently do offer. On the other hand, although the *Agenda* also recognizes this main objective of industrialization, it does not recommend that it be pursued at any cost, particularly as manufacturing constitutes "only a small sector in Africa and can make only a modest . . . contribution to development." On the whole, the *Agenda* gives a marginal role to industrial development and therefore discusses it under "other productive sectors."

With regard to trade in all commodities, the broad objectives of ECOWAS, as detailed in the Community's trade liberalization scheme, and those of the *Lagos Plan* under the subject of "Intra-African trade expansion," are quite similar.[17] On the contrary, the *Agenda* broadly favors the African trade status quo; thus, by implication, unduly tying African economies to extra-African influences. Generally however, the three documents--the *LPA*, the *Agenda*, and ECOWAS--equally draw considerable attention to the transport and communications sector as constituting one of the greatest impediments for the acceleration of development of African countries.

In short, although the *LPA* and the *Agenda* are responses to the continental African crisis, the former attempts to learn from past mistakes and therefore "advocates a break with past policies and present problems," while the latter hardly seeks to offer any substantial "departure from orthodox assumptions and prescriptions." Its advocacy of reduced self-reliance, especially in food production, is at best risky and at worst a recipe for mass starvation. In brief, the Berg Report is not, taken by itself, a safe guide for action.[18] To a great extent, therefore, the strategies and approaches to development espoused in the *Agenda* are generally inconsistent with those of ECOWAS. ECOWAS is indeed committed to the principles of self-reliance and regional cooperation, two of the most fundamental building blocks of the *Lagos Plan*. The Community seeks to provide the necessary instruments for the implementation of the *Plan* in the sub-region. Its adoption of a single trade liberalization scheme at the Conakry summit is evidently in keeping with the *LPA*, which envisages the setting up of an African common market by the year 2000.

Of the subjects covered by the three documents, perhaps the one that is most pressing and therefore calls for immediate action is that of food self-sufficiency. And the question that poses itself is this: to what extent have the ECOWAS countries implemented the *LPA* food and agriculture strategy? Although both the *LPA* and ECOWAS food strategies were adopted in 1980, many West African countries are still without an explicit food policy. And no attempts would seem to have been made to build the bridge between recognition of problems and the policy measures and resources required for their solution. Specifically, no effort has so far been initiated in setting up sub-regional food security arrangements and in undertaking the feasibility of establishing an African Food Relief Support Scheme which when set up is to assist ECOWAS countries in times of food emergency. Besides, very little has been accomplished in giving fillip to intercountry cooperative agronomic research programs as required by the *LPA*.

In view of the serious food shortages in the sub-region--13 out of the 26 seriously affected countries in Africa[19]--it is high time the West African countries attempted to transform the concepts of the *LPA* from political slogans into a framework for policy and action. Food policy should be of paramount concern to economic development efforts of the ECOWAS countries for at least the next two decades. This policy should encompass the collective efforts of governments of the 16 countries to influence the decision-making environment of food producers, food consumers, and food marketing agents in order to further social objectives. In the course of implementing their food policy, ECOWAS members must be reminded of Amartya Sen's recent succinct statement that there is "no such thing as an apolitical food problem."[20] To reverse the current trend of declining food self-sufficiency and achieve greater national and collective self-reliance in food would no doubt require major changes in policies and shifts in the allocation of development resources in favor of agriculture. New attitudes with regard to food planning and strong political commitment to develop agriculture and the rural areas would be an important aspect of the whole program. ECOWAS governments should have the capacity to confront, as Lofchie once put it, "the economic primacy of the export sector, and the political primacy of the vested interests which support it."[21]

On the whole, the ECOWAS food strategy reviewed here is an expression of the concern of West African governments for policy change and an indication of what they are prepared to undertake in order to implement their *LPA* commitments in the food sector. The results cannot be expected in all cases to come easily, quickly, and smoothly. Agricultural development is a slow and evolutionary process. Breakthroughs are infrequent and never instant. What is important is that the key priority areas for policy change toward food self-sufficiency in most of the ECOWAS countries are now basically accepted.

ECOWAS: SOME LIMITATIONS

Although ECOWAS has been created as a means of promoting the development of the West African sub-region, it should not be regarded as a single, all-inclusive means of achieving that end for there are limits, very great limits, to what the Community can contribute or accomplish. Economic integration, it has been stressed, is not a panacea for the complex problems of the sub-region; its success is crucially dependent on a number of factors, in particular domestic reforms. A number of bottlenecks to development cannot be directly affected by integration. Among these is the high illiteracy rate and the inadequacy of the educational system in the countries of the sub-region, which are obstacles to industrial development. Effective implementation of the Community's industrial program, for instance, would require a trained labor force, qualified personnel in the field of technology, competent technocrats, and a corps of persons prepared to occupy management positions and well equipped to negotiate on behalf of the Community with external firms and agencies operating in the sub-region. As long as the necessary trained manpower is lacking or is available to only a limited extent, there is a built-in check on industrial development. Similarly, as long as educational opportunities are restricted, the segment of the population most in need of employment opportunities--the lower classes--will not have them. Illiteracy and various inadequacies in the educational system of the member countries of the Community have to be tackled independently of ECOWAS and at least to some extent before the Community can have much prospect of achieving the objectives being sought through it.

Closely related to this is another obstacle to industrial development: the disturbing health problems throughout the ECOWAS countries. A people ravaged by disease or weakened by malnutrition do not constitute anything approaching an ideal, or even satisfactory, industrial labor force. Fundamental to the betterment of health and the furnishing of health care is the provision of doctors. A *United Nations Statistical Yearbook* (1978) and *World Development Report* (1981) have revealed all too plainly the very limited number of physicians in so many Third World countries, particularly in the poorest of them, the majority of which are in the West African sub-region. According to these sources, the number of people per physician in the ECOWAS countries in 1977 ranged from 7,571 (Guinea-Bissau); 10,310 (Ghana); 14,814 (Nigeria); 15,234 (Ivory Coast), 17,066 (Senegal), 47,300 (Niger); 57,130 (Burkina Faso); 58,400 (Mali). During that year (1977), the developed world had 500 to 800 people per doctor, the middle-income developing countries at worst had 11,000 to 15,000 people per doctor, and many of the poorest countries above 20,000, the worst being Ethiopia with 75,000.

These figures underline the poor provision of health care for millions of the population in the ECOWAS countries, and this is a situation that cannot quickly be rectified. It takes several years to train a physician: it is expensive in monetary terms and demanding in levels of education and intelligence (to mention only two necessary attributes) and these are severely limiting factors to the poor ECOWAS countries that are currently struggling to lay the foundation of free primary education for all. Health problems, like educational problems, have to be overcome independently of the ECOWAS scheme. Alternatively, these two closely related problems may be tackled at the Community level through coordination or harmonization of the educational and health systems of member states, taking advantage, also, of Article 31, which enjoins ECOWAS members to "provide places for training in their educational and technical institutions of Community citizens."

Perhaps what must constantly be borne in mind is that neither economic integration nor economic progress can be attained in West Africa without more dynamic policies and better planned strategies of national and regional development designed to tackle the most crucial and most urgent economic and social problems.

In the absence of such reforms, the Treaty of Lagos and the procedures that it has set in motion are bound to remain sterile and unproductive. For, as Maritano once warned, "a common market of beggars or destitute masses remains still a poor market."[22] Thus it is only a common market that would bring with it formulation of dynamic policies of profound structural, economic, social, and even cultural transformations that would be a successful enterprise. ECOWAS will not give the countries of West Africa an easy road to higher living standards or render unnecessary the painful adjustments that the political and social circumstances of the subregion have shown to be necessary. It can increase the power of the economic forces of development, once these forces are well and truly mobilized; it can never substitute for them.

One other limit to economic integration is what is normally described as "the time factor." The kind of economic transformation that is possible through integration may not come about either quickly or easily. The process of community-building is a long one, which is not kinder to seekers of short-cuts. Thus a viable West African economic integration scheme will not be built in a day, or in a decade, or even perhaps the fifteen-year transition period indicated in the ECOWAS Treaty. It will be built through daily, concrete, national, and sub-regional achievements in the spirit of sub-regional solidarity and international cooperation. For despite the rational appeal of the arguments for regional economic grouping, its implementation might be impeded by deep-seated distrust and hostility, refusal to sacrifice what is perceived as short-term self-interest to achieve longer term benefits, and aversion to paying the necessary costs and taking the inherent risks. It is the question of hastening slowly. For there is a certain danger in the "myth of quickness." The myth leads to expectations that cannot be realized. The resulting possibility is that expectations, even if they are unrealistic ones, may lead to a withdrawal of support for the regional grouping or cooperation. Progress and accomplishment may be judged in terms of the "myth of quickness" and may be found wanting. This may probably be the case in West Africa, where because of the limited legitimacy and endemic instability of the polities, the leaders' preoccupation with survival may lead them to make excessively short-term calculations of interest. Therefore, it must always be stressed that integration, particularly under conditions of underdevelopment, is a long-term process. The actual impact of policies can only play a very small role in the overall assessment of ECOWAS. Rather, attention should be directed mainly at the adoption of integrative measures to respond to problems of development and dependence, and the perceptions of the adequacy of the policies as a key element in negotiating coalitions. Finally, the success of the development programs of ECOWAS that have been reviewed in this chapter would very much require a steadily increasing commitment. ECOWAS members must be able to depend upon their neighbors to fulfill their commitments in a spirit of give-and-take between and among themselves.

NOTES

1. Rafael Vargas-Hidalgo, "The Crisis of the Andean Pact," *Journal of Common Market Studies*, vol. 8, no. 3 (March 1979):224.
2. Lateef Adebite, "Need for Integration of Legal Systems Among ECOWAS States" (Paper presented at the international conference on ECOWAS, Lagos, August 1976).
3. *West Africa*, 19 November 1984.
4. Ibid, 8 June 1981. See also, Julius E. Okolo, "Securing West Africa: the ECOWAS Defence Pact" *The World Today*, vol. 39, no. 5 (May 1983):177-84.
5. See Charles S. Stevenson, "African Armed Forces," *Military Review*, vol. 47, no. 3 (March 1970):19-23.
6. Ibid, p. 71.
7. "Guinea-Sierra Leone Union in Sight?," *Africa* (London), July 1971.
8. Gerald Helleiner, "Aid and Dependence in Africa: Issues for recipients," in *The Politics of Africa: Dependence and Development*, ed. T. M. Shaw and K. Heard (Canada: Dalhousie University Press, 1979), pp. 285.
9. See *Developing Local Technical and Managerial Capabilities for Dealing with Transnational Corporations in Africa* (A note by the ECA Secretariat, ST/ECA/CTNC/3, 10 July 1981).
10. Constantine V. Vaitsos, *The Role of Transnational Enterprises in Latin American Integration Efforts*, UNCTAD Round Table, TAD/E SEM. 5/2, Lima, Peru, 15 May 1978.
11. Ali A. Mazrui, *The African Condition: A Political Diagnosis* (London et al.: Cambridge University Press, 1983), p. 82.
12. Much of this discussion is drawn upon the analysis of Hugh M. Arnold, "Africa and the New International Economic Order," *Third World Quarterly*, vol. 11, no. 2 (April 1980):295-304.
13. UN Economic and Social Council, *Survey of Economic Conditions in Africa 1974*, E/5682 (13 May 1975), p. 13. See also

Ervin Laszlo et al., *The Obstacles to the New International Economic Order* (New York: Pergamon, 1980).

14. Arnold, "Africa and the New International Economic Order," p. 289.

15. *Co-operation and Trade in Food Crop Products in the ECOWAS Sub-Region*, Joint ECA/FAO report, ECW/TRAD/3, Lagos 1980.

16. See T. Mkandawire, "The Lagos Plan of Action (LPA) and the World Bank on Food and Agriculture: A Comparison," *Africa Development*, vol. 7, nos. 1, 2 (1982):169-70.

17. For details see A. Diaby-Ouattara, "ECOWAS in the Context of the Lagos Plan of Action" (Paper presented at the meeting of Directors of Social Science Institutions on the implementation of the Lagos Plan of Action, Addis Ababa, March 1982).

18. C. Allison and R. Green, "Stagnation and Decay in Sub-Saharan Africa: Dialogues, Dialectics and Decay," *IDS Bulletin* (Sussex), vol. 14, no. 1 (January 1983):6; also Jane I. Guyer, "The World Bank's Prescriptions for Rural Africa," *Review of African Political Economy* 27/28 (February 1984):187.

19. *South* 14 (March 1984):11. Conscious of the magnitude of the economic crisis that has been afflicting Africa and, especially the sub-region, the November 1984 ECOWAS summit passed a resolution on economic recovery in West Africa: A/RES/3/11/84, *Final Communique*, ECW/HSG/VII/6/Rev. 1, Lome (November 1984).

20. Amartya Sen, "The Food Problem: Theory and Policy," *Third World Quarterly*, vol. 4, no. 3 (July 1982):459.

21. Michael F. Lofchie, "Political and Economic Origins of African Hunger," *Journal of Modern African Studies*, vol. 13, no. 4 (1975):566.

22. Ninon Maritano, *A Latin American Economic Community* (Notre Dame: University of Notre Dame Press, 1970), p.xiii.

9

CONCLUSION:
TOWARDS A NEW FUTURE

The general conclusion toward which this study tends is that by establishing ECOWAS the countries of the West African sub-region have been firmly set on the road to the fulfilment of their commonly held aspirations for greater effective cooperation and integration. It is an expression of their awareness of the fact that in the present international economic system, no country will be able to stand alone. The realities of today require wider units of cooperation. Through ECOWAS the irrationality of the national boundaries drawn up by the former colonial powers can be mitigated and corrected. Thus in ECOWAS, the countries of West Africa have now found "a new future" in the world that is increasingly becoming small and interdependent. The ultimate objective is to move toward an evolution of a West African community. Among the most essential ingredients of the movement toward this community many must be found at the human level.

The main concern of this concluding chapter, therefore, is to stress not only the importance of commitment of political will at the highest level, but also, and perhaps more significantly, the supportive role of the human factor. For the success of any regional strategy for collective self-reliance hinges on a common political will of national governments, which in turn requires backing from societal leaders and citizens generally. In this regard, ECOWAS institutions should be more rooted in the minds of the citizens of West Africa, who should be constantly taught and reminded that whenever they use the telephone, cablegram, or enter any West African country free from visa requirements, and are permitted to reside in this country and even establish some business, they are using services and enjoying rights and facilities that are cheaply, freely, and efficiently provided by the Community of West African States. By emphasizing the functional aspects of the Community to the peoples of West Africa, and by making them participate in the development process of the Community, a more definite and functional sense of commitment to regional coopera- tion can be enhanced.

It has already been argued that what appears to be lacking in the West African integration movement is a group or a popular dynamic supporting integration: pressure groups for the mobiliza- tion of public opinion in the direction of the Community and their almost total noninvolvement in the Community's institutions. The group or popular dynamic means a "momentum propelling integration forward." It means, as well, an attachment or commit- ment to integration and action to give effect to the attachment or commitment. Indeed, it is the dynamic that would provide the motivation for actions to promote integration, and support for ac- tions taken. And as long as groups in the West African sub- region remain more or less on the sidelines or as limited partici- pants, there would be little or no dynamic propelling and support- ing the movement toward evolution of a West African community. Hence though ECOWAS may be a powerful means for achieving a West African community and the acceleration of development in the sub-region, in the final analysis, as Abangwu has rightly con- cluded, "man is both the means and the end. The best study of the strategy of economic integration is man."[1]

For the techniques or mechanisms of integration reviewed in this study will not be enough. Unless the peoples of West Africa are themselves aware of the integration process, and are interested in, and enthusiastic to make an effort, all the fine paper schemes outlined in the Lagos Treaty may come to nil. While the national governments of the sub-region must no doubt be in control of the commanding heights of the economy and must lay down policies and guide the direction of change, ample opportunities should be provided for the active participation of the people in the develop- ment process--that is, in the conception, planning and program- ming, and implementation.[2] In sum, therefore, the consolidation of West African Community may depend, to a large extent, on the support its programs obtain from social, economic, and political groups that consider the community to be convenient for their in- terests and ideas.

In this regard, it can be said that, apart from political, legal, and technical obstacles to regional cooperation, there is also the importance of public apathy and opposition. A strong opposition to a major ECOWAS policy by the business community of a member state, for example, can have some dangerous implications such as the cessation of that state's contribution to the Community, the formal withdrawal of the state, or even the eventual disintegration of the grouping. This could happen if certain domestic business groups, for instance, prevail upon a major resource-producing nation to reduce the price of its primary resource well below that of the producers' association to which it belongs. Thus, a participation of a state becomes precarious when its economic actors perceive that increasing regional cooperation seriously threatens their interests, at least in the short run.

Briefly then, the effective mobilization of public support should be regarded as a crucial ingredient in recipes for implementing and maintaining regional cooperation and integration oriented toward collective self-reliant, endogenous, and self-sustaining development. Therefore, what is needed in West Africa as a precondition to ECOWAS' development efforts is the mobilization of human resources: governments, entrepreneurs, farmers, religious groups, and what one might broadly describe as the agents of socio-economic activity--business, industrial, and financial enterprises and institutions and their organized associations like the chambers of commerce and industry, and professional associations. The reality of the West African community may probably rest largely in the hands of these groups. There should, therefore, be deliberate efforts on the part of the Community to create an active, supporting integration constituency among, in particular, socio-economic groups in the populations.

The trade unions in the member states, for example, can play an important role through coordination of their own activities at international level, including the maintenance of joint liaison bureaus at the ECOWAS Secretariat in Lagos for contact with the Community. Along this line, a pan-West African labor movement should be encouraged rather than discouraged, as such a movement will go a long way toward fostering a spirit of comradeship between the workers of the various countries. Then, too, an adequate representation for labor on some of the institutions of the Community may be a step in the right direction. This may be responsible for general economic and collective bargaining questions, industrial economic questions, and social affairs.

As the experience of the EEC has shown, it is true that trade union role may be strictly limited inasmuch as ECOWAS does not act as an employer (except of course, for its own staff in Lagos and Lome), and has no jurisdiction in a general sense over the wages or terms or conditions of employment of employees in

ECOWAS countries. Nevertheless, the involvement of the trade unions at the Community level through consultation by appropriate bodies on aspects of economic and social policy may be necessary. The trade unions in West Africa may be responsible for broadly-based and organized popular opinion favorable to the Community. Their support will be dictated by the fact that it is through common economic efforts at the Community level that the standards of living in West Africa may be raised and full employment secured. Apart from articulating popular support, the unions may, when properly organized, be in advance of some of the member governments in giving priority to Community over national interests when some elements of choice occurs.

Besides the trade unions, the employers' organizations in West Africa should be given the requisite encouragement to enable them to play a valuable role in the development of the Community. These organizations "can be significant vehicles for the transfer or introduction of technologies which are both growth and employment generating, either directly or indirectly."[3] Indeed, the importance of technology in a production, distribution, or consumption process can hardly be disputed. And, by playing such a role, West African employers' organizations would no doubt be contributing to the efforts being directed by the Community at diminishing the ties of dependency of ECOWAS countries on external forces and thus strengthening national independence. To enable the West African employers' organizations to play this role, they should be encouraged to be involved in the administration of foreign investment laws and regulations with the ultimate aim of ensuring that there is proper screening of types of technology being introduced into the sub-region. Employers could also help in the harmonization of foreign investment policies and instruments, particularly as they relate to grounds for accepting new investments, as did their counterparts in Latin America during the enactment in 1971 of the Andean Community foreign investment code or Decision 24. And like the West African Federation of Chambers of Commerce, employers' organizations in West Africa can be accorded an observer status at ECOWAS meetings. It would be necessary for the Community to cultivate the support particularly of employers and industrialists who are the ones who benefit the most from regional economic integration, given the new investment opportunities that the program creates. These agents of socio-economic activity, as well as other professional bodies, should be created where they do not exist and should be induced to function across national boundaries.

In recent years, however, ECOWAS would seem to have recognized the major role that the business community has to play in achieving some of its objectives. Hence the representation of an ECOWAS delegation at the 1981 annual meeting of the Federation of West African Chambers of Commerce and Industry. Another manifestation of the interaction between the ECOWAS Secretariat and the Secretariat of the Federation was the inclusion of an official of the Federation on the ECOWAS delegation that went on a study tour of the ASEAN region in July 1981. The ECOWAS Secretariat is also in the process of establishing some close contact with the journalist association of the sub-region whose activities should prove to be an additional means of promoting the ideals of ECOWAS. Similarly, since its inauguration in April 1978, the West African Economic Association, comprising mostly economists in the academic fields in West Africa, has maintained close relations with the ECOWAS Secretariat which, in turn, has been participating actively in the association's series of biannual conferences in Lagos (1978), Abidjan (1980), and Freetown (1982). Indeed, there is on the whole, the dire need in West Africa for an "integration spirit" or "integration" ideology to stimulate responses from the industrial, commercial, agricultural, labor, elite, and student leaders. This is required to limit the intensity or efficacy or overcome the national sovereignty concepts prevalent in the sub-region and, one might add, traditional, conservative, short-sighted attitudes about business investment.

Apathy toward ECOWAS by the citizens of the Community may perhaps spring from insufficient information about the overall benefits of the organization. Generally, also, public skepticism about and opposition to economic regionalism is exacerbated by what Thomas Jones describes as "the perceived differences among developing partner states."[4] There may be, for example, differences in possession of valuable natural resources, stages of technological development, level and distribution of income, political power, geographical size and location, population size and composition, language, level of education, and ideology--all these encourage popular misunderstandings and suspicion of foreigners, thus hampering programs aimed at collective self-reliance. There is, therefore, the need for disseminating relevant information about ECOWAS via, for instance, the educational system and communication media, supplemented by group discussions. Dissemination of information can show people from different social strata and institutional settings how the proposed changes could benefit them. Furthermore, instances of a successful regional economic grouping like the EEC could be pointed out to counter "fatalistic pessimism," and also show how people in various walks of life can facilitate such cooperation. All these may be necessary in order to dispel apathy arising from insufficiency of information about ECOWAS, its aims and objectives.

The Community must, in addition, encourage and devote some of its resources to the foundation of integration journals and promotion of research and seminars in the field of integration. Such an undertaking would in no small measure contribute to the broadening of outlook of West African socio-economic groups as well as the enlargement of their regional understanding, all of which would help to create a favorable nationwide climate for the development of integration movement in the sub-region.[5] As a corollary of this, in order to infuse among the younger generation of West Africans, "a tradition of integrative spirit and thinking," a course on economic integration should be taught as an independent branch of study in all research institutes, schools, colleges, and higher institutions in West Africa. And to facilitate communication between the various cultural and linguistic groups, the study of French and English, and possibly Portuguese, should be made compulsory in all secondary schools and colleges. All this would help create a long-lasting intellectual foundation for the movement toward West African community.

And to drive these points home further, a conscious attempt should be made to promote the ECOWAS ideal in all the member states of the Community in other different ways. For example, as part of the effort toward this end, there should be established, perhaps on nonofficial basis, in every important city or urban center in West Africa ECOWAS associations, like the various associations connected with the League of Nations or the United Nations. The activities of these associations should take on the form of an integration lobby, with clearly defined immediate and long-term objectives. These associations could arrange regular meetings at which ECOWAS issues could be freely discussed. They could act as a countervailing force against uninformed integration obstructionists, in particular, and raise the consciousness of the nation in general, as to the meaning and advantages of ECOWAS as a regional grouping. The integration lobby in each member state should coordinate its activities with its counterparts in the other countries within the Community. As Abangwu has rightly asserted, this general "infiltration of the body politic with the ideology of regional integration and rousing of mass consciousness" would appear to be the fundamental precondition "for both the successful inception and continued functioning of an integration scheme. . . ."[6] Furthermore, May 28, the day on which the

ECOWAS Treaty was signed could be set aside for an annual celebration of "ECOWAS Day" throughout West Africa. To this may be added harmonization of a number of commonly used products producing something such as "Ecobeer" or "Ecobread." The recent introduction of the ECOWAS Games is a desirable function to which all member states should commit themselves unequivocally. If successful, these lobbies and functions would help in mobilizing popular support for the Community, and in exercising pressure on national governments to make definite and positive commitments in its favor. In a region such as West Africa where national sovereignty is very jealously guarded, the importance of such activities cannot be overemphasized.

On the whole, what this final chapter has sought to stress is that, in the final analysis, no amount of foreign aid or foreign trade, and no form and dimension of international cooperation or of technical assistance from the United Nations specialized agencies, for example, can substitute for West African national and subregional determination and effort to develop and to achieve the objectives of ECOWAS. Nor can any crisis created by the international economic system be so great and disturbing that it can prevent the march toward West African community if the governments of ECOWAS and their peoples show sufficient vision, dynamism, and determination. Hence to create a West African community, the governments of West Africa must first establish a community of social and economic interest in their respective countries, and then induce international cooperation. Needless to add that any program of mutual cooperation formulated by the Community should be based on the principle that we are all West Africans, regardless of whether from the Francophone, Anglophone, or Lusophone. The guiding principle--or the watchword-- of the Community should therefore be "West Africaphone" or "Africaphone." Yesterday's prejudices and differences fostered and sustained by colonialism are not viable in today's world of technological, social, and economic interdependence.

Despite the efforts that have been made to make the Community operational since 1977 and the potentials that exist in the sub-region, there is still need for caution in assessing ECOWAS and looking at its future. Some scholars would even consider it foolhardy to attempt to predict the future of the Community at this early stage of its existence.[7] For the path that the West African countries have charted since May 1975 is not an easy one, and there is the possibility of problems arising and the development of conflict or disagreement among the member states. To achieve the objectives they have set, the partner states will be compelled to engage in intense, high-level collaboration with one another which will impose many significant limits on national freedom of action. It is an open question whether domestic nationalism, concern with national development, and domestic political realities will permit the required collaboration, limitation on national freedom of action, and willingness to sacrifice to aid fellow members.

For it is difficult to assume that the movement toward West African community will prove strong enough to modify, in a short period, the ideas of national sovereignty that have hitherto formed a fundamental part of the ideology of the member states of the Community. It is not simply a matter of willingness of the national governments to cooperate with one another. More serious is the fact that the promotion of economic development calls for considerable government initiative in many directions. Mounting social pressures are bound to make any dynamic government reluctant to postpone action until its programs and policies have been dovetailed with those of other, possibly less vigorous, governments. There is an undeniable danger that insistence on a sub-regional approval, and on the harmonization of economic development plans, could paralyze government thinking and action and, indeed, provide a convenient justification for doing nothing. Even if all ECOWAS members were equally anxious to promote the development of their countries, the process of reaching inter-governmental agreement not merely on whether to do certain things but on how to do them would inevitably be a long and arduous one. It would be dangerous to underestimate the political difficulties involved in securing prompt joint action by a group of independent governments--which, moreover, differ to some extent, in political orientation and ideology--even if they all act with the best will in the world. The utmost political ingenuity will be required in working out forms and procedures for inter-governmental cooperation that will make it possible to advance on a regional level without holding back progress nationally.

And finally, if the major factors promoting a West African economic community and those setting it apart from the other African regional integrative efforts prevail, if the potential problems reviewed in this study do not become real and overwhelming, then ECOWAS is likely to go farther, much farther, toward meeting the objective of African regional integration movements--development, especially industrial development--than any other regional economic grouping in Africa. If so, ECOWAS might both revitalize African regional integration movements which, as the experience of the East African Community has shown, are now in something of a period of stagnation if not decline, and serve as a model for other groupings of developing countries, African and non-African.

In conclusion, though the odds were hardly favorable at the decisive decade of the 1970s--the global crises syndrome symbolized by the collapse of the Bretton Woods Agreement, the OPEC oil shock, the energy crunch, and continuing stagflation coupled with the rising crescendo of the demand for a NIEO-- when the move toward the creation of ECOWAS was launched, it is up to us in West Africa to determine whether the 1980s will set the seal on our economic, social, and political decline or, instead, represent the dawn of our human renaissance. We have all the keys in our hands. ECOWAS, as our regional approach to collective self-reliance, self-improvement, to mutual understanding and cooperation, and to joint planning of the future, is an essential key. We must learn how to use it without delay and without hesitation.

NOTES

1. George C. Abangwu, "Systems Approach to Regional Integration in West Africa," *Journal of Common Market Studies*, vol. 13, nos. 1,2 (1975):133.
2. Adebayo Adedeji, "Development and Economic Growth in Africa to the Year 2000," in *Alternative Futures for Africa*, ed. Timothy M. Shaw (Boulder, Colo.: Westview Press, 1982), p. 297.
3. James Nti, "Economic Co-operation of West African States" (Talk presented to Inter-territorial Conference of Employers' Organisations in English-Speaking West Africa, Accra, Ghana, 17 September 1980).
4. Thomas Jones, "Regionalism: The Problem of Public Support," in *Regionalism and the New International Economic Order*, ed. Davidson Nicol et al. (New York: Pergamon Press, 1981), p. 219.
5. Abangwu, "Systems Approach to Regional Integration," p. 132.
6. Ibid., p. 131.
7. John P. Renninger, *Multinational Cooperation for Development in West Africa* (New York: Pergamon Press, 1979), p. 97.

APPENDIX

TREATY OF THE ECONOMIC COMMUNITY OF WEST AFRICAN STATES (ECOWAS)

Preamble

The President of the Republic, Head of State, Head of the Revolutionary Military Government, and President of the National Council of the Revolution of Dahomey
The President of the Republic of Gambia
The Head of State and Chairman of the National Redemption Council of the Republic of Ghana
The Head of State and Commander-in-Chief of the People's Revolutionary Armed Forces, President of the Republic of Guinea
The President of the Republic of Guinea Bissau
The President of the Republic of Ivory Coast
The President of the Republic of Liberia
The Chairman of the Military Committee of National Liberation, President of the Republic of Mali
The President of the Islamic Republic of Mauritania
The Head of State and President of the Supreme Military Council of the Republic of Niger
The Head of the Federal Military Government, Commander-in-Chief of the Armed Forces of the Federal Republic of Nigeria
The President of the Republic of Senegal
The President of the Republic of Sierra Leone

The President of the Togolese Republic
The President of the Republic of Upper Volta
CONSCIOUS of the overriding need to accelerate, foster and
encourage the economic and social development of their states in
order to improve the living standards of their peoples;
CONVINCED that the promotion of harmonious economic
development of their states calls for effective economic cooperation largely through a determined and concerted policy of
self-reliance;
RECOGNISING that progress towards sub-regional economic
integration requires an assessment of the economic potential and
interests of each state;
ACCEPTING the need for a fair and equitable distribution of the
benefits of co-operation among Member States;
NOTING that forms of bilateral and multilateral economic cooperation existing in the sub-region give hope for wider cooperation;
RECALLING the Declaration of African Co-operation,
Development and Economic Independence adopted by the Tenth
Assembly of Heads of State and Government of the Organisation
of African Unity;
BEARING IN MIND that efforts at sub-regional co-operation
should not conflict with or hamper similar efforts being made to
foster wider co-operation in Africa;
AFFIRMING as the ultimate objective of their efforts accelerated
and sustained economic development of their states and the
creation of a homogeneous society, leading to the unity of the
countries of West Africa, by the elimination of all types of
obstacles to the free movement of goods, capital and persons:
DECIDE for the purpose of the foregoing to create an Economic
Community of West African States, and AGREE AS FOLLOWS:

Chapter 1
Principles
Article 1
Establishment and Membership of the
Community

1. By this Treaty the HIGH CONTRACTING PARTIES establish
among themselves an Economic Community of West African States
(ECOWAS), hereinafter referred to as "the Community".
2. The members of the Community, hereinafter referred to as
"the Member States", shall be the States that ratify this Treaty and
such other West African States as may accede to it.

Article 2
Aims of the Community

1. It shall be the aim of the Community to promote co-operation and development in all fields of economic activity particularly in the fields of industry, transport, telecommunications, energy, agriculture, natural resources, commerce, monetary and financial questions and in social and cultural matters for the purpose of raising the standard of living of its peoples, of increasing and maintaining economic stability, of fostering closer relations among its members and of contributing to the progress and development of the African continent.

2. For the purposes set out in the preceding paragraph and as hereinafter provided for in this Treaty, the Community shall by stages ensure:

   (a) the elimination as between the Member States of customs duties and other charges of equivalent effect in respect of the importation and exportation of goods;

   (b) the abolition of quantitative and administrative restrictions on trade among the Member States;

   (c) the establishment of a common customs tariff and a common commercial policy towards third countries;

   (d) the abolition as between the Member States of the obstacles to the free movement of persons, services and capital;

   (e) the harmonisation of the agricultural policies and the promotion of common projects in the Member States notably in the fields of marketing, research and agro-industrial enterprises;

   (f) the implementation of schemes for the joint development of transport, communication, energy and other infrastructural facilities as well as the evolution of a common policy in these fields;

   (g) the harmonisation of the economic and industrial policies of the Member States and the elimination of disparities in the level of development of Member States;

   (h) the harmonisation, required for the proper functioning of the Community, of the monetary policies of the Member States;

   (i) the establishment of a Fund for Co-operation, Compensation and Development; and

   (j) such other activities calculated to further the aims of the Community as the Member states may from time to time undertake in common.

Article 3
General Undertaking

The Member States shall make every effort to plan and direct their policies with a view to creating favourable conditions for the achievement of the aims of the Community; in particular, each Member State shall take all steps to secure the enactment of such legislation as is necessary to give effect to this Treaty.

Chapter II
Institutions of the Community
Article 4
Institutions

1. The institutions of the Community shall be:
   (a) the Authority of Heads of State and Government;
   (b) the Council of Ministers;
   (c) the Executive Secretariat;
   (d) the Tribunal of the Community; and
   (e) the following Technical and Specialised Commissions:
   -- the Trade, Customs, Immigration, Monetary and Payments Commission;
   -- the Industry, Agriculture and Natural Resources Commission;
   -- the Transport, Telecommunications and Energy Commission;
   -- the Social and Cultural Affairs Commission;

and such other Commissions or bodies as may be established by the Authority of Heads of State and Government or are established or provided for by this Treaty.

2. The institutions of the Community shall perform the functions and act within the limits of the powers conferred upon them by or under this Treaty and by Protocols thereto.

Article 5
Authority of Heads of State and Government
Establishment, Composition and Functions

1. There is hereby established the Authority of Heads of State and Government of the Member States referred to in this Treaty as "the Authority" which shall be the principal governing institution of the Community.

2. The Authority shall be responsible for, and have the general direction and control of the performance of the executive functions of the Community for the progressive development of the Community and the achievement of its aims.

3. The decisions and directions of the Authority shall be binding on all institutions of the Community.

4. The Authority shall meet at least once a year. It shall determine its own procedure including that for convening its meetings, for the conduct of business thereat and at other times, for the annual rotation of the office of Chairman among the members of the Authority.

Article 6
Council of Ministers
Establishment, Composition and Functions

1. There is hereby established a Council of Ministers which shall consist of two representatives of each Member State.
2. It shall be the responsibility of the Council of Ministers:
    (a) to keep under review the functioning and development of the Community in accordance with this Treaty;
    (b) to make recommendations to the Authority on matters of policy aimed at the efficient and harmonious functioning and development of the Community.
    (c) to give directions to all subordinate institutions of the Community; and
    (d) to exercise such other powers conferred on it and perform such other duties assigned to it by this Treaty.
3. The decisions and directions of the Council of Ministers shall be binding on all subordinate institutions of the Community unless otherwise determined by the Authority.
4. The Council of Ministers shall meet twice a year and one of such meetings shall be held immediately preceding the annual meeting of the Authority. Extraordinary meetings of the Council of Ministers may be convened as and when necessary.
5. Subject to any directions that the Authority may give, the Council of Ministers shall determine its own procedure including that for convening its meetings, for the conduct of business thereat and at other times, and for the annual rotation of the office of Chairman among the members of the Council of Ministers.
6. Where an objection is recorded on behalf of a Member State to a proposal submitted for the decision of the Council of Ministers, the proposal shall, unless such objection is withdrawn, be referred to the Authority for its decision.

Article 7
Decisions of the Authority and the Council
of Ministers

The Authority shall determine the procedure for the dissemination of its decisions and directions and those of the Council of Ministers and for matters relating to their coming into effect.

Article 8
The Executive Secretariat

1. There shall be established an Executive Secretariat of the Community.

2. The Executive Secretariat shall be headed by an Executive Secretary who shall be appointed by the Authority to serve in such office for a term of four (4) years and be eligible for reappointment for another term of four (4) years only.

3. The Executive Secretary shall only be removed from office by the Authority upon the recommendation of the Council of Ministers.

4. The Executive Secretary shall be the principal executive officer of the Community. He shall be assisted by two Deputy Executive Secretaries who shall be appointed by the Council of Ministers.

5. In addition to the Executive Secretary and the Deputy Executive Secretaries, there shall be a Financial Controller and such other officers in the Executive Secretariat as the Council of Ministers may determine.

6. The terms and conditions of service of the Executive Secretary and other officers of the Executive Secretariat shall be governed by regulations that may be made by the Council of Ministers.

7. In appointing officers to offices in the Executive Secretariat due regard shall be had, subject to the paramount importance of securing the highest standards of efficiency and technical competence, to the desirability of maintaining an equitable distribution of appointments to such posts among citizens of the Member States.

8. The Executive Secretary and officers of the Executive Secretariat, in the discharge of their duties, owe their loyalty entirely to the Community.

9. The Executive Secretary shall be responsible for the day to day administration of the Community and all its institutions.

10. The Executive Secretary shall:
    (a) as appropriate, service and assist the institutions of the Community in the performance of their functions;
    (b) keep the functioning of the Community under continuous examination and, where appropriate, report the results of its examination to the Council of Ministers;
    (c) submit a report of activities to all sessions of the Council of Ministers and all meetings of the Authority; and
    (d) undertake such work and studies and perform such services relating to the aims of the Community as may be assigned to him by the Council of Ministers and also

make such proposals thereto as may assist in the efficient and harmonious functioning and development of the Community.

Article 9
Technical and Specialised Commissions
Establishment, Composition and Functions

1. There shall be established the following Commissions:
   (a) the Trade, Customs, Immigration, Monetary and Payments Commission;
   (b) the Industry, Agriculture and Natural Resources Commission;
   (c) the Transport, Telecommunications and Energy Commission; and
   (d) the Social and Cultural Affairs Commission.

2. The Authority may from time to time establish other Commission as it deems necessary.

3. Each Commission shall consist of representatives designated one each by the Member States. Such representatives may be assisted by advisers.

4. Each Commission shall:
   (a) submit from time to time reports and recommendations through the Executive Secretary to the Council of Ministers either on its own initiative or upon the request of the Council of Ministers or the Executive Secretary; and
   (b) have such other functions as are imposed on it under this Treaty.

5. Subject to any directions which may be given by the Council of Ministers, each Commission shall meet as often as necessary for the proper discharge of its functions and shall determine its own procedure, including that for convening its meetings and the conduct of business thereat and at other times.

Article 10
External Auditor

1. There shall be an External Auditor of the Community who shall be appointed and removed by the Authority on the recommendation of the Council of Ministers.

2. Subject to the provisions of the preceding paragraph, the Council of Ministers shall make regulations governing the terms and conditions of service and powers of the External Auditor.

Article 11
Tribunal of the Community

1. There shall be established a Tribunal of the Community which shall ensure the observance of law and justice in the interpretation

of the provisions of this Treaty. Furthermore, it shall be charged with the responsibility of settling such disputes as may be referred to it in accordance with Article 56 of this Treaty.

2. The composition, competence, statutes and other matters relating to the Tribunal shall be prescribed by the Authority.

Chapter III
Customs and Trade Matters
Article 12
Liberalization of Trade

There shall be progressively established in the course of a transitional period of fifteen (15) years from the definitive entry into force of this Treaty, and as prescribed in this Chapter, a Customs Union among the Member States. Within this Union, customs duties or other charges with equivalent effect on imports shall be eliminated. Quota, quantitative or like restrictions or prohibitions and administrative obstacles to trade among the Member States shall be removed. Furthermore, a common customs tariff in respect of all goods imported into the Member States from third countries shall be established and maintained.

Article 13
Customs Duties

1. Member States shall reduce and ultimately eliminate customs duties and any other charges with equivalent effect except duties notified in accordance with Article 17 and other charges which fall within that Article, imposed on or in connection with the importation of goods which are eligible for Community tariff treatment in accordance with Article 15 of this Treaty. Any such duties or other charges are hereinafter referred to as "import duties".

2. Within a period of two (2) years from the definitive entry into force of this Treaty, a Member State may not be required to reduce or eliminate import duties. During this two-year period, Member States shall not impose any new duties and taxes or increase existing ones and shall transmit to the Executive Secretariat all information on import duties for study by the relevant institutions of the Community.

3. Upon the expiry of the period of two (2) years referred to in paragraph 2 of this Article and during the next succeeding eight (8) years, Member States shall progressively reduce and ultimately eliminate import duties in accordance with a schedule to be recommended to the Council of Ministers by the Trade, Customs, Immigration, Monetary and Payments Commission. Such a schedule shall take into account, inter alia, the effects of the reduction and elimination of import duties on the revenue of

Member States and the need to avoid the disruption of the income they derive from import duties.

4. The Authority may at any time, on the recommendation of the Council of Ministers, decide that any import duties shall be reduced more rapidly or eliminated earlier than is recommended by the Trade, Customs, Immigration, Monetary and Payments Commission. However, the Council of Ministers shall, not later than one calendar year preceding the date in which such reductions or eliminations come into effect, examine whether such reductions, or eliminations shall apply to some or all goods and in respect of some or all the Member States and shall report the result of such examination for the decision of the Authority.

Article 14
Common Customs Tariff

1. The Member States agree to the gradual establishment of a common customs tariff in respect of all goods imported into the Member States from third countries.

2. At the end of the period of eight (8) years referred to in paragraph 3 of Article 13 of this Treaty and during the next succeeding five (5) years, Member States shall gradually, in accordance with a schedule to be recommended by the Trade, Customs, Immigration, Monetary and Payments Commission, abolish existing differences in their external customs tariffs.

3. In the course of the same period, the above-mentioned Commission shall ensure the establishment of a common customs nomenclature and customs statistical nomenclature for all the Member States.

Article 15
Community Tariff Treatment

1. For the purposes of this Treaty, goods shall be accepted as eligible for Community tariff treatment if they have been consigned to the territory of the importing Member State from the territory of another Member State and originate in the Member States.

2. The definition of products originating from Member States shall be the subject of a protocol to be annexed to this Treaty.

3. The Trade, Customs, Immigration, Monetary and Payments Commission shall from time to time examine whether the rules referred to in paragraph 2 of this Article can be amended to make them simpler and more liberal. In order to ensure their smooth and equitable operation, the Council of Ministers may from time to time amend them.

Article 16
Deflection of Trade

1. For the purpose of this Article, trade is said to be deflected if,
   (a) imports of any particular product by a Member State from another Member state increase,
       (i) as a result of the reduction or elimination of duties and charges on that product, and
       (ii) because duties and charges levied by the exporting Member State on imports of raw materials used for manufacture of the product in question are lower than the corresponding duties and charges levied by the importing Member State; and
   (b) this increase in imports causes or would cause serious injury to production which is carried on in the territory of the importing Member State.

2. The Council of Ministers shall keep under review the question of deflection of trade and its causes. It shall take such decisions, as are necessary, in order to deal with the causes of this deflection.

3. In case of deflection of trade to the detriment of a Member State resulting from the abusive reduction or elimination of duties and charges levied by another Member State, the Council of Ministers shall study the question in order to arrive at a just solution.

Article 17
Revenue Duties and Internal Taxation

1. Member States shall not apply directly or indirectly to imported goods from any Member State fiscal charges in excess of those applied to like domestic goods or otherwise impose such charges for the effective protection of domestic goods.

2. Member States shall eliminate all effective internal taxes or other internal charges that are made for the protection of domestic goods not later than one (1) year after the period of two (2) years referred to in paragraph 2 of Article 13 of this Treaty. Where by virtue of obligations under an existing contract entered into by a Member State and such a Member State is unable to comply with the provisions of this Article, the Member State shall duly notify the Council of Ministers of this fact and not extend or renew such contract at its expiry.

3. Member States shall eliminate progressively all revenue duties designed to protect domestic goods not later than the end of the period of eight (8) years referred to in paragraph 3 of Article 13 of this Treaty.

4. Each Member State shall, not later than the end of the period of two (2) years referred to in paragraph 2 of Article 13 of this Treaty, notify the Council of Ministers of any duty it wishes to apply under the provisions of paragraph 3 of the aforementioned Article.

Article 18
Quantitative Restrictions on Community Goods

1. Except as may be provided for or permitted by this Treaty, each of the Member States undertakes to relax gradually and to remove ultimately in accordance with a schedule to be recommended by the Trade, Customs, Immigration, Monetary and Payments Commission and not later than ten (10) years from the definitive entry into force of this Treaty, all the then existing quota, quantitative or like restrictions or prohibitions which apply to the import into that State of goods originating in the other Member States and thereafter refrain from imposing any further restrictions or prohibitions.

2. The Authority may at any time, on the recommendation of the Council of Ministers, decide that any quota, quantitative or like restrictions or prohibitions shall be relaxed more rapidly or removed earlier than is recommended by the Trade, Customs, Immigration, Monetary and Payments Commission.

3. A Member State may, after having given notice to the other Member States of its intention to do so, introduce or continue to execute restrictions or prohibitions affecting:

    (a) the application of security laws and regulations;
    (b) the control of arms, ammunition and other war equipment and military items;
    (c) the protection of human, animal or plant health or life, or the protection of public morality;
    (d) the transfer of gold, silver and precious and semi-precious stones; or
    (e) the protection of national treasures; provided that a Member State shall not so exercise the right to introduce or continue to execute the restrictions or prohibitions conferred by this paragraph as to stultify the free movement of goods envisaged in this Article.

Article 19
Dumping

1. Member States undertake to prohibit the practice of dumping goods within the Community.

2. For the purposes of this Article, "dumping" means the transfer of goods originating in a Member State to another Member State for sale:

(a) at a price lower than the comparable price charged for similar goods in the Member States where such goods originate (due allowance being made for the differences in the conditions of sale or in taxation or for any other factors affecting the comparability of prices); and

(b) under circumstances likely to prejudice the production of similar goods in that Member State.

Article 20
Most Favoured Nation Treatment

1. Member States shall accord to one another in relation to trade between them the most favoured nation treatment and in no case shall tariff concessions granted to a third country under an agreement with a Member State be more favourable than those applicable under this Treaty.

2. Copies of such agreements referred to in paragraph 1 of this Article shall be transmitted by the Member State which are parties to them, to the Executive Secretariat of the Community.

3. Any agreement between a Member State and a third country under which tariff concessions are granted, shall not derogate from the obligations of that Member State under this Treaty.

Article 21
Internal Legislation

Member States shall refrain from enacting legislation which directly or indirectly discriminates against the same or like products of another Member State.

Article 22
Re-exportation of Goods and Transit Facilities

1. Where customs duty has been charged and collected on any goods imported from a third country into a Member State such goods shall not be re-exported into another Member State except as may be permitted under a Protocol to this Treaty entered into by the Member States.

2. Where goods are re-exported under such a Protocol, the Member States from whose territory such goods are re-exported shall refund to the Member State into whose territory such goods are imported the customs duties charged and collected on such goods. The duties so refunded shall not exceed those applicable on such goods in the territory of the Member State into which such goods are imported.

3. Each Member State, in accordance with international regulations, shall grant full and unrestricted freedom of transit through its territory of goods proceeding to or from a third country indirectly through that territory to or from other Member

States; and such transit shall not be subject to any discrimination, quantitative restrictions, duties or other charges levied on transit.

4. Notwithstanding paragraph 3 of this Article,
   (a) goods in transit shall be subject to the customs law; and
   (b) goods in transit shall be liable to the charges usually made for carriage and for any services which may be rendered, provided such charges are not discriminatory.

5. Where goods are imported from a third country into one Member State, each of the other Member States shall be free to restrict the transfer to it of such goods whether by a system of licensing and controlling importers or by other means.

6. The provisions of paragraph 5 of this Article shall apply to goods which, under the provisions of Article 15 of this Treaty, fail to be accepted as originating in a Member State.

Article 23

Customs Administration

Member States shall, upon the advice of the Trade, Customs, Immigration, Monetary and Payments Commission, take appropriate measures to harmonise and standardise their customs regulations and procedures to ensure the effective application of the provisions of this chapter and to facilitate the movement of goods and services across their frontiers.

Article 24

Drawback

1. Member States may, at or before the end of the period of eight (8) years referred to in paragraph 3 of Article 13 of this Treaty, refuse to accept as eligible for Community tariff treatment, goods in relation to which drawback is claimed or made use of in connection with their exportation from the Member States in the territory of which the goods have undergone the last process of production.

2. For the purposes of this Article:
   (a) "drawback" means any arrangement, including temporary duty-free admission, for the refund of all or part of the duties applicable to imported raw materials, provided that the arrangement, expressly or in effect, allows such refund or remission if goods are exported but not if they are retained for home use;
   (b) "remission" includes exemption from duties for goods imported into free ports, free zones or other places which have similar customs privileges; and
   (c) "duties" means customs duties and any other charges with equivalent effect imposed on imported goods, except the nonprotective element in such duties or charges.

Article 25
Compensation for Loss of Revenue
1. The Council of Ministers shall, on the report of the Executive Secretary and recommendation by the appropriate Commission or Commissions, determine the compensation to be paid to a Member State which has suffered loss of import duties as a result of the application of this Chapter.
2. A protocol to be annexed to this Treaty shall state precisely the methods of assessment of the loss of revenue suffered by Member States as a result of the application of this chapter.

Article 26
Safeguard Clause
1. In the event of serious disturbances occurring in the economy of a Member State following the application of the provisions of this chapter, the Member State concerned shall after informing the Executive Secretary and the other Member States take the necessary safeguard measures pending the approval of the Council of Ministers.
2. These measures shall remain in force for a maximum period of one year. They may not be extended beyond that period except with the approval of the Council of Ministers.
3. The Council of Ministers shall examine the method of application of these measures while they remain in force.

Chapter IV
Freedom of Movement and Residence
Article 27
Visa and Residence
1. Citizens of Member States shall be regarded as Community citizens and accordingly Member States undertake to abolish all obstacles to their freedom of movement and residence within the Community.
2. Member States shall by agreements with each other exempt Community citizens from holding visitors' visas and residence permits and allow them to work and undertake commercial and industrial activities within their territories.

Chapter V
Industrial Development and Harmonisation
Article 28
General Principles
For the purpose of this chapter, Member States shall achieve their industrial development and harmonisation in the three stages as set out in Articles 29, 30 and 31.

Article 29
Stage I: Exchange of Information on Major Industrial Projects

Member States undertake to:
  (a) furnish one another with major feasibility studies and reports on projects within their territories;
  (b) furnish one another, on request, reports, on the performance of prospective technical partners who have developed similar projects in their territories;
  (c) furnish one another, on request, reports on foreign business groups operating in their territories;
  (d) furnish one another, on request, with reports on their experiences on industrial projects and to exchange industrial research information and experts;
  (e) commission, where appropriate, joint studies for the identification of viable industrial projects for development within the Community; and
  (f) finance, where appropriate, joint research on the transfer of technology and the development of new products through the use of raw materials common in some or all of the Member States and on specific industrial problems.

Article 30

Stage II: Harmonisation of Industrial Incentives and Industrial Development Plans

Member States undertake to:
  (a) harmonise their industrial policies so as to ensure a similarity of industrial climate and to avoid disruption of their industrial activities resulting from dissimilar policies in the fields of industrial incentives, company taxation and Africanisation; and
  (b) co-operation with one another by exchanging their plans so as to avoid unhealthy rivalry and waste of resources.

Article 31

Stage III: Personnel Exchange. Training and Joint Ventures

Member States shall:
  (a) exchange, as may be necessary, skilled, professional and managerial personnel in the operation of projects within the Community;
  (b) provide places for training in their educational and technical institutions for Community citizens; and
  (c) engage, where appropriate, in joint development of projects including those which entail the execution of complementary parts of such projects in different Member States.

Article 32
Remedial Measures

1. The Council of Ministers shall keep under constant review in the implementation of the provisions of this Chapter, the disparity in the levels of industrial development of the Member States and may direct the appropriate Commission of the Community to recommend measures to remedy such disparity.

2. In the implementation of the aims of the Community, the Council of Ministers shall recommend measures designed to promote the industrial development of Member States and shall take steps to reduce gradually the Community's economic dependence on the outside world and strengthen economic relations among themselves.

3. The Council of Ministers shall further recommend measures designed to accelerate the industrial integration of the economies of the Member States.

Chapter VI
Co-operation in Agriculture and Natural Resources
Article 33
Co-operation among Member States

Member States shall co-operate as set out in this Chapter in the development of their natural resources particularly agriculture, forestry, animal husbandry and fisheries.

Article 34

Stage I: Harmonisation of Agricultural Policies

1. Member States undertake to work towards the harmonisation of their internal and external agricultural policies in their relations with one another;

2. Member States shall exchange regularly information on experiments and results of research being carried out in their respective territories and on existing rural development programmes; and

3. Member States shall formulate, as appropriate, joint programmes for both basic and in-service training in existing institutions.

Article 35

Stage II: Evolution of a Common Agricultural Policy

Member States undertake to take all measures necessary for the creation of a common policy especially in the fields of research, training, production, processing and marketing of the products of agriculture, forestry, animal husbandry and fisheries. For this purpose, the Industry, Agriculture and Natural Resources Commission shall, as soon as possible, after its establishment meet to make recommendations to the Council of Ministers for the harmonisation and exploitation of natural resources of the Member States.

Chapter VII
Co-operation in Monetary and Financial Matters
Article 36
Co-operation in Monetary and Fiscal Matters

1. It shall be the responsibility of the Trade, Customs, Immigration, Monetary and Payments Commission, among other things, to:

    (a) as soon as practicable, make recommendations on the harmonisation of the economic and fiscal policies of the Member States;

    (b) give its constant attention to the maintenance of a balance of payments equilibrium in the Member States; and

    (c) examine developments in the economies of the Member States.

2. The recommendations of the Trade, Customs, Immigration, Monetary and Payments Commission under this Article shall be made to the Council of Ministers.

Article 37
Settlement of Payments Between Member States

The Trade, Customs, Immigration, Monetary and Payments Commission shall make recommendations to the Council of Ministers on the establishment, in the short term, of bilateral systems for the settlement of accounts between the Member States and, in the long term, of a multilateral system for the settlement of such accounts.

Article 38
Committee of West African Central Banks

1. For the purpose of overseeing the system of payments within the Community, there is hereby established a Committee of West African Central Banks, which shall consist of the Governors of the Central Banks of the Member States or such other persons as may be designated by Member States. This Committee shall, subject to this Treaty, determine its own procedures.

2. The Committee of West African Central Banks shall make recommendations to the Council of Ministers from time to time on the operation of the clearing system of payments and on other monetary issues of the Community.

Article 39
Movement of Capital and Capital Issues Committee

1. For the purpose of ensuring the free flow of capital between the Member States consistent with the objectives of this Treaty,

there is hereby established a Capital Issues Committee, which shall consist of representatives designated one each by the Member States and shall, subject to this Treaty, determine its own procedure.

2. The Member States, in designating their representatives referred to in paragraph 1 of this Article, shall designate persons with financial, commercial, banking or administrative experience or qualifications.

3. In the exercise of its functions under paragraph 1 of this Article, the Capital Issues Committee shall:

   (a) seek to achieve the mobility of capital within the Community through the interlocking of any capital markets and stock exchanges;

   (b) ensure that stocks and shares floated in the territory of a Member State are quoted on the stock exchanges of the other Member States;

   (c) ensure that nationals of a Member State are given the opportunity of acquiring stocks, shares and other securities or otherwise investing in enterprises in territories of other Member States;

   (d) establish a machinery for the wide dissemination in the Member States of stock exchange quotations of each Member State;

   (e) organise and arrange the quotation of prices, timing, volume and conditions of issue of new enterprises in the Member States;

   (f) ensure the unimpeded flow of capital within the Community through the removal of controls on the transfer of capital among the Member States in accordance with a time-table, to be determined by the Council of Ministers; and

   (g) seek to harmonise the rates of interest on loans prevailing in the Member States so as to facilitate the investment of capital from a Member State in profitable enterprises elsewhere within the Community.

4. The capital envisaged in the provisions of this Article is that of Member States or their citizens.

5. With regard to capital other than that referred to in paragraph 4 of this Article, the Capital Issues Committee shall determine its movement within the Community.

Chapter VIII
Infrastructural Links in the Fields of Transport and
Communications
Article 40
Common Transport and Communications Policy

Member States undertake to evolve gradually common transport
and communications policies through the improvement and expansion of their existing transport and communications links and the
establishment of new ones as a means of furthering the physical
cohesion of the Member States and the promotion of greater
movement of persons, goods and services within the Community.

Article 41
Roads

The Transport, Telecommunications and Energy Commission shall
formulate plans for a comprehensive network of all-weather roads
within the Community with a view to promoting social and unimpeded commercial intercourse between the Member States through
the improvement of existing roads to, and the construction of new
ones of international standards. In the formulation of these plans,
the Transport, Telecommunications and Energy Commission shall
give priority to a network of roads traversing the territories of the
Member States.

Article 42
Railways

The Transport, Telecommunications and Energy Commission shall
for the purpose of connecting the railways of the Member States
formulate plans for the improvement and reorganisation of such
railways.

Article 43
Shipping and International Waterways

1. The Transport, Telecommunications and Energy Commission
shall formulate plans for the harmonisation and rationalisation of
policies on shipping and international waterways of the Member
States.
2. Member States undertake to do their utmost to form multinational shipping Companies for both maritime and river navi-
gation.

Article 44
Air Transport

Member States shall use their best endeavour to bring about the
merger of their national airlines in order to promote efficiency
and profitability in the air transportation of passengers and goods
within the Community by aircraft owned by the Governments of
the Member States and/or their citizens. To this end, they shall

co-ordinate the training of their nationals and policies in air transport and standardize their equipment.

Article 45
Telecommunications

1. Member States shall reorganise and improve, where necessary, their national telecommunications network to meet standards required for international traffic.
2. Member States undertake to establish a direct, modern, efficient and rational system of telecommunications among themselves.

Article 46
Pan-African Telecommunications Network

The Transport, Telecommunications and Energy Commission shall make urgent recommendations for the rapid realisation in the West African Section of the Pan-African Telecommunications network and, in particular, the establishment of links necessary for the economic and social development of the Community. Member States shall co-ordinate their efforts in this field and in the mobilisation of national and international financial resources.

Article 47
Postal Services

1. The Transport, Telecommunications and Energy Commission shall study and make recommendations to the Council of Ministers on proposals for speedier, cheaper and more frequent postal services within the Community.
2. Member States undertake to:
    (a) promote close collaboration among their postal administrations;
    (b) harmonise routes of mails; and
    (c) establish among themselves a system of postal remittances and preferential tariffs which are more favourable than those envisaged by the Universal Postal Union.

Chapter IX
Energy and Mineral Resources
Article 48
Co-operation in Energy and Mineral Resources

1. The Transport, Telecommunications and Energy Commission shall engage in consultations on, and the co-ordination of the policies and activities of the Member States in the field of energy and submit its recommendations to the Council of Ministers.
2. Member States undertake to:
    (a) co-operate, consult on and co-ordinate their policies, regarding energy and mineral resources;
    (b) harmonise their energy and mineral resources policies especially as regards the production and distribution of

energy, research, production and processing of mineral resources;

(c) exchange information on the results of research being carried out;

(d) plan joint programmes for training technicians and personnel; and

(e) formulate a common energy and mineral policy especially in the fields of production, distribution of energy, research, production and processing of mineral resources.

Chapter X
Social and Cultural Matters
Article 49
Co-operation in Social and Cultural Matters

Subject to any directions that may be given by the Council of Ministers, the Social and Cultural Affairs Commission shall examine ways of increasing exchange of social and cultural activities among the Member States and of developing them, provide a forum for consultation generally on social and cultural matters affecting the Member States and make recommendations to the Council of Ministers.

Chapter XI
Fund for Co-operation, Compensation and Development
Article 50
Establishment

There is hereby established a Fund to be known as the Fund for Co-operation, Compensation and Development hereinafter referred to as "the Fund".

Article 51
Resources of the Fund

1. The Fund shall derive its resources from:

(a) contributions of Member States;

(b) income from Community enterprises;

(c) receipts from bilateral and multilateral sources as well as other foreign sources; and

(d) subsidies and contributions of all kinds and from all sources.

2. The contributions of Member States referred to in sub-paragraph (a) of the preceding paragraph shall be determined by the Council of Ministers and shall be of such minimum and maximum amounts as the Council of Ministers may determine.

3. The method of determining the contribution to be paid by Member States, the regulations governing the payment and the currencies in which they shall be effected, the operation, organisation, management, status of the funds and matters related and

incidental thereto shall be the subject of a protocol to be annexed to this Treaty.

Article 52
Uses of the Fund

The Fund shall be used to:

    (a) finance projects in Member States;

    (b) provide compensation to Member States which have suffered losses as a result of the location of Community enterprises;

    (c) provide compensation and other forms of assistance to Member States which have suffered losses arising out of the application of the provisions of this Treaty on the liberalisation of Trade within the Community;

    (d) guarantee foreign investments made in Member States in respect of enterprises established in pursuance of the provisions of this Treaty on the harmonisation of industrial policies;

    (e) provide appropriate means to facilitate the sustained mobilisation of internal and external financial resources for the Member States and the Community; and

    (f) promote development projects in the less developed Member States of the Community.

Chapter XIII
Financial Provisions
Article 53
Budget of the Community

1. There shall be established a budget of the Community.

2. All expenditures of the Community, other than those in respect of the Fund for Co-operation, Compensation and Development, established under Chapter XI of this Treaty, shall be approved in respect of each financial year by the Council of Ministers and shall be chargeable to the budget.

3. Resources of the budget shall be derived from annual contributions by Member States and such other sources as may be determined by the Council of Ministers.

4. The budget shall be in balance as to revenues and expenditures.

5. A draft budget for each financial year shall be prepared by the Executive Secretary and approved by the Council of Ministers.

6. There shall be special budgets to meet extraordinary expenditures of the Community.

Article 54
Contributions by Member States
1. A protocol to be annexed to this Treaty shall state the mode by which the contribution of Member States shall be determined and the currencies in which the contribution is to be paid.
2. The Member States undertake to pay regularly their annual contributions to the budget of the Community.
3. Where a Member State is in arrears at the end of the financial year in the payment of its contributions for reasons other than those caused by public or natural calamity or exceptional circumstances that gravely affect its economy, such Member States may, by a resolution of the Authority be suspended from taking part in the activities of the institutions of the Community.

Article 55
Financial Regulations
The Council of Ministers shall make financial regulations for the application of the provisions of this chapter.

Chapter XIII
Settlement of Disputes
Article 56
Procedure for the Settlement of Disputes
Any dispute that may arise among the Member States regarding the interpretation or application of this Treaty shall be amicably settled by direct agreement. In the event of failure to settle such disputes, the matter may be referred to the Tribunal of the Community by a party to such disputes and the decision of the Tribunal shall be final.

Chapter XIV
General and Final Provisions
Article 57
Headquarters of the Community
The Headquarters of the Community shall be determined by the Authority.

Article 58
Official Languages
The official languages of the Community shall be such African languages declared official by the Authority and English and French.

Article 59
Relations with other Regional Associations and Third Countries
1. Member States may be members of other regional or sub-regional associations, either with other Member States or non-Member States, provided that their membership of such associations does not derogate from the provisions of this Treaty.

2. The rights and obligations arising from agreements concluded before the definitive entry into force of this Treaty between one or more Member States on the one hand, and one Member State and a third country on the other hand, shall not be affected by the provisions of this Treaty.

3. To the extent that such agreements are not compatible with this Treaty, the Member State or States concerned shall take all appropriate steps to eliminate the incompatibilities established. Member States shall, where necessary, assist each other to this end and shall, where appropriate, adopt a common attitude.

4. In applying the agreements referred to in paragraph 1 of this Article, Member States shall take into account the fact that the advantages accorded under this Treaty by each Member State form an integral part of the establishment of the Community and are thereby inseparably linked with the creation of common institutions, the conferring of powers upon them and the granting of the same advantages by all the other Member States.

Article 60
Status, Privileges and Immunities

1. The Community, as an international organization, shall enjoy legal personality.

2. The Community shall have in the territory of each Member State:
   (a) the legal capacity required for the performance of its functions under this Treaty; and
   (b) power to acquire, hold or dispose of movable or immovable property.

3. In the exercise of its legal personality under this Article, the Community shall be represented by the Executive Secretary.

4. The privileges and immunities to be granted to the officials of the Community at its Headquarters and in the Member States shall be the same as are accorded to diplomatic persons at the Headquarters of the Community and in the Member States. Similarly, the privileges and immunities granted to the Secretariat at the Headquarters of the Community shall be the same as granted to diplomatic missions at the Headquarters of the Community and in the Member States. Other privileges and immunities to be recognised and granted by the Member States in connection with the Community shall be determined by the Council of Ministers.

Article 61
Setting up of the Institutions

1. The Authority shall at its first meeting after the entry into force of this Treaty:
   (a) appoint the Executive Secretary;

(b) determine the Headquarters of the Community; and

(c) give such directions to the Council of Ministers and other institutions of the Community as are necessary for the expeditious and effective implementation of this Treaty.

2. Subject to the provisions of the preceding paragraph, the Council of Ministers shall, within two months of the entry into force of this Treaty, hold its first meeting to:

(a) appoint persons to offices in the Executive Secretariat in accordance with the provisions of this Treaty;

(b) give directions to other subordinate institutions;

(c) give directions to the Executive Secretary as to the implementation of the provisions of this Treaty; and

(d) perform such other duties as may be necessary for the expeditious and effective implementation of this Treaty.

Article 62
Entry into Force, Ratification and Accession

1. This Treaty and the protocols which shall be annexed and which shall form an integral part of the Treaty shall respectively enter into force provisionally upon the signature by Heads of State and Government and definitely upon ratification by at least seven signatory States in accordance with the constitutional procedures applicable for each signatory State.

2. Any West African state may accede to this Treaty on such terms and conditions as the Authority may determine. Instruments of accession shall be deposited with the Federal Military Government of Nigeria which shall notify all other Member States. This Treaty shall enter into force in relation to an acceding state on such date as its Instrument of accession is deposited.

Article 63
Amendments and Revisions

1. Any Member State may submit proposals for the amendment or revision of this Treaty.

2. Any such proposals shall be submitted to the Executive Secretary who shall communicate them to other Member States not later than thirty days after the receipt of such proposals. Amendments or revisions shall be considered by the Authority after Member States have been given one month's notice thereof.

Article 64
Withdrawal

1. Any Member State wishing to withdraw from the Community shall give to the Executive Secretary one year's written notice. At the end of this period of one year, if such notice is not withdrawn, such a State shall cease to be a member of the Community.

2. During the period of one year referred to in the preceding paragraph, such a Member State shall nevertheless observe the provisions of this Treaty and shall remain liable for the discharge of its obligations under this Treaty.

Article 65
Depository Government

The present Treaty and all Instruments of ratification and accessions shall be deposited with the Federal Military Government of Nigeria which shall transmit certified true copies of this Treaty to all Member States and notify them of the dates of deposits of the Instruments of ratification and accession and shall register this Treaty with the Organisation of African Unity, the United Nation's Organisation and such other Organisations as the Council of Ministers shall determine. IN FAITH WHEREOF, WE, THE HEADS OF STATE AND GOVERNMENT IN WEST AFRICA, HAVE SIGNED THIS TREATY DONE AT Lagos this 28th Day of May, 1975 in single original in the English and French languages, both texts being equally authentic.

THE INAUGURAL ADDRESS BY GENERAL YAKUBU GOWON, HEAD OF THE FEDERAL MILITARY GOVERNMENT OF NIGERIA

Opening Address by his Excellency General Yakubu Gowon, Head of the Federal Military Government, Commander-in-Chief of the Armed Forces of the Federal Republic of Nigeria at the formal opening session of the meeting of Heads of State of the Economic Community of West African States (ECOWAS) in Lagos on Tuesday, 27th May, 1975

Brother Heads of State and Government, Honourable Ministers and Commissioners, Your Excellencies, Distinguished Guests, Ladies and Gentlemen:

It gives me great pleasure, on this historic occasion, to acknowledge the rare honour bestowed on Nigeria to be host to this meeting of Heads of State and Government of West African countries, and to welcome you, Excellencies and dear Brothers, on behalf of myself, the Government and people of the Federal Republic of Nigeria, to Lagos, our capital city. It is my fervent hope that Your Excellencies' stay among us will be pleasant and memorable. It is also my sincere hope that our deliberations at this meeting will set us firmly on the road to the fulfilment of our commonly held aspirations for greater effective co-operation of the countries of West Africa, and a more cohesive and prosperous sub-region, as part of, and contributing to, a progressive and equally prosperous continent. I am particularly gratified to note that the great leader of the heroic and brotherly people of the Republic of Guinea-Bissau who, about a year ago, liberated themselves after such a prolonged and arduous struggle from the shackles of foreign domination, is present in our midst today along with his charming consort. I feel sure that I speak the minds of all present here at this gathering when I extend to him, his wife, to the Government and people of Guinea-Bissau, our sincere and very special welcome in our midst.

This is a momentous day, marking as it does the fulfilment of many hopes; the result of persistent efforts on the part of the leaders from all corners of West Africa; another major and concrete step in giving practical effect to aspirations which we all share and which, in various previous meetings, conferences and groups, we have all endeavoured since the beginning of the last decade, to bring to fruition. The Governments of this sub-region have met, sometimes in smaller or larger numbers, sometimes with representatives from all countries in the area. They have met in various capitals sometimes at the level of Heads of State, sometimes at the level of Ministers or experts. The most significant fact is that in spite of what appeared to be discouraging and even insurmountable obstacles, we have moved along the hard and difficult road to our gathering here today. It is particularly gratifying that we have been able to follow, consistently, the programme which our representatives laid down at the meeting of Ministers which took place in Lome in December 1973. Then, the time-table or programme of action towards the evolution of an economic community for all the States in our West African sub-region was mapped out and determined.

It is a credit to the vision of the leaders of Africa that we are gathered here today, to open a conference that could provide the basis for the practical realisation of this cherished goal. For, it is no longer a matter for doubt or argument that, in the world today, the steps we are meeting to consider are in conformity with the trends which govern the relations of closely connected countries in various regions and various parts of the world. It is also no longer in dispute that the realities of today require wider units of co-operation at a time when even the most developed and highly industrialised nations are themselves forging such closer bonds of practical co-operation through larger economic units. Indeed, this lesson was amply demonstrated recently in the mutually advantageous terms obtained through the Lome Convention with the European Economic Community, by a united group of nations from diverse parts of the earth, comprising African, Pacific and Caribbean countries. It remains our firm belief that the degree of cohesion we show will determine the measure of success we achieve in dealing effectively, and with strength, in regard to multinational and transnational organisations, and other formations of a like nature in the more developed countries of the world.

Poverty

I do not need to emphasise the urgent necessity to promote economic co-operation, bearing in mind the level of poverty in Africa which has the disheartening record of harbouring 16 out of the 25 countries classified by the United Nations as the least developed countries of the world. Economic integration will hasten economic and social development on the continent. The slow pace of economic growth and development in many countries make economic co-operation an urgent necessity. Indeed, the benefits from economic co-operation are so self-evident and the role that such co-operation can play in the development of our respective countries so fundamental, that whatever may be the initial difficulties, we must be united in our determination to succeed. Throughout the developing world, the fact has been brought home to countries associated with the giant economic groupings in the developed world that, in spite of such association, the industrialised countries continue to maintain restrictive policies against the imports of manufactured and semi-manufactured goods from the developing countries.

We cannot give a boost to inter-African trade, which is at present infinitesimal in global terms, unless we create bigger markets to allow viable and optimum utilization and allocation of our resources; we must also examine how to introduce arrangements which would ensure that goods manufactured locally in our own countries have relatively greater advantage over foreign goods produced by the modern cost-saving equipment and machineries. An economic community will surely accelerate intra-African trade, and create more job opportunities among all our peoples. It will also be a base on which to build a prosperous and vigorous export trade beyond our own regional frontiers. At this juncture, may I express our great satisfaction with the bold initiative taken by the businessmen in our West African subregion who have given a practical demonstration of our hopes and aspirations by forming the Association of West African Chambers of Commerce. They deserve our fullest support.

The universal trend towards some form of regional economic co-operation in both developed and developing countries is due to the realisation of the importance of economic inter-dependence for the promotion of the economic well-being of the peoples of these countries. This general awareness has found expression in the attempts by the United Nations to encourage regional economic integration. Indeed the United Nations Resolution on the International Development Strategy for the Second Development Decade urged developing countries to continue their efforts "to negotiate and promote schemes for regional and sub-regional integration among themselves so as to achieve the objectives of the new economic order namely, collective self-reliance and growing co-operation among developing countries which will further strengthen their role in the new international economic order." The same spirit animated the African Economic Charter prepared at the historic meeting held in Abidjan two years ago and approved by the Organisation of African Unity Heads of State and Government in Addis Ababa.

The underlying philosophy behind these declarations prompted, despite earlier unsuccessful attempts at economic co-operation in the sub-region, the initiative taken by our dear Brother and Friend, His Excellency President Gnassingbe Eyadema and ourselves in April 1972, to revive the idea of an Economic Community which cuts across linguistic and cultural barriers. Because of the practical difficulties that have been experienced in the past, and drawing lessons from previous efforts, we agreed on the principles which would guide our efforts. These were the adoption of a pragmatic and flexible approach, the pursuit of objectives capable of early realisation, the adoption of an open-door policy which would enable all the countries in our sub-region to become members of the Community and the setting up of necessary institutions to deal with specific issues that require immediate attention. The adoption of these principles, no doubt, reflected an understanding of the need to fashion instruments which would be workable in our peculiar circumstances, and not necessarily those that have proved admirable in the sophisticated economies of the industrialised world.

Pragmatism

These principles guided the efforts of our various functionaries in the sub-region who prepared the treaty now before us. Our Ministers have not attempted in the document to provide precise answers to all possible questions that may arise from time to time. The Economic Community which we are striving to establish will be a living organism evolving in its own unique way and growing over the years. Pragmatism is, indeed a word enshrined in the treaty. By providing a flexible and working instrument able to accommodate all our differences, our doubts and our reservations, we believe the treaty has attempted to come to terms with the realities of our sub-region.

Your Excellencies, the draft that we are about to consider takes cognisance of the realities of historical development in this sub-region since the beginning of the last decade when our various Governments, aware of the benefits of economic co-operation, however limited, established inter-Government bodies for the promotion of common economic objectives in very limited fields in economic or geographic terms. Within the sub-region attempts are being currently made to establish tariff preferential zones or economic unions for the mutual benefit of all the participating countries. The draft treaty takes account of these developments and guarantees their organic growth, provided such growth does not impede the success of this momentous and exciting adventure on which we are now embarked.

The establishment of this Economic Community of West African States should be a step towards greater economic integration and co-operation in areas neighbouring to West Africa, and in the continent as a whole. Indeed, this should be our goal, although prudence and practical realities dictate that the movement towards this ideal must be gradual in order to achieve success. We cannot confine ourselves to our little corner of our continent. Our responsibilities, our final goal and our vision must extend beyond the confines of this sub-region. As we consolidate our success, and as we march forward towards greater achievement, cohesion and solidarity, we will, at the same time, begin the bridge building and the infrastructure necessary for the eventual integration of the economies of our continent.

Wisdom

Excellencies and dear Brothers, your presence here today attests to the wisdom and vision of African leaders, and their ability to overcome their artificial and superficial obstacles to the wider fulfilment of the destinies of their people. I fervently hope that our deliberations will be frank and friendly in the best tradition of our practice and values so that, at the end, we will be able to sign the treaty which will usher the Economic Community of West

African States for progress, prosperity and well-being of all our peoples.

Distinguished Heads of State and Government, Honourable Ministers, Excellencies, Ladies and Gentlemen, it now remains for me and it is now my great honour to declare open this Economic Community of West African States meeting of the Heads of State and Government of the countries of West Africa. I wish us all God's guidance and blessings in our deliberations and future undertakings.

BIBLIOGRAPHY

PRINTED PRIMARY SOURCES

ECOWAS Documents

ECOWAS. Comments on the ECA Study Report *Proposals for Strengthening Economic Integration in West Africa*, ECW/1GO/ 1/5, March 1984, Lagos.

---. *Development of the Community: The First Five Years.* ECW/DEVE/C/7781, 1981, Lagos.

---. *News.*

---. *Official Journal* (Protocols, Decisions and Directives). Vols. 1-5: June 1979-June 1984.

---. *Work Programme 1981-1986.* ECW/WORK/P/8186.

Executive Secretary's Reports. Annual Report 1978-1979. ECW/HSG 11/5, May 1979, Dakar.

---. Annual Report 1980-1981. ECW/CM/IX/2, May 1981, Rev. 1, Freetown.

---. Annual Report 1981-1982. ECW/CM/XI/2, May 1982, Cotonou.

---. Annual Report 1982-1983. ECW/HSG/VI/2, May 1983, Conakry.

---. Council of Ministers. ECW/CM/VI/2, November 1979, Dakar.

---. Council of Ministers. ECW/CM/VII/2, May 1980, Lome.

---. Council of Ministers. ECW/CM/VIII/2/Rev. 1, November 1980, Lome.

---. Council of Ministers. ECW/CM/XII/2, November 1982, Cotonou.

---. Council of Ministers. ECW/CM/XV/13/Rev. 1, July 1984, Lagos.

---. Council of Ministers. ECW/CM/XVI/2, November 1984, Lome.

Final Communiques of ECOWAS Summit Meetings. Communique. Fifth Meeting of the Authority of Heads of State and Government. ECW/HSG/V/4, May 1982, Cotonou.

---. Communique. Sixth Meeting of the Authority of Heads of State and Government. ECW/HSG/VI/4/Rev. 1, May 1983, Conakry.

---. Seventh Meeting of the Authority of Heads of State and Government. ECW/HSG/VIII/6/Rev. 1, November 1984, Lome.

ECOWAS Fund. Report. 5th Meeting of Board of Directors. Document F-BD/CA-5-79-2, October 1979, Lome.

---. Report. 7th Meeting of Board of Directors. May 1981, Banjul, The Gambia.

---. *Statement of General Policy and Procedures for Loans, Investments, Backings and Subsidies* (undated).

---. *General Conditions Applicable to Loan, Guarantee and Counter-Guarantee Agreements* (undated).

---. *Rules and Regulations of the Special Fund for the Development of Telecommunications in ECOWAS Member States* (undated).

---. *Quarterly Newsletters*, March 1982.

ECOWAS: Special Studies. *Assignment Report and Studies Prepared for the ECOWAS Secretariat on Customs and Rules of Origin Questions.* Prepared by UNDP and UNCTAD, December 1979.

---. *Co-operation and Trade in Food Crop Products in the ECOWAS Sub-Region* (1 Main Report). Prepared by joint ECA/FAO Agriculture Division, January 1980, ECW/TRAD/3, 1980, Lagos.

---. *Critical Appraisal of the Economic and Social Conditions in the West Africa Sub-Region* (Industrial Development, Appendix iv). Study conducted by the Nigerian Institute of Social and Economic Research (NISER) and the Ivorian Centre for Economic and Social Research (CIRES), March 1979.

---. *Critical Appraisal of the Economic and Social Conditions in the West Africa Sub-Region* (International Assistance, Appendix viii).

---. *Currency Convertibility in the Economic Community of West African States* (ECOWAS Monetary Co-operation Programme Study Project 2). Prepared by the IMF, November 1980, ECW/MONEP/2, 1980, Lagos.

---. *Preliminary Report on Trade Liberalization Options and Issues for the ECOWAS.* Prepared by UNCTAD, January 1979, ECW/TRAD/11, 1980, Lagos.

---. *Preliminary Study on Approaches to Fiscal Co-operation and Harmonization in ECOWAS.* Prepared by UNDP and UNCTAD, ECW/FISC/1, 1980, Lagos.

---. *The Profiles and Potential of External Trade of Members of the Economic Community of West African States Vol. I* (ECOWAS Trade Customs and Monetary Study Project, Study No. 3: Part II). Prepared by the International Trade Centre, UNCTAD/GATT, December 1979, Geneva.

---. *The Profiles and Potential of External Trade of Members of the Economic Community of West African States Vol. II* (Information on Selected Manufactured Products). ECW/TRAD/9, 1980, Lagos.

---. *Unrecorded Trade Flows Within ECOWAS.* Prepared by the ECA and United Nations Economic and Social Council, August 1979, ECW/TRAD/2, 1980, Lagos.

United Nations Documents

United Nations. Resolutions Adopted by the General Assembly on the Declaration on the Establishment of a New International Economic Order. A/RES/3201 (S-vi), 9 May 1974.

---. Programme of Action on the Establishment of a New International Economic Order. A/RES/3202 (S-vi), 16 May 1974.

Economic Commission for Africa (ECA). "Administrative and Institutional Machinery for Economic Cooperation in Africa." In African Association for Public Administration and Management, *Regional Cooperation in Africa: Problems and Prospects* (Addis Ababa: 1977).

---. *Directory of Intergovernmental Co-operation Organisations in Africa.* E/CN.14/CEC/1/REV.2, June 1976.

---. *Economic Bulletin for Africa.* (Addis Ababa: 1961).

---. *Elements of Model Convention for Sub-Regional Common Markets in Africa.* E/CN, 14 WP1/I, 1965, Addis Ababa.

---. *Extraordinary Meeting of the Council of Ministers of the ECA MULPOC for West Africa.* ECA/MULPOC/NIA/VII/XLVIX, June 1984, Addis Ababa.

---. *Proposals for Strengthening Economic Integration in West Africa* (undated).
---. *Report of the ECA Mission on the Evaluation of UDEAC.* 1981, Libreville.
---. *Report of the Sub-regional Meeting on Economic Co-operation in West Africa, Niamey.* 1966, E/CN, 14/366, 1966.
---. *Report of the West African Industrial Co-operation Mission.* E/CN, 14/246, 7 January 1965.
---. *Report of the West African Sub-regional Conference on Economic Co-operation.* E/CN, 14/399, 1968.
---. *Statistical and Economic Information Bulletin for Africa No. 9.* UN, E/CN, 14/SE IB. 9.
---. *West African Sub-regional Conference on Economic Co-operation, Accra, 1967.* E/CN. 14/399, 1967.
United Nations Conference on Trade and Development (UNCTAD). *The Distribution of Benefits and Costs in Integration Among Developing Countries.* TD/13/413, September 1972.
---. *Trade Expansion and Economic Integration Among Developing Countries: A Report of the Secretariat.* UN Publication, Sales No. 67, 11 D. 20, 1967, New York.
---. "Current Problems of Economic Integration: The Role of Institutions in Regional Integration among Developing Countries." TD/B/422, 1974.
---. Vaitsos, Constantine V., *The Role of Transnational Enterprises in Latin American Economic Integration Efforts: Who Integrated and with Whom, How and for Whose Benefit?* UNCTAD Round Table on the "Role of Transnational Enterprises in the Latin American Integration Process." TAD/E SEM.5/2, Lima, Peru, 15 May 1978.

ECOWAS Papers (Unpublished papers presented at the International Conference on the Economic Community of West African States, Lagos, 23-27 August 1976.)

Adedeji, Adebayo. "Collective Self-Reliance in Developing Africa: Scope, Prospects and Problems."
Adebite, Lateef. "Need for Integration of Legal Systems Among ECOWAS States."
Adeniyi, Eniola O. "The Economic Community of West African States Within the Framework of the New International Economic Order."
Ajayi, E. A. "Towards Economic Co-operation in West Africa."

Cukwurah, Oye A. "ECOWAS: Obstacles to Labour Migration and Residence."

Ebiefie, E. O. "Central Provisions of the Treaty of Economic Community of West African States."

Fajemirokun, Henry. "The Role of West African Chambers of Commerce in the Formation of ECOWAS."

Markham, Theodore K. "Economic Community of West African States [ECOWAS]: A Theoretical Appraisal of Gains, Problems and Prospects."

Odusanya, T. O. "Trade in the West African Sub-Region."

Ojo, Folayan. "Trade Expansion and Economic Cooperation in West Africa: The Role of ECOWAS."

Palmer, E., and C. C. Edordu. "Issues Relating to Customs Union Theory."

Udeobo, M. A. "Trade and Other Restrictions in the West African Sub-Region."

Other Unpublished Papers

Adedeji, Adebayo. "The Evolution of a West African Economic Community." Text of an address presented at the Ministerial Council on ECOWAS, December 10-16, 1973, Lome, Togo.

Akpan, M. B. "Neo-colonialism: The Political Economy of Combating Dependent Modernisation in West Africa." Paper presented at the Conference on the New International Economic Order, September 1977, Lagos, Nigeria.

Asante, S. K. B. "Development and Regional Integration Since 1980: Progress Report and Prospects." Paper presented at the international conference on the Lagos Plan of Action and Africa's Future International Economic Relations: Projections and Implications for Policy Makers, ECA/Dalhousie University, November 1984, Halifax, Canada.

---. "Economic Community of West African States: Problems and Prospects." Paper presented at the international seminar on Planning Economic Integration: Experiences, Policies, and Models, November 1979, West Berlin.

---. "The European Community, the Lome Conventions, and the North-South Dialogue." Paper presented at the international colloquium on Relations between Europe and African within the Framework of North-South Dialogue, March 1982, Lome, Togo.

---. "Expectations and Reality: Transnational Corporations and Regional Self-Reliance Objective of the Lagos Plan of Action." Paper presented at the international conference on OAU/ECA,

Lagos Plan of Action and the Future of Africa, March 1984, University of Ife, Nigeria.

---. "The New International Economic Order and the Problem of Controlling Multinational Corporations in Africa." Paper presented at the international conference on the Future of Africa and the New International Economic Order, June 1982, University of Ife, Nigeria.

---. "Political Economy of Regulations: Africa and the Challenges of Transnational Corporations in the 1980s." Paper presented at the fifth biannual conference of African Association of Political Science, June 1983, Dakar, Senegal.

---. "The Politics of Regionalism in Africa: The Case of ECOWAS." Seminar paper, Africa Research Programme, April 1984, Harvard University, Cambridge, Mass.

---. "The Role of the Organization of African Unity in Promoting Peace, Development and Regional Security in Africa." Paper presented at the United Nations University Seminar on Peace, Development and Regional Security in Africa, January 1985, Addis Ababa, Ethiopia.

Castro, A. "The ASEAN Experience in Economic Cooperation." Paper presented at the international seminar on Planning Economic Integration: Experiences, Policies, and Models, November 1979, West Berlin.

Diabby-Ouattara, A. "ECOWAS and Regional Economic Cooperation." Address to Nigeria's principal representatives abroad, July 1979, Lagos.

---. "ECOWAS in the Context of the Lagos Plan of Action." Paper presented at the meeting of Directors of Social Science Institutions on the implementation of the Lagos Plan of Action, March 1982, Addis Ababa.

Diouf, Makhtar. "Approaches to Economic Integration in Black Africa: Assessment and Suggestions." Paper presented at the international seminar on Planning Economic Integration: Experiences, Policies, and Models, November 1979, West Berlin.

Eze Osita, C. "ECOWAS: Hopes and Illusion." Paper presented at the conference of African Association of Political Science, September 1977, Rabat, Morocco.

Gambari, Ibrahim Agboola. "The Politics and Economics of Regional Cooperation in West Africa." Paper presented at the 18th Annual Meeting of the African Studies Association, 29 October-1 November 1975, San Francisco.

Mahmood, Mamdani. "The Breakup of the East African Community: Some Lessons." Paper presented at the fifth biannual conference of African Association of Political Science, June 1983, Dakar, Senegal.

Ndongko, W. A. "Regional Economic Integration of French-Speaking Countries in Africa: The Case of the West African Economic Community (CEAO)." Paper presented at the International Conference on Law and Economy in Africa, February 1982, Ife, Nigeria.

Nti, James. "Economic Co-operation of West African States." A Talk to Inter-territorial Conference of Employers' Organisations in English-Speaking West Africa, 17 September 1980, Accra, Ghana.

---. "ECOWAS: An Approach to Regional Economic Co-operation." A Talk at the 18 Induction Course for Newly Recruited Foreign Service Officers, July 1980, Lagos.

Obadan, Idi Michael. "Regional Trade of the ECOWAS: Characteristics, Problems and Prospects." Paper presented at the third biannual conference of the West African Economic Association, April 1982, Freetown.

Tubman, Robert C. "Cooperation between EEC and ECOWAS." Paper presented at the international colloquium on Relations between Europe and Africa Within the Framework of North-South Dialogue, March 1982, Lome, Togo.

---. "ECOWAS as a Sub-Regional Institution and its Relations with the EEC." Paper presented at the international colloquium on the Lome Conventions: Underlying Principles, Practical Applications and Prospects, November 1982, Lome, Togo.

Udokang, Okon. "Nigeria and ECOWAS: Economic and Political Implications of Regional Integration." Paper presented at the conference on Nigeria and the World, 27-30 January 1976, Lagos.

Official Publications

Bank of Sierra Leone. *West African Cooperation: Problems and Possibilities*, Occasional Paper No. 1 (n.d.).

Common Crisis, North-South: Co-operation for World Recovery (Brandt Commission Report), [London: Pan, 1983].

IBRD. *Accelerated Development in Sub-Saharan Africa: an Agenda for Action*. Washington, D.C.: 1981.

---. *World Development Report 1983*. New York: Oxford University Press, 1983.

North-South: A Programme for Survival. Report of the Independent Commission on International Development Issue (Brandt Commission Report). London: Pan, 1980.

Organisation of African Unity. *Lagos Plan of Action for the Economic Development of Africa, 1980-2000.* Geneva: International Institute for Labour Studies, 1981.

Report by a Commonwealth Expert Group (confidential). *Towards A New International Economic Order.* Ottawa: July 1975.

Third World Forum. Occasional Paper No. 4, 1979.

UN Centre on Transnational Corporations. *Transnational Corporations in World Development: Third Survey.* New York: United Nations, 1983.

West Africa Finds A New Future. Lagos: Federal Government Publication, 1975.

SECONDARY SOURCES: BOOKS

Ake, Claude. *A Political Economy of Africa.* London: Longman, 1981.

Akintan, S. A. *The Law of International Economic Institutions in Africa.* Leyden: A. W. Sijhoff, 1977.

Asante, S. K. B. *Pan-African Protest: West Africa and the Italo-Ethiopian Crisis 1934-1941.* London: Longman, 1977.

Axline, W. A. *Caribbean Integration: The Politics of Regionalism.* New York: Nichols, 1979.

Balassa, Bela. *The Theory of Economic Integration.* Homewood, Ill.: Richard D. Irwin, 1961.

Beever, Colin R. *Trade Unions and Free Labour Movement in the EEC.* London: Chatham House, PEP. 1969.

Berger, M. *Industrialisation Policies in Nigeria.* Munich: Afrika Studien, No. 88, Institut fur Wirtschaftsforschung, 1975.

Boateng, E. A. *A Political Geography of Africa.* Cambridge: Cambridge University Press, 1978.

Bracewell-Milnes, Barry. *Economic Integration in East and West.* London: Croom Helm, 1976.

Browne, Robert S., and Robert J. Cummings. *The Lagos Plan of Action Vs. The Berg Report: Contemporary Issues in African Economic Development.* Lawrenceville: Brunswick, 1984.

Church, Harrison R. J. *West Africa.* London: Longman, 1963.

Cochrane, James D. *The Politics of Regional Integration: The Central American Case.* New Orleans: Tulane University Press, 1969.

Cohen, Dennis, and John Daniel, eds. *Political Economy of Africa: Selected Readings.* London: Longman, 1981.

Colman, David, and Frederick Nixson. *Economics of Change in Less Developed Countries.* Oxford: Philip Allan, 1978.

Cowan, L. Gray. *The Dilemmas of African Independence.* New York: Columbia University Press, 1965.

Denton, G. R., ed. *Economic Integration in Europe.* London: Weidenfeld and Nicolson, 1969.

Diejomaoh V. P., and Milton A. Iyoha, eds. *Industrialization in the Economic Community of West African States (ECOWAS).* Ibadan: Heinemann, 1980.

Fagan, Stuart I. *Central American Economic Integration: The Politics of Unequal Benefits.* Berkeley: University of California Press, 1970.

Fontaine, Roger W. *The Andean Pact: A Political Analysis.* Beverly Hills/London: The Washington Papers, vol. 5, Sage Publications, 1977.

Frey-Wouters, Ellen. *The European Community and the Third World: The Lome Convention and Its Impact.* New York: Praeger, 1980.

Fyfe, Christopher. *Africanus Horton: West African Scientist and Patriot 1835-1883.* London: OUP, 1972.

Ghai, D., ed. *Economic Independence in Africa.* Nairobi, Kampala and Dar es Salaam: East African Literature Bureau, 1973.

Green, R. H., and K. G. Krishna. *Economic Cooperation in Africa: Retrospect and Prospect.* Nairobi: OUP, 1967.

Gruhn, Isebill V. *Regionalism Reconsidered: The Economic Commission for Africa.* Boulder: Westview Press, 1979.

Haas, E. B. *The Unity of Europe: Political, Social and Economic Forces 1950-57.* Stanford: Stanford University Press, 1958.

Harris, Richard, ed. *The Political Economy of Africa.* Cambridge: Schenkman, 1975.

Hazlewood, Arthur. *Economic Integration: The East African Experience.* London: Heinemann, 1975.

Jalloh, Abdul A. *The Politics and Economics of Regional Integration in Equatorial Africa.* Berkeley: University of California Press, 1973.

Kahnert, F., et al. *Economic Integration Among Developing Countries.* Paris: OECD Centre, 1969.

Kerr, Anthony J. C. *The Common Market and How It Works.* New York: Pergamon Press, 1977.

Laszlo, E. *RCDC: Regional Cooperation Among Developing Countries.* New York: Pergamon, 1981.

Laszlo, E. et al. *The Obstacles to the New International Economic Order*. New York: Pergamon, 1980.

Lawson, Roger, and Bruce Reed. *Social Security in the European Community*. London: Chatham House, PEP, 1975.

Leys, Colin. *Underdevelopment in Kenya: The Political Economy of Neo-Colonialism*. Berkeley: University of California Press, 1975.

Lindberg, L. N. *The Political Dynamics of European Economic Integration*. Stanford: Stanford University Press, 1963.

Long, Frank, ed. *The Political Economy of EEC Relations With African, Caribbean and Pacific States: Contributions to the Understanding of the Lome Convention on North-South Relations*. Oxford: Pergamon Press, 1980.

Mabogunje, Akin L. *Regional Mobility and Resource Development in West Africa*. Montreal: McGill University Press, 1972.

Maritano, Ninon. *A Latin American Economic Community: History, Policies and Problems*. Notre Dame, Ind.: University of Notre Dame Press, 1970.

Maritano, Ninon, and Antonio Obaid. *An Alliance For Progress: the Challenge and the Problems*. Minneapolis: T. S. Denision, 1963.

Mattis, Ann, ed. *A Society for International Development: Prospects 1984*. Durham: Duke University Press, 1983.

Mazuri, Ali A. *The African Condition*. London: Cambridge University Press, 1983.

Mazuri, Ali A., and Hasu H. Patel, eds. *Africa: The Next Thirty Years*. London: Julian Friedmann, 1974.

Mazzeo, D., ed. *African Regional Organizations*. Cambridge: Cambridge University Press, 1984.

Morawetz, David. *The Andean Group: A Case Study in Economic Integration Among Developing Countries*. Cambridge, Mass.: M.I.T. Press, 1974.

Mutharika, Bingu W. T. *Toward Multinational Economic Cooperation in Africa*. New York: Praeger, 1972.

Mytelka, Lynn K. *Regional Development in a Global Economy: The Multinational Corporation, Technology, and Andean Integration*. New Haven and London: Yale University Press, 1979.

Ndegwa, P. *The Common Market and Development in East Africa*. Nairobi: East African Publishing House, 1965.

Nixon, F. I. *Economic Integration and Industrial Location: An East African Case Study*. London: Longman, 1973.

Nkrumah, Kwame. *Africa Must Unite*. London: Panaf Books, 1963.

Nyerere, Julius K. *Non-Alignment in the 1970s.* Dar-es-Salaam: Government Printing Press, 1970.

Onwuka, R. I. *Development and Integration in West Africa: The Case of the Economic Community of West African States (ECOWAS).* Ife: University of Ife Press, 1982.

Plessz, Nicolas. *Problems and Prospects of Economic Integration in West Africa.* Montreal: McGill University Press, 1968.

Renninger, John P. *Multinational Cooperation for Development in West Africa.* New York: Pergamon Press, 1979.

Rimmer, Douglas. *The Economies of West Africa.* London: Weidenfeld and Nicholson, 1984.

Robson, Peter. *Integration, Development and Equity: Economic Integration in West Africa.* London: George Allen and Unwin, 1983.

Rothchild, D., and R. L. Curry, Jr. *Scarcity, Choice, and Public Policy in Middle Africa.* Berkeley: University of California Press, 1975.

Schmitter, Philippe C. *Autonomy or Dependence as Regional Integration Outcomes: Central America.* Berkeley: Research Series No. 17, Institute of International Studies, University of California, 1972.

Seers, Dudley, ed. *Dependency Theory: A Critical Reassessment.* London: Frances Pinter, 1981.

Spero, Joan E. *The Politics of International Economic Relations.* London: George Allen and Unwin, 1977.

Swann, Dennis. *The Economics of the Common Market.* Harmondsworth: Penguin, 1975.

Uka, Ezenwe. *ECOWAS and the Economic Integration of West Africa.* London: C. Hurst, 1983.

Viner, Jacob. *The Customs Union Issue.* New York: Carnegie Endowment for International Peace, 1950.

Wallace, Helen, et al. *Policy-Making in the European Community.* New York: John Wiley and Sons, 1978.

Waterston, Albert. *Development Planning: Lessons of Experience.* Baltimore: The John Hopkins Press, 1965.

Zartman, William I., ed. *The Political Economy of Nigeria.* New York: Praeger, 1983.

Zuvekas, Clarence. *Economic Development: An Introduction.* London: Macmillan Press, 1971.

ARTICLES

Abangwu, George C. "Systems Approach to Regional Integration in West Africa." *Journal of Common Market Studies* 13 (1975).

Aboyade, O. "The Economy of Nigeria." In *The Economics of Africa*, edited by P. Robson and D. A. Luri. London: George Allen and Unwin, 1969.

Adamolebun, Ladipo. "Cooperation or Neo-colonialism--Francophone Africa." *Africa Quarterly* 18 (July 1978).

Adedeji, Adebayo. "Development and Economic Growth in Africa to the Year 2000: Alternative Projections and Policies." In *Alternative Futures for Africa*, edited by Timothy M. Shaw. Boulder, Colo.: Westview Press, 1982.

---. "Economic Cooperation of West African States: Ideals and Realities." *The Nigerian Trade Journal* 22 (April-June 1975).

---. "The Need for Concrete Action." In African Association for Public Administration and Management, *Regional Cooperation in Africa: Problems and Prospects*, Addis Ababa: 1977.

---. "Prospects of Regional Economic Cooperation in West Africa." *Journal of Modern African Studies* 8 (1970).

Ake, Claude. "Explanatory Notes on the Political Economy of Africa." *Journal of Modern African Studies* 14 (1976).

Allison C., and R. Green. "Stagnation and Decay in Sub-Saharan Africa: Dialogues, Dialectics and Decay." *IDS Bulletin* 14 (January 1983).

Amin, Samir. "Capitalism and Development in the Ivory Coast." In *African Politics and Society*, edited by I. L. Markovitz. New York: Free Press, 1970.

Anglin, Douglas G. "Economic Liberation and Regional Cooperation in Southern Africa: SADCC and PTA." *International Organization* 37 (Autumn 1983).

Arnold, Hugh M. "Africa and the New International Economic Order." *Third World Quarterly* 11 (April 1980).

Asante, S. K. B. "Restructuring Transnational Mineral Agreements." *American Journal of International Law* 73 (July 1979).

Asante, S. K. B. "CEAO-ECOWAS: Conflict and Cooperation in West Africa." In *The Future of Regionalism in Africa*, edited by R. I. Onwuka and A. Sesay. London: Macmillan, 1984.

---. "Economic Integration in West Africa: Some Crucial Issues." *Africa Development* 5 (1980).

---. "ECOWAS, the EEC, and the Lome Convention." In *African Regional Organisations*, edited by D. Mazzeo. Cambridge: Cambridge University Press, 1984.

---. "ECOWAS: Towards Autonomy or Neo-colonialism?" In *In-dependence, Dependence and Interdependence*, edited by Timothy M. Shaw and R. I. Onwuks. London: George Allen and Unwin, 1983.

---. "The Experience of the EEC: Relevant or Impediment to ECOWAS Regional Self-Reliance Objective?" *Afrika Spectrum* 17 (1982/3)

---. "International Assistance and International Capitalism: Supportive or Counter-Productive?" In *African Independence: The First 25 Years*, edited by Gwendolen M. Carter and Patrick O'Meara. Bloomington: University of Indiana Press, 1985.

---. "Kwame Nkrumah and Pan-Africanism: The Early Phase 1945-1961." *Universitas* (New Series) 3 (October 1973).

---. "The Lome Convention: Towards Perpetuation of Depen-dence or Promotion of Interdependence." *Third World Quar-terly* 3 (October 1981).

---. "Politics of Regional Integration: The Case of the Economic Community of West African States (ECOWAS)." *Universitas* 7 (May 1978).

Assisi Asobie, H. "Nigeria and the EEC, 1970-1980: An Analysis of the Processes and Implications of Nigeria's Association with the EEC under the First Lome Convention." *Africa Development* 7 (1982).

Avery, William P. "Oil, Politics, and Economic Decision Making: Venezuela and the Andean Common Market." *International Organization* 30 (Autumn 1976).

Avery, William, and J. D. Cochrane. "Innovation in Latin American Regionalism: The Andean Common Market." *Inter-national Organization* 27 (Spring 1973).

Axline, W. Andrew. "Underdevelopment, Dependence, and Inte-gration: The Politics of Regionalism in the Third World." *International Organization* 31 (Winter 1977).

Balassa, Bela. "Types of Economic Integration." In *Economic Integration: Worldwide, Regional, Sectoral*, edited by Fritz Machlup. London: Macmillan Press, 1978.

Barbour, K. M. "Industrialization in West Africa--The Need for Sub-Regional Groupings within an Integrated Economic Com-munity." *Journal of Modern African Studies* 10 (1972).

Bayliss, B. T. "Competition and Industrial Policy." In *The Economics of the European Community*, edited by A. M. El-Agra. Oxford: Philip Allan, 1980.

Bergsten, Fred C., R. O. Keohane, and J. S. Nye, Jr. "Inter-national Economics and International Politics: Framework for Analysis." *International Organization* 29 (Winter 1975).

Bond, Robert D. "Regionalism in Latin America: Prospects for the Latin American Economic System (SELA)." *International Organization* 32 (Spring 1978).

Bergsten, Fred C., R. O. Keohane, and J. S. Nye, Jr. "International Economics and International Politics: Framework for Analysis." *International Organization* 29 (Winter 1975).

Bond, Robert D. "Regionalism in Latin America: Prospects for the Latin American Economic System (SELA)." *International Organization* 32 (Spring 1978).

Brewster, H., and Y. Thomas Clive. "Aspects of the Theory of Economic Integration." *Journal of Common Market Studies* 8 (December 1969).

Cherol, R. L., and Jose N. del Arco. "Andean Multinational Enterprises: A New Approach to Multinational Investment in the Andean Group." *Journal of Common Market Studies* 21 (June 1983).

Collins, C. D. C. "History and Institutions of the EEC." In *The Economics of the European Community*, edited by A. M. El-Agra. Oxford: Philip Allan, 1980.

Corea, Gamani. "UNCTAD and the New International Economic Order." *International Affairs* 53 (April 1977).

Cox, Thomas S. "Northern Actors in a South-South Setting: External Aid and East African Integration." *Journal of Common Market Studies* 21 (March 1983).

Diejomaoh, V. P. "State, Structure and Nature of Manufacturing Production in the Economic Community of West African States (ECOWAS)." In *Industrialization in the Economic Community of West African States (ECOWAS)*, edited by V. P. Diejomaoh and Milton A. Iyoha. Ibadan: Heinemann, 1980.

Dressel, Klaus. "Latin American Economic Integration: Between Standstill and Progress." *Development and Cooperation* (May 1977).

Drummond, S. "ASEAN: The Growth of an Economic Dimension." *The World Today* 35 (January 1979).

Ewusi, Kodwo. "Scope, Structure and State of Industrialization in Ghana." In *Industrialization in the Economic Community of West African States (ECOWAS)*, edited by V. P. Diejomaoh and Milton A. Iyoha. Ibadan: Heinemann, 1980.

Ezenwe, Uka. "Trade and Growth in West Africa in the 1980s." *The Journal of Modern African Studies* 20 (1982).

Feld, Werner. "National Interest Groups and Policy Formation in the EEC." *Political Science Quarterly* 81 (September, 1966).

Fischlowitz, Estanislau. "A Labour Common Market." *Americas* 14 (August 1962).

Floto, Edgardo A. "Economic Integration and Collective Self-Reliance." In *Third World Forum*, Occasional Paper, 4 (1979).

Furnish, Dale B. "The Andean Common Market's Common Regime for Foreign Investment." *Vanderbilt Journal of Transnational Law* 5 (Spring 1972).

Green, R. H. "Economic Independence and Economic Cooperation." In *Economic Independence in Africa*, edited by D. Ghai. Nairobi, Kampala, Dar es Salaam: East African Literature Bureau, 1973.

Gruhn, Isebill V. "The Lome Convention: Inching Towards Interdependence." *International Organization* 30 (Spring 1976).

Guyer, Jane I. "The World Bank's Prescriptions for Rural Africa." *Review of African Political Economy* 27/28 (February 1984).

Haas, Ernst B. "The Study of Regional Integration: Reflections on the Joy and Anguish of Pretheorizing." *International Organization* 24 (Autumn 1970).

Hansen, Roger D. "Regional Integration: Reflections on a Decade of Theoretical Efforts." *World Politics* 21 (January 1969).

Hazlewood, Arthur. "The End of the East African Community: What are the Lessons for Regional Integration Schemes?" *Journal of Common Market Studies* 18 (September 1979).

Helleiner, Gerald. "Aid and Dependence in Africa: Issues for Recipients." In *The Politics of Africa: Dependence and Development*, edited by Timothy M. Shaw and K. Heard. Canada: Dalhousie University Press, 1979.

Hill, Christopher R. "Regional Co-operation In Southern Africa." *African Affairs* 82 (April 1983).

Hodges, Michael. "Industrial Policy: A Directorate-General in Search of a Role." In *Policy-Making in the European Communities*, edited by Helen Wallace, William Wallace, and Carole Webb. New York: John Wiley and Sons, 1978.

Jacobs, Francis G. "The Free Movement of Persons Within the EEC." In *Current Legal Problems*, edited by Lord Lloyd of Hampstead, et al. London: Steven and Sons, 1977.

Jalloh, Abdul A. "Regional Integration in Africa: Lessons from the Past and Prospects for the Future." *Africa Development* 1 (1976).

Jones, Thomas. "Regionalism: The Problem of Public Support." In *Regionalism and the New International Economic Order*, edited by Davidson Nicol, et al. New York: Pergamon Press, 1981.

Kisanga, E. J. "Regional Co-operation--A Challenge for the Continent." *Africa Now* 36 (April 1984).

Kuehn, Rainer, and Frank Seelow. "ECOWAS-CEAO: Regional Cooperation in West Africa." *Development and Cooperation* 3 (May/June 1980).

Lipsey, R. G. "The Theory of Customs Union: A General Survey." *Economic Journal* 70 (September 1960).

Lodge, J., and V. Herman. "The Economic and Social Committee in the EEC Decision-Making." *International Organization* 34 (Spring 1980).

Lofchie, Michael L. "Political and Economic Origins of African Hunger." *Journal of Modern African Studies* 13 (1975).

Mkandawire, Thandika. "The Lagos Plan of Action and the World Bank on Food and Agriculture: A Comparison." *Africa Development* 7 (1982).

Mutharika, B. W. T. "A Case Study of Regionalism in Africa." In *Regionalism and the New International Economic Order*, edited by Davidson Nicol, et al. New York: Pergamon Press, 1981.

Mytelka, Lynn K. "Fiscal Politics and Regional Redistribution: Bargaining Strategies in Asymmetrical Integrative System." *Journal of Conflict Resolution* 19 (March 1975).

---. "A Geneology of Francophone West and Equatorial African Regional Organization." *Journal of Modern African Studies* 12 (June 1974).

Nye, Joseph S., Jr. "Comparing Common Markets: A Revised Neo-Functionalist Model." *International Organization* 24 (Autumn 1970).

---. "Comparing Regional Integration: Concept and Measurement." *International Organization* 22 (Autumn 1968).

O'Brien, Rita Cruise. "Factors of Dependence: Senegal and Kenya." In *Decolonisation and After: The British and French Experience*, edited by W. H. Morris-Jones and Georges Fischer. London: Frank Cass, 1980.

Ojo, Folayan. "Economic Integration: The Nigerian Experience since Independence." *Nigerian Journal of Economic and Social Studies* 18 (July 1976).

Ojo, Olatunde J. B. "Nigeria and the Formation of ECOWAS." *International Organization* 34 (Autumn 1980).

Ollawa, P. E. "On a Dynamic Model for Rural Development in Africa." *Journal of Modern African Studies* 15 (1977).

Olofin, Sam. "ECOWAS and the Lome Convention: An Experiment in Complementary or Conflicting Customs Union Arrangements?" *Journal of Common Market Studies* 14 (September 1977).

Onitiri, H. M. A. "Towards a West African Economic Community." *Nigerian Journal of Economic and Social Studies* 5 (March 1963).

Onwuka, Ralph I. "The ECOWAS Protocol on the Free Movement of Persons: A Threat to Nigerian Security?" *African Affairs* 81 (April 1982).

---. "Transnational Corporations and Regional Integration in West Africa." In *Africa and the International Political System*, edited by Timothy M. Shaw and 'Sola Ojo. Washington D.C.: University Press of America, 1982.

Osoba, Segun. "The Deepening Crisis of Nigerian National Bourgeoisie." *Review of African Political Economy* 13 (May-August 1978).

Pentland, Charles. "The Regionalism of World Politics: Concepts and Evidence." *International Journal* 30 (Autumn 1975).

Pinder, John. "Positive and Negative Integration: Some Problems of Economic Union in the EEC." *The World Today* 24 (March 1968).

Ramsay, Robert. "UNCTAD'S Failures: The Rich Get Richer." *International Organization* 38 (Spring 1984).

Ravenhill, John. "Regional Integration and Development in Africa: Lessons from the East African Community." *Journal of Commonwealth and Comparative Politics* 17 (1979).

Renninger, John P. "The Future of Economic Cooperation Schemes in Africa, with Special Reference to ECOWAS." In *Alternative Futures for Africa*, edited by Timothy M. Shaw. Boulder, Colo.: Westview Press, 1982.

Rothchild, Donald. "The Political Implications of the Treaty." *East African Economic Review* 3 New Series (December 1967).

Ruggie, J. "Collective Good and Future of International Collaboration." *American Political Science Review* 66 (September 1972).

Sen, Amartya. "The Food Problem: Theory and Policy." *Third World Quarterly* 4 (July 1982).

Sesay, Amadu. "Conflict and Collaboration: Sierra Leone and Her West African Neighbours." *Afrika Spectrum* 2 (1980).

Shaw, Timothy M. "EEC-ACP Interactions and Images as Redefinitions of Euro-Africa: Exemplary, Exclusive and/or Exploitative?" *Journal of Common Market Studies* 17 (December 1979).

---. "Regional Cooperation and Conflict in Africa." *International Journal* 30 (Autumn 1975).

---. "From Dependence to Self-reliance: Africa's Prospects for the Next Twenty Years." *International Journal* 35 (Autumn 1980).

Shaw, Timothy M., and Malcolm J. Grieve. "Dependence as an Approach to Understanding Continuing Inequalities in Africa." *Journal of Developing Areas* 13 (April 1979).

Sloan, John W. "The Strategy of Developmental Regionalism: Benefits, Distribution, Obstacles and Capabilities." *Journal of Common Market Studies* 10 (December 1971).

Streeten, Paul. "Costs and Benefits of Multinational Enterprises in Less Developed Countries." in *The Multinational Enterprise*, edited by J. H. Dunning. London: George Allen and Unwin, 1972.

Sunkel, Osvaldo. "National Development Policy and External Dependence in Latin America." In *Contemporary Inter-American Relations*, edited by Yale Ferguson. Englewood Cliffs, N.J.: Prentice-Hall, 1972.

Tella, Quido Di. "Regional Cohesion and Incoherence in Latin America." *The World Today* (December 1974).

Tunteng, P-Kiven. "External Influences and Sub-imperialism in Francophone West Africa." In *The Political Economy of Contemporary Africa*, edited by Peter C. W. Gutkind and Immanuel Wallerstein. Beverly Hills/London: Sage, 1976).

Uri, Pierre. "Industrial Policy: Location, Technology, Multinational Firms, Competition and Integration of Product Markets." In *Economic Integration: Worldwide, Regional, Sectoral*, edited by Friz Machlup. London: Macmillan Press, 1978.

Vaitsos, Constantine V. "Crisis in Regional Economic Cooperation [Integration] Among Developing Countries." *World Development* 6 (June 1978).

Vargas-Hidalgo, Rafael. "The Crisis of the Andean Pact: Lessons for Integration Among Developing Countries." *Journal of Common Market Studies* 17 (March 1979).

Wallace, Helen. "National Bulls in the Community China Shop: The Role of National Governments in Community Policy-Making." In *Policy-Making in the European Communities*, edited by Helen Wallace, et al. New York: John Wiley and Sons, 1978.

Williams, Gavin. "Nigeria: The Neo-colonial Political Economy." In *Political Economy of Africa: Selected Readings*, edited by Dennis Cohen and John Daniel. London: Longman, 1981.

INDEX

INDEX

ABOUT THE AUTHOR

SAMUEL K. B. ASANTE is presently Visiting Professor and African Area Studies Consultant in the Department of Political Science through the Center for African Studies, University of Florida, Gainesville. A former chairman of the Department of Political Science, University of Ghana, Legon, Dr. Asante received his B.A. from the University of Ghana, Legon, M.Sc. (Economics), and Ph.D. from the London School of Economics, University of London. He has taught previously at the University of Ghana, University of Calabar, Nigeria, State University of New York at Brockport, and served on two occasions as Senior Research Fellow of the Friedrich Ebert Foundation in the Federal Republic of Germany.

Trained in higher university administration and management in the Universities of Manchester, Nottingham, Leicester, and Southhampton (England), Dr. Asante was a former university administrator in the University of Ghana, Legon, and a civil servant in the Ghana Civil Service. He has held various extracurricular positions in the public sector, including directorship of Ghana Diamond Marketing Corporation and of the New Times Corporation, as well as chairmanship of various high school and college management committees.

Dr. Asante is the author of *Pan-African Protest: West Africa and the Italo-Ethiopian Crisis*, many book chapters and monographs, and dozens of articles in scholarly journals, including *Third World Quarterly*, *African Affairs*, *Africa Development*, *Universitas*, and *Race*. A regular contributor to the bi-weekly *Legon Observer* (University of Ghana publication) and the London-based weekly, *West Africa*, Dr. Asante's latest contributions on regionalism and pan-Africanism, peace and security, development and food policies in contemporary Africa are forthcoming in the UNESCO General History of Africa (volume 8), the United Nations University publication on *Peace, Development and Regional Security in Africa*, the University of Florida volume on *Food in Africa* and the ECA/Dalhousie University illuminating study of the *Lagos Plan of Action* and African development.

267